T0408853

Explaining SUCCESSES in Africa

Explaining SUCCESSES in Africa

Things Don't Always Fall Apart

Erin Accampo Hern

BOULDER
LONDON

Published in the United States of America in 2023 by
Lynne Rienner Publishers, Inc.
1800 30th Street, Suite 314, Boulder, Colorado 80301
www.rienner.com

and in the United Kingdom by
Lynne Rienner Publishers, Inc.
Gray's Inn House, 127 Clerkenwell Road, London EC1 5DB
www.eurospanbookstore.com/rienner

Library of Congress Cataloging-in-Publication Data
Names: Hern, Erin Accampo, 1987– author.
Title: Explaining successes in Africa : things don't always fall apart / Erin Accampo Hern.
Description: Boulder, Colorado : Lynne Rienner Publishers, Inc., 2023. | Includes bibliographical references and index. | Summary: "Analyzes the performance of African countries that have achieved political and economic successes"—Provided by publisher.
Identifiers: LCCN 2022039029 (print) | LCCN 2022039030 (ebook) | ISBN 9781955055789 (hardcover) | ISBN 9781955055796 (paperback) | ISBN 9781685852658 (ebook) | ISBN 9781685852795 (ebook)
Subjects: LCSH: Comparative government. | Africa—Politics and government—1960– | Africa—Economic conditions. | Africa—Social conditions.
Classification: LCC DT30.5 .H475 2023 (print) | LCC DT30.5 (ebook) | DDC 960.3/2—dc23/eng/20220817
LC record available at https://lccn.loc.gov/2022039029
LC ebook record available at https://lccn.loc.gov/2022039030

British Cataloguing in Publication Data
A Cataloguing in Publication record for this book is available from the British Library.

Printed and bound in the United States of America

The paper used in this publication meets the requirements of the American National Standard for Permanence of Paper for Printed Library Materials Z39.48-1992.

5 4 3 2 1

Contents

Tables and Figures

Tables

Figures

Acknowledgments

In March 2020, the novel coronavirus brought the world to a standstill. Over the next months and years, we all grappled with the strange circumstances of our new reality and struggled to make sense of a once-in-a-hundred-years pandemic. For those of us whose work includes traveling across borders and talking to people face-to-face, it demanded a total recalibration. This book was born of that moment and reflects a need for a project that was at once hopeful and possible to complete without travel or face-to-face contact.

I am grateful for grant funding from Syracuse University's Maxwell School Dean's Office and Intelligence Community Center for Academic Excellence to kickstart this project. This early support enabled excellent research assistance from Nneka Eke, who helped put together an initial bibliography across the sprawling topics covered in the book. I owe a big thank you to Anita Venter for her time corresponding with me about environmentalism in Bloemfontein, which sent me down a deep rabbit hole of local politics in South Africa. Tom Mowle provided excellent editorial feedback on the first draft of the book manuscript, helping me strengthen the arguments and identifying the gaps in the evidence. Thank you to Lynne Rienner for believing in the concept of the book and encouraging me throughout the writing process. Relatedly, I am indebted to two anonymous reviewers whose helpful critiques greatly strengthened the book. Thank you to Tom, Jess, Elinor, Bob, and Sonia for thinking this was a good idea and periodically reminding me of that.

Finally, and most important, thank you to Coco, for reluctantly letting me work, and Turtle, for giving me a firm deadline. Kathryn Grody says that having a child is an act of radical optimism. That statement feels especially true now. This book is dedicated to you two, my children, in the radical hope that the world tomorrow will be better than today.

1

Explaining Successes in Africa: Why and How

When I teach undergraduate African politics, I often begin the course by asking my students to write the first thing that comes to mind when they think about Africa. Most students provide terms that have a negative connotation: poverty, famine, war, colonialism. This is not surprising. The media generally portray Africa as an undifferentiated space where bad things happen. African countries typically make the news because something terrible has occurred. Ebola in Sierra Leone, famine and war in Ethiopia, child soldiers in Uganda, kidnappings in Nigeria—these are the stories deemed newsworthy. More than 120 years after Joseph Conrad popularized the notion of Africa as a "dark continent," many people still think of it that way.

Academic courses and research do not always offer the best antidote to these media portrayals. In the field of comparative politics, African countries often appear as case studies on corruption, failed economic policy, political instability, or ethnic violence. Countries that do perform well in certain areas are often described as "miracles" or "darlings," highlighting their performance as the exception rather than the rule (e.g., Bratton 1998; Brautigam 1999; Jerven 2010). There are two problems with this characterization. First, presenting these success stories as outliers suggests that they are so exceptional that other countries cannot learn from their experiences. Second, the label "miracle" creates an unrealistic impression that the country is problem-free. The "exceptional" label then often provokes a rush to find examples of failure to prove that the title is undeserved (see Kasenally 2011; Taylor 2006). While these academic analyses are rooted in fact, their result is to focus on ongoing challenges rather than successes. Thus, the general tenor of work on Africa, to borrow Chinua Achebe's (1994) characterization, is that "things fall apart."[1]

It is easy to find things that are going poorly on the African continent, just as it is easy to find things are going poorly elsewhere. However, in the case of Africa, the narrative presented to the public is almost exclusively negative. This narrative belies the dramatic continent-wide progress across multiple fronts over the past three decades. Sometimes things do fall apart—but not always. Since 1990, poverty rates have decreased, driven partly by rapid economic growth.[2] The average quality of governance across the continent has improved, with more countries adopting democratic elections and protecting civil liberties.[3] The percentage of women elected to national legislatures has more than doubled.[4] Rates of malaria and other diseases have plummeted.[5] While the continent will face major challenges related to climate change, rapid technological innovation offers hope.

My goal in highlighting success stories is not to sweep ongoing challenges under the rug. It is critically important to continue to address the economic, social, and political challenges that people living in African countries face—just as it is important to highlight those same issues on other continents. This book is an optimistic complement to the singular attention to places where things fall apart; it is an invitation to focus on countries where things are going well so that other countries might learn from their experiences.

With that in mind, I designed this book around three goals. The first is to present success stories from African countries that have performed very well in certain areas, described subsequently, and inject some optimism into the narrative about Africa. My second goal is to highlight Africa's diversity and showcase African countries that receive less attention. Much of the social science research published about Africa focuses on a handful of countries. Research in the field of economics, for example, is mostly confined to just five countries: Kenya, South Africa, Ghana, Uganda, and Malawi (Porteous 2022). This book includes case studies of eighteen countries in sub-Saharan Africa, many of which (like Equatorial Guinea and Gabon) are rarely featured in academic work. My third goal is to apply the logic, methods, and theories of comparative politics to African countries. Many dominant theories within this subdiscipline of political science are derived from the experience of European and North American countries, while African countries are underrepresented. Examining these theories through an African lens enables a deeper understanding of how the world works and illuminates which political theories may have universal traction and which are regionally specific.

Scope of This Book

This book includes five substantive chapters, each concentrated on an outcome of interest in comparative politics: economic development, governance, gender equality, public health, and climate resilience. This list is by no means an exhaustive accounting of the topics that are important in comparative politics. Rather, as explained subsequently, they are topics that residents of African countries identify as most important to them. Each chapter is dedicated to understanding variation in the outcome it considers. Some countries do well, while others fare poorly. The goal of each chapter is to try to understand what the best-performing countries did to achieve their success.

To approach this question—"What explains success?"—each chapter presents dominant theories in comparative politics that might offer some insight. While each chapter presents a different set of theories, they all fall into familiar theoretical families. For example, some theories address institutions, such as the form of government, while others focus on agency, the role that individuals might play in achieving the outcome. Each theory corresponds to a testable hypothesis, and each chapter evaluates these hypotheses to determine the most plausible explanation for success. The list of theories and hypotheses is certainly not exhaustive, but space does not allow the inclusion of all possibilities. Instead, each chapter applies theories that are dominant and likely to hold some explanatory value.

The chapters evaluate these hypotheses through comparative case analysis, as detailed in the next section. Each chapter addresses a single topic and explores four cases. The main cases are two countries that have achieved a high level of success, while two shadow cases present details from countries that have not performed as well. The chapters use these cases to evaluate whether any of the hypotheses hold for all four cases: Does the theory provide a plausible explanation for the two successful countries, while also explaining what was lacking in the two less successful countries? Such case comparison is good for ruling out the theories that do not match the details of the cases. The remaining theories are plausible explanations for success.

The cases are drawn from sub-Saharan Africa, excluding the five countries of North Africa (Morocco, Algeria, Tunisia, Libya, and Egypt). Why exclude North Africa? These countries are often grouped with the Middle East because of their shared history, geographical linkages, and cultural exchange. Ultimately, the dividing lines between sub-Saharan and North Africa are somewhat arbitrary, particularly when it comes to categorizing countries of the Sahel, like Chad and Sudan: the Sahara Desert is not the barrier some imagine it to be (Lydon 2005). While this distinction between Africa north and south of the Sahara has been characterized as arbitrary, racist, and Eurocentric, it is also very old and has influenced how countries experienced trade, colonialism, state formation, and integration into the international arena after World War II (Lydon 2015). I focus on sub-Saharan Africa not to reinforce this constructed distinction but out of recognition that it has political consequences that shaped these countries' trajectories. These countries share many circumstances, while also exhibiting a great deal of diversity (Englebert and Dunn 2019, 13).

The information for these case studies comes from scholarly publications, government documents, newspaper articles, reports from nongovernmental organizations, and publicly available data from sources like the Afrobarometer, the World Bank, the Varieties of Democracy Project, and Interparliamentary Union. Each of these data sources is described in the appendix. The cases are a synthetic analysis and are not based on original data collection; their conclusions are therefore limited by the availability and comprehensiveness of existing work. The analytic leverage behind the arguments thus relies on the logic of the comparative method.

The Comparative Method

In political science, we use theories (broad conceptual explanations) to generate hypotheses (testable propositions that, if true, provide support for the broad theory). In comparative politics, a subdiscipline of political science, researchers often employ the comparative method to test hypotheses and evaluate the plausibility of theories. Derived from John Stuart Mill's *System of Logic* (2020), the comparative method is a way of selecting and comparing cases in research so that one can be as confident as possible in the conclusions one draws. In any kind of research, if you evaluate theories within a single case, there is no way of knowing which of the factors under investigation contributed to the outcome. For the sake of simplicity, consider the example of training a dog. Let's say you want to know what enables a dog to be trained quickly and effectively. You theorize that three things matter: the dog's age, the dog's breed, and the experience of the trainer. You hypothesize that dogs are trained most quickly when they are under nine months old, they are a hunting breed (like hounds and retrievers), and they have a trainer with at least five years of experience. You get a golden retriever puppy and enroll her at four months old in a class with a trainer who boasts ten years of experience. Your clever puppy is fully trained in six weeks. Based on this single experience (a single case), can you conclude which of your theories was correct?

No, you can't. The problem, of course, is that since your puppy had all three factors—the right age, the right kind of breed, and an experienced trainer—there is no way of knowing whether one, two, or all three of those factors mattered. To figure out which of your theories offers the best explanation in general, you need to compare. For example, say you found another puppy from the same litter and enrolled her with the same trainer when she was eighteen months old. That puppy does poorly in the class. Based on this comparison, you could conclude that age is the important factor: the younger puppy of the same breed with the same trainer did much better than the older dog. You still wouldn't be sure, however, whether breed and the experience of the trainer matter. Are they totally irrelevant? Or just less important than age? You would need to complete additional comparisons to find out.

Of course, this story about puppy training is overly simplistic. What if different combinations of characteristics matter? What if hunting dogs like golden retrievers are best trained when young, but hyperenergetic breeds like chihuahuas are best trained when they are a little older and calmer? What if the experience of the trainer matters more with older, stubborn dogs than it does with docile puppies? To figure these nuances out, you would need to do many comparisons.

The goal of comparison is to evaluate which hypotheses find support across the most cases, thereby offering evidence supporting the theory. The more structured comparisons a researcher can complete, the more convincing are the findings. However, the real world is messy. Each case has unique features, and there are always outliers that do not behave as expected. With cleverly structured comparisons, however, a researcher can use evidence to determine which theory has the most real-world support. In this book, I use two ways to structure comparisons: most-different case analysis and most-similar case analysis.

Most-Different Case Analysis

Most-different case analysis entails selecting two or more cases that are as different as possible but have the same outcome. What they have in common possibly explains the outcome. Returning to the puppy training example: to apply this method, you would find two dogs that seem to be very different but were both successfully trained. Then, you would try to figure out what they have in common that can explain their shared success. Your theories help you to figure out what features to focus on. For this example, let's say you selected an English pointer that was trained at six months by an inexperienced trainer and a Maltese that was trained at five months by an experienced trainer. These two dogs are very different, but they

Table 1.1 Example of Most-Different Case Analysis

Theory	Dog 1: English Pointer (Succeeded)	Dog 2: Maltese (Succeeded)	Conclusion
Breed	Hunting dog	Nonhunting dog	*Theory unsupported:* being a hunting dog is not necessary for successful training.
Trainer experience	Inexperienced	Experienced	*Theory unsupported:* trainer experience does not determine successful training.
Age	Less than nine months	Less than nine months	*Supports theory:* young age may contribute to successful training.

were both successfully trained. Comparison across each relevant characteristic can illuminate which theory best explains their success. In this case, the two dogs are different breeds—the pointer is a hunting dog, but the Maltese is not, so breed cannot explain their training success. The pointer had an inexperienced trainer while the Maltese had an experienced one, so trainer experience cannot explain their shared success. These two hypotheses are unsupported, so the theories are unsubstantiated. The only hypothesis with support was training at a young age, so this is the only theory with supporting evidence. This logic is outlined in Table 1.1.

Most-Similar Case Analysis

Most-similar case analysis rests on the inverse of the logic of most-different analysis. Using this approach, you would select two or more cases that are as similar as possible but have different outcomes. Whatever differs between the two cases possibly explains why one succeeded while the other did not. To apply this method, you would find two dogs that were very similar but had different training outcomes. Then, you would use the theories to generate testable hypotheses to determine what differed between the two dogs that might explain why one was easier to train than the other. The initial example of selecting two dogs from the same litter and sending them to the same trainer is a most-similar case approach. In this case, the dogs are the same breed (and are even siblings) and have the same training experience. Therefore, those hypotheses are unsupported—these theories cannot explain why one dog trained more easily than the other. The only difference between the two dogs was

Table 1.2 Example of Most-Similar Case Analysis

Theory	Dog 1: Golden Retriever (Succeeded)	Dog 2: Golden Retriever (Failed)	Conclusion
Breed	Hunting dog	Hunting dog	*Theory unsupported:* being a hunting dog does not guarantee successful training.
Trainer experience	Experienced	Experienced	*Theory unsupported:* trainer experience does not guarantee successful training.
Age	Less than nine months	More than nine months	*Supports theory:* young age may contribute to successful training.

that one was trained at a much older age than the other. That hypothesis finds support and is the theory that we cannot rule out—it is a plausible difference that explains the younger dog's training success. This example is summarized in Table 1.2.

These are simple examples, and there are many other things that might be theoretically important for explaining a dog's training success. When applying any version of the comparative method during research, it is important to consider as many theories as are plausible. Otherwise, you might unintentionally omit the most important factor, such as the owner's commitment to training.

Additionally, pay attention to the language used here and in the conclusion columns of the tables. The comparative method allows a researcher to evaluate hypotheses to determine whether theories have support. However, it does not allow a researcher to claim that any theory is confirmed. The distinction between supporting and confirming a theory is important. Using the comparative method in this way allows the researcher to narrow down which theories remain plausible explanations of the cases. But additional methods—which I do not deploy in this book—are necessary to provide more evidence that a theory is definitively correct or that one thing causes another. There is always the possibility that something omitted from the analysis is the true cause of the outcome. Social sciences are a process, and each study or analysis builds evidence that can support or undermine theories, while new information makes researchers reconsider old findings.

The Comparative Method in This Book

In each chapter in this book, I employ a two-step comparison to evaluate hypotheses and determine which theories most plausibly explain the outcome on which the chapter focuses. First, a most-different case analysis features two African countries that have had success in a particular area. This most-different analysis is the main case comparison of the chapter. It serves to determine what these very different countries have in common that might explain why they were both able to achieve success. However, in a most-different case comparison, there is always the risk that something held in common by the two successful countries also occurs in countries that were less successful. For example, two countries that achieved economic success may have both implemented structural adjustment as prescribed by the International Monetary Fund. One might thus conclude that structural adjustment contributed to these countries' success. However, if other countries experienced massive economic declines after structural adjustment, it cannot be the cause of success. It may even be that the two success stories achieved economic growth despite structural adjustment.

To address that issue, I pair each most-different case analysis with a most-similar case analysis. The most-different case analysis tests hypotheses and finds support for one or a few theories. These factors may have contributed to these countries' shared success. It is important to ensure that those factors do not also appear in countries that did poorly, in which case the theory would be undermined. An extension of the dog training example illustrates this idea.

Let's say you repeat the pointer/Maltese most-different comparison, but this time you also want to consider whether the owner's commitment to the training process is important. You find that, in addition to being close in age, both the pointer and the Maltese had owners who were committed to the training process. As Figure 1.1 summarizes, this most-different comparison allows you to conclude that to explain training success, the theories about breed and trainer experience have no support, but the theories about the dog's age and the owner's commitment to the process do have support. However, it is possible that other dogs train poorly even at young ages or with committed owners. To check, you complete a set of most-similar analyses: one with another puppy from the pointer's litter that used the same trainer, and another with a puppy from the Maltese's litter that used the same trainer. In this case, the second pointer and the second Maltese both struggled with training. You find out that they both trained when they were young, but they both had owners who did not keep up with the training process. As Figure 1.1 illustrates, by adding this second set of comparisons, you realize that the age of the puppy is not as important as you had thought. Some young puppies still struggle with their training. Instead, owner commitment is the only theory that finds support across all four cases.

Each chapter in this book completes a two-step comparison. First, a most-different case analysis examines two very different countries that were both successful in the given area. The goal of the first analysis is to determine which theories find support to explain their joint success. Next, each of those countries is matched with a most-similar country that was less successful. The goal of this second step of analysis is to see whether any of the theories that found support in the first stage also find support in the second stage. This approach cannot prove a theory correct, but it can determine which theories lack support and which remain plausible. Tables 1.3 and 1.4 provide an example of this two-stage analysis.

Selecting Cases: Theory vs. Practice

In practice, selecting appropriate most-similar and most-different cases can be challenging. Sometimes, in the pool of countries available for comparison, few countries are obviously "most similar" or "most different." In this book, in each chapter I identify a pool of relevant countries (based on performance on each indicator) and then select countries that are as different or as similar as possible given the pool. When the available country pairings are less helpful for eliminating theories, more case analysis is required.

Each chapter follows the same decision rules for selecting countries. First, I identify the pool of countries that are most successful. For some topics, a clear group of countries stands out relative to the rest of the continent. For others, performance is distributed more evenly, in which case I

Table 1.3 Example of Stage One Most-Different Comparison

Theory	Dog 1: English Pointer (Succeeded)	Dog 2: Maltese (Succeeded)	Conclusion
Breed	Hunting dog	Nonhunting dog	Theory unsupported
Trainer experience	Inexperienced	Experienced	Theory unsupported
Age	Less than nine months	Less than nine months	Supports theory
Owner commitment	Yes	Yes	Supports theory

Table 1.4 Example of Stage Two Most-Similar Comparisons

Most Similar Pointers			
Theory	Successful Pointer	Failed Pointer	Conclusion
Breed	Hunting dog	Hunting dog	Theory unsupported
Trainer experience	Inexperienced	Inexperienced	Theory unsupported
Age	Less than nine months	Less than nine months	Theory unsupported
Owner commitment	Yes	No	Supports theory
Most Similar Maltese			
Theory	Successful Maltese	Failed Maltese	Conclusion
Breed	Nonhunting dog	Nonhunting dog	Theory unsupported
Trainer experience	Experienced	Experienced	Theory unsupported
Age	Less than nine months	Less than nine months	Theory unsupported
Owner commitment	Yes	No	Supports theory

consider the top ten. Within that group, I eliminate countries that already appear in other chapters and then select countries that are as different from each other as possible based on region, colonial history, ethnodemographic characteristics, and political institutions. Sometimes there is more than one pairing that could be considered most different within the pool. In those cases, my selection is based on the goal of including countries across a broad geographic spread and highlighting those that appear less often in the academic literature on Africa.

Next, I select two cases that are most similar (or as similar as possible) to the cases in the most-different country pair. To do so, I identify a pool of regional neighbors (or other islands, for the island countries) with similar colonial histories, ethnodemographic characteristics, and political institutions. From that pool of most-similar countries, I select the one that has the poorest performance in order to accentuate the difference in outcome between it and the more successful comparison country. In some cases, all regional neighbors perform similarly, requiring me to relax that criterion and look more widely to find a state that has poor performance but is as similar as possible to its comparison state. The decision criteria for each chapter are detailed in the appendix.

Limitations of the Comparative Method

While the comparative method is effective at highlighting which theories have support across multiple countries, it also has shortcomings. First, it only enables researchers to test the theories they think of (or deem most important). There is no such thing as a comprehensive case analysis—there will always be factors a researcher failed to consider, which may turn out to be important for explaining an outcome. In this book, each chapter presents theories that are prevalent in the literature, but I do not claim to include every theory that exists to explain each outcome. Continuing to develop and test new theories (and retest old ones) is an essential part of the ongoing project of social science.

Next, the comparative method as employed in this book is not adept at identifying the way different factors may interact with each other. Other social science methodologies (for example, statistical analysis with interaction terms, or case analysis employing Boolean algebra) have tools that can assess complex interactions, determining whether a certain factor is necessary or sufficient for an outcome, or whether a factor is more likely to lead to an outcome when other conditions are in place. Qualitative analysis of the comparative cases can suggest the way different factors may interact with each other, but the methods employed here do not systematically test interactions.

Similarly, as noted previously, the comparative method as employed here can provide evidence that supports or undermines a theory, but it cannot provide definitive proof that a factor causes an outcome. Rather, it can provide evidence that a factor tends to be present when an outcome occurs (correlation). Again, other methods in social sciences (e.g., experiments and process tracing) are more adept at identifying causal relationships between variables.

Finally, a note on measurement: In each chapter, determining how well each country performs requires making decisions about how to measure the outcomes and other variables involved. Because this book is a synthetic analysis, I rely on datasets compiled by experts (detailed in the appendix) that produce indicators. These indicators are useful because they allow comparison across countries. However, scholars have reasonable disagreements about the best way things should be measured. While cross-country datasets are useful for comparison, they do not replace the thick, contextualized information that comes from in-country study. In this book, I am transparent about the measures I use, understanding that other scholars may make different decisions about the best way to measure concepts.

To say that a method is limited, however, does not make it useless. All methods are limited, and social science advances most fruitfully when researchers approach questions from different angles, applying different theories, with different methods and measurements. Each well-designed study improves our collective knowledge. The comparative method enables researchers to ask big, important questions, take on broad comparisons, and seek generalizations—even if the conclusions are necessarily tentative.

Theories in Comparative Politics

As described previously, the comparative method enables researchers to examine whether theories that explain a certain outcome find support across multiple cases. In each of the chapters that follow, I present theories grouped into categories. These categories are an organizational tool that indicate what type of factor the theory highlights as important in leading to an outcome. However, while theories within each category focus on a different type of explanation, they are not mutually exclusive (more than one type can be true for explaining an outcome). The boundaries between these categories are blurry, and I present them primarily as an organizational tool. Each chapter includes theories from several of the following categories.

Agency-based theories are those that focus on the power of individuals, usually leaders or key decisionmakers. These theories indicate that the decisions and will of these individuals have a disproportionate impact on outcomes. Theories that focus on civil society highlight the importance of people acting in a coordinated manner through groups to make an impact on society, politics, or policy. Sociocultural theories examine the way features of society as a whole—such as religiosity, ethnic demographics, or belief systems—might shape outcomes. Policy-based theories look at how government policies can change outcomes. Institutional theories examine the impact of broader institutions—the formal "rules of the game," like constitutions, the legal system, or form of government—on outcomes, often by shaping the incentives that face leaders, constraining the policy that can be enacted, or shaping the possibilities for civil society activity. Structural theories focus on the broad, underlying structures that are impossible (or very difficult) to change, such as geographical or climatic features. Sometimes, historical legacies are treated as structures. Finally, international theories consider the way that international actors—other countries, multilateral institutions, donors—shape outcomes within countries.

Outline of the Book

Areas of Focus

In each of the five substantive chapters of this book I focus on a different topic: economic development, governance, public health, climate adaptation, and gender equality. These topics are areas of importance in comparative politics, but they are also issues of primary concern for people living in African countries. Within each topic, each chapter focuses on one or two indicators that measure performance related to the topic: the Human Development Index (for economic growth), the World Governance Indicator (for governance), malaria incidence (for public health), progress under the Global Covenant of Mayors (for climate adaptation), and a combination of the V-Dem's Women Political Empowerment Index and the United Nations Development Program's Gender Inequality Index (for gender equality). Understanding variation in these outcomes—why some countries do better than others—is critically important both as an academic question and as a quality-of-life issue for hundreds of millions of people.

The Afrobarometer, a massive survey that collects nationally representative samples from over thirty African countries, asks people to identify the most important problems facing their country. The question is open ended, and people can identify up to three problems, which the Afrobarometer then groups into categories such as "poverty" and "drought." Figure 1.1 shows the distribution of these responses, with the categories grouped by theme.[6]

Figure 1.1 Distribution of Categories Identified as "Most Important" in Afrobarometer

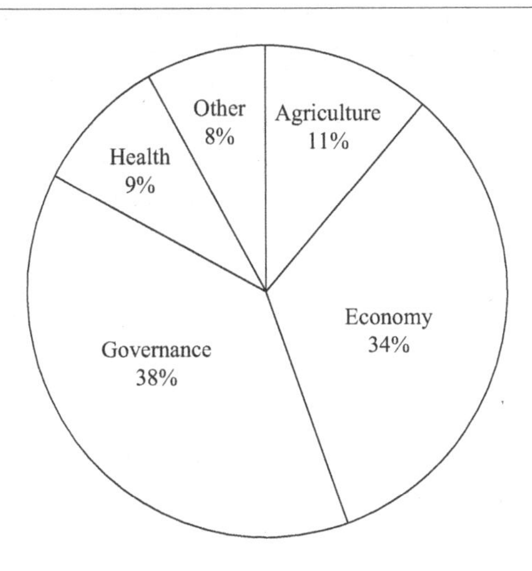

The most common theme in these responses is the economy, the focus of Chapter 2. Africans are worried about unemployment, stagnant wages, and other economic issues affecting their daily lives. Chapter 3 addresses the second most common theme, governance, which includes political issues like corruption and rights, as well as a country's ability to develop a political system that is responsive and effective at providing basic public goods. Health care, the most frequently cited public good, is the subject of Chapter 4. This chapter focuses on the specific public health challenge of malaria, which takes hundreds of thousands of lives in African countries annually, mostly those of young children. Chapter 5 concentrates on adaptation to climate change. While "climate" was not a common response to this Afrobarometer question, many respondents listed agricultural concerns that will be dramatically affected by a changing climate, including food shortage and drought. Finally, Chapter 6 addresses gender equality. Like climate, this issue was not one that many people directly identified in the Afrobarometer survey. However, gender inequalities mark every other area of importance: women in Africa hold less wealth (McFerson 2010), are underrepresented in government (Tripp 2016), bear the brunt of public health failures through their caring responsibilities (Hunter 2012), and will be disproportionately affected by climate change (Makina and Moyo 2016). This is far from an exhaustive list of the important topics in comparative politics, but it reflects the issues that are of greatest importance to Africans.

Country Cases

Chapter 2 focuses on economic development as measured by the Human Development Index. The most-different analysis features Seychelles and Gabon, both of which have achieved impressive levels of economic growth, though in different ways and with different resources. For the second stage of analysis, Seychelles is paired with the most-similar case of Sao Tome and Principe, and Gabon is paired with Equatorial Guinea. The analysis highlights that both Seychelles and Gabon pursued policies of directed development that may explain their shared success, while Sao Tome and Principe and Equatorial Guinea did not.

Chapter 3 examines governance, as conceptualized by the World Governance Index. This chapter examines Botswana and Mauritius as the most-different successful countries. The second stage of analysis pairs Botswana with Uganda and Mauritius with Comoros. Through these comparisons, the chapter provides evidence that Botswana and Mauritius achieved strong governance because of their modes of historical institutional development and the quality of leadership in the countries' early days of independence.

Chapter 4 examines public health through countries' ability to respond to malaria. The two most-different countries that have done well at reducing malaria incidence are Guinea-Bissau and Malawi. The second stage of analysis compares Guinea-Bissau to Sierra Leone and Malawi to Mozambique. The chapter concludes that the most plausible explanation for Guinea-Bissau and Malawi's shared success is that international agencies were able to engage local actors with a national reach more effectively there than they were in Sierra Leone and Mozambique.

Chapter 5 addresses climate adaptation. This chapter differs from the others in that, instead of using countries as cases, it focuses on cities. This chapter conceptualizes success as a city's progress through the Global Covenant of Mayors program, which issues badges to cities that achieve planning benchmarks related to climate mitigation and adaptation. Two most-different cities that have excelled in this program are Lagos, Nigeria, and Durban, South Africa. The second stage of comparison pairs Lagos with Abuja, Nigeria, and Durban with Bloemfontein, South Africa. The chapter concludes that the most plausible explanation for Lagos's and Durban's shared success was that climate-related focus events put climate issues on the agenda, and a local champion within the government was able to promote adaptation policies over a long duration.

Chapter 6 focuses on gender equality, as measured by the United Nations Development Program's Women's Empowerment Index. Rwanda and Senegal are the most-different countries that have demonstrated success in this area. The second stage of analysis pairs Rwanda with Burundi and Senegal with Guinea. The chapter concludes that in Rwanda and Senegal (but not Burundi and Guinea), women in the legislature, supported by the president, were able to advance legislation that supported women and changed people's minds about women in power.

Finally, a concluding chapter synthesizes the thematic and theoretical lessons across these five topics.

Notes

1. Title taken from William Butler Yeats's poem "The Second Coming."

2. World Bank's "poverty headcount ratio," which estimates the percentage of the population living on less than $1.90/day (purchasing power parity; PPP), declined from 55.1 percent in 1990 to 40.4 percent in 2018.

3. The Varieties of Democracy Project's Additive Polyarchy Index, a measure of the quality of democracy, increased from 0.41 in 1990 to 0.65 in 2020.

4. According to the Interparliamentary Union, the average percentage of women in parliament rose from 10.2 percent in 1997 to 25.6 percent in 2021.

5. The World Bank estimates that the incidence of malaria decreased from 350 to 219 per 1,000 people from 2000 to 2018.

6. "Economy" includes the categories economic management, wages, unemployment, poverty, taxes, and credit. "Governance" includes the political categories of corruption, political violence, political instability, discrimination, gender issues, and democracy, as well as the public service categories of infrastructure, education, housing, electricity, water, homelessness, services, and agricultural marketing. "Health" includes health, AIDS, and illness; "agriculture" includes agriculture, food shortage, drought, and land. "Other" includes assorted categories including security, communication, and other.

2

Overcoming Obstacles to Economic Growth

Why are some countries so much wealthier than others, and what does it take for a poor country to achieve economic development? These questions are particularly consequential for African countries. While the continent has achieved impressive levels of economic growth in the twenty-first century, much of this wealth has remained concentrated in the hands of a few while poverty remains entrenched. Persistent rates of poverty in Africa are particularly striking considering the reduction of poverty elsewhere—between 1990 and 2015, rates of extreme poverty in other regions plummeted (World Bank 2018). The World Bank estimated that, in 2015, "nearly every low-income country is in sub-Saharan Africa," and that across the region an average of 41 percent of people live below the international poverty line (2018, 29). Nevertheless, some African countries have outperformed their neighbors and achieved sustained economic growth alongside improving development indicators.

Economic growth is not an end in itself; rather, it enables broad improvements in people's quality of life, including better health, education, food security, and standard of living. One way of measuring these improvements is the human development index (HDI), calculated annually by the United Nations Development Program (UNDP), which combines income, health, and education in each country.[1] As Figure 2.1 illustrates, most countries in sub-Saharan Africa score below the world average of 0.737. Only two countries—Seychelles and Mauritius—score better than the world average, and only three more countries—South Africa, Botswana, and Gabon—score above the UNDP's threshold of 0.7 to achieve a "high" level of human development.

Figure 2.1 HDI in African Countries, 2019

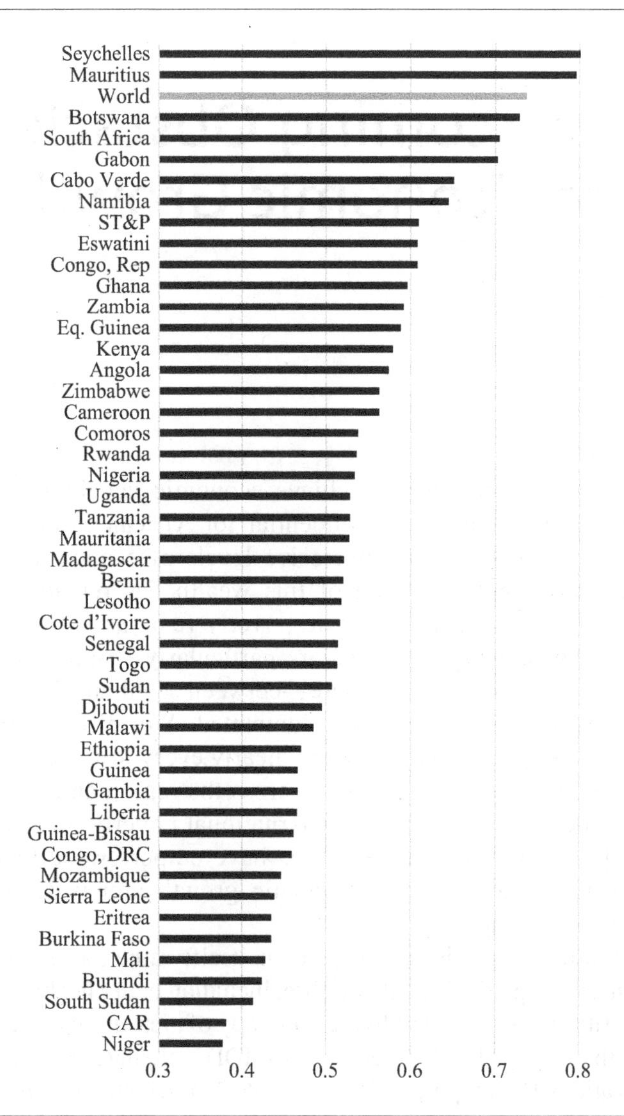

This chapter uses the HDI as a metric for economic development out of recognition that increasing gross domestic product (GDP) alone does not necessarily improve a population's standard of living. The HDI incorporates measures of life expectancy and education, which reflect investment in health and education systems alongside economic growth. Its measure of GDP per capita in purchasing power parity (PPP) helps to adjust for inflation and other economic distortions—it measures not just how much money people have, but how far it goes.

This chapter analyzes economic performance in four countries, drawing on their experiences to understand why some African countries have performed well while others have floundered. It begins by outlining ten possible theories that may explain why some countries perform better than others. Next, a most-different case comparison of Seychelles and Gabon investigates what they have in common that might explain their shared success. Then, two most-similar case analyses compare Seychelles against Sao Tome and Principe (STP), another small island nation with a similar history but a much lower degree of economic development, and Gabon against Equatorial Guinea, a neighboring country with similar economic resources but less economic success. Through this two-stage analysis, the chapter will consider what Seychelles and Gabon have in common that can explain their shared success as well as what features absent from STP and Equatorial Guinea may explain their relative lack of success. More detail on the case selection rationale is in the appendix.

Theories of Economic Performance

There are many theories in political science and economics as to why some countries are wealthier than others. This section describes some of the most prominent, organized into four categories: structural/historical, institutional, policy/performance, and sociocultural. These theories are not mutually exclusive—more than one can be correct. However, each family of theories emphasizes a different factor as being most important for economic growth.

Structural / Historical

Structural theories include some of the oldest economic explanations for why some countries are wealthier than others. In this context, "structures" are preexisting features over which people or countries have little control. This chapter considers three interrelated structural factors that may influence long-run economic development: geography, colonial history, and a country's position in the world economic system. While these factors are all related to one another, they each have corresponding theories that offer distinct predictions about which countries will be better able to achieve economic growth.

Geography, which includes things like topography, location, climate, and resource endowments, can influence economic development through both direct and indirect pathways. Geography most directly influences economic development through logistical accessibility and the disease environment (Rodrik 2012). Places with coastlines featuring natural harbors or capes and without challenging features like dense jungle, high mountains, or large deserts were better poised to become major commercial centers during the early days of global trade (Ricart-Huguet 2022). Now, countries with fewer logistical challenges have fewer costs associated with building infrastructure or moving goods. Additionally, some argue that different climatic bands have an independent impact on economic development, particularly tropical locations adjacent to the equator, where endemic diseases like malaria take an economic toll (Gallup, Sachs, and Mellinger 1999). It therefore follows that countries with favorable geography—those that are the most accessible and do not have a tropical environment—are better positioned to achieve economic development.

Historically, geographical factors such as rainfall and raw resources like timber and metals were important for economic production. While it is intuitive to assume that resources—sometimes called factor endowments—would continue to influence economic development over time, the relationship between resources and economic development is unclear. Some places with abundant resources that were comparatively wealthy hundreds of years ago are among the poorest today (Acemoglu, Johnson, and Robinson 2002; Sokoloff and Engerman 2000). Additionally, there is evidence that some valuable resources are bad for long-term economic development through a phenomenon known as the resource curse. This argument typically applies to oil, minerals, and other high-value resources (Ross 2012, 2015). While counterintuitive, high-value resources can lead to economic decline when a country's economy becomes reliant on one major export. Economies that lack diversification are vulnerable to price shocks, leading to dramatic swings in GDP. If the industry does not require a large amount of labor, like oil and some other extractive industries, then GDP can be deceptively high while employment rates are low. An economy pegged to oil or other high-value resources can cause "Dutch disease": export of the resource increases the relative value of the country's currency, which in turn makes its other exports too expensive to compete in an international market (Corden 1984). If a country cannot rely on the export of a single high-value good, it is forced to invest strategically in other sectors that yield better, more diverse returns over time. The resource curse also extends to political institutions, as access to revenue like oil rents can sometimes enable corruption and poor governance (Dunning 2008; Ross 2015). Most studies indicate that the resource curse is most pronounced when the resources are discovered in a country with weak institutions

(Abdulahi, Shu, and Khan 2019; Epo and Nochi Faha 2020). This chapter focuses on the economic consequences of the resource curse, while Chapter 3 explores the political side of the resource curse further, and corruption and institutional quality are discussed separately in subsequent sections.

Geography also influences economic development indirectly through its influence on historical events, specifically the nature and extent of colonialism (Nunn 2009). Nearly every country in Africa experienced colonialism at the hands of a European country, but the nature and intensity of colonialism varied. To understand the impact of the nature of colonialism, most analyses distinguish between settler and extractive colonialism. Settler colonialism (as in the United States or Australia) tended to occur in places with lower population density and fewer high-value resources like metals and ores. Typically, settler colonialists arrived, decimated existing populations, established new settlements, and developed their own political and economic institutions over time. While devastating for indigenous populations, settler colonialism tended to produce institutional arrangements that allowed long-term economic growth (Acemoglu, Johnson, and Robinson 2002). Extractive colonialism was more common in places where high-value resources were readily evident. Put simply, such colonialism involved a great power invading and occupying another region and taking its resources (both material resources and people). Colonialism produced the resources that fueled industrialization and rapid economic development in colonizing countries while diminishing the wealth of the colonized (Rodney 1982). At a minimum, the experience of colonialism boosted economic development for colonizers while delaying it for the colonized. In some places, it also changed the economic trajectory of colonized countries.

Extractive colonial economies were oriented around the export of raw materials, like timber or minerals, with little local industrial processing. Instead, these raw materials were sent to Europe, where they were processed and manufactured into higher value products. Once former colonies gained their independence, they inherited economies built around the export of lower-value raw materials (Gunder Frank 1978). Because other former colonies exported similar goods, competition was intense and prices remained low (Wallerstein 2004). Meanwhile, with little domestic industry or manufacturing, these countries had to import processed goods from wealthier countries—often their former colonizer. In the 1960s and 1970s, many former colonies were stuck in a cycle of exporting unprocessed raw materials and importing high-value processed goods, which made economic development challenging (Infante-Amate and Krausmann 2019). This cycle was hard to break because these countries had to compete on the international market with older, better established industrial and manufacturing sectors elsewhere. Therefore, the lingering economic impact of colonialism depends in part on how extractive it was, specifically, whether a country emerged from colonialism with an economy oriented around the export of raw materials and limited domestic manufacturing.

Other analyses of the impact of colonialism highlight the importance of the identity of the colonizer. In Africa, the British and French were the primary colonizers, while the Portuguese, Spanish, Belgians, and Germans had minor colonial holdings. British colonialism tended to be indirect, meaning the colonial administration relied heavily on local leaders and pre-existing political structures to rule. By contrast, the French preferred direct rule, destroying local political institutions and replacing them with colonial institutions (Muller-Crepon 2020).[2] Indirect rule may have been less harmful than direct rule for long-run economic development because it was less disruptive and preserved more local political structures (Letsa and Wilfahrt 2020). In addition to the nature of colonial rule, the identity of the colonizer influenced the type of legal institutions in the newly independent countries, as they tended to adopt the legal systems of their former colonizers. Some have argued that the British common law system, with its strong protection of property rights, leads to better economic outcomes than French civil law (La Porta, Lopez-De-Silanes, and Shleifer 2008). Compared to the British and the French, the other minor colonial powers in Africa tended to be highly interventionist and brutal, rendering worse long-term outcomes.

Another way that the identity of the colonizer matters is in the way a country becomes integrated into the world economic system after independence. Many formerly colonized countries entered the world economic system in a position of dependency, meaning that they primarily export low-value raw materials and must rely on wealthier countries to import higher value processed materials and as a source of credit and investment. Often, economic links are strongest between a country and its former colonizer, which often has retained business interests in the new country. In some cases, these links may be helpful, if a former colony gains access to preferential trade terms. However, they can also be pernicious, with characteristics of neocolonialism. France in particular was reluctant to let go of its economic influence over its former African colonies, setting up a system in its former West and Central African holdings that some refer to as *francafrique*. In short, this collection of former French colonies all share a currency—the CFA franc—that was pegged to the French franc and systematically overvalued. As Ian Taylor (2019, 1067–1068) describes,

> The net result has been that the CFA franc has helped entrench its member countries' dependent positions as relatively low-priced sources of raw materials. This has been primarily because the two CFA currencies were (and continue to be) set at an unreasonably high level, which limited the price competitiveness of exports onto global world markets (except when these exports went to the French market). Thus, 'the parity was engineered in such a way as to make France's market the exclusive outlet for her former colonies' raw materials: cocoa, coffee, cotton, rubber, uranium, among others.' Continued underdevelopment and dependency has been the net result.

Thus, the legacies of colonialism can operate through multiple pathways to continue to influence economic development. The general expectation is that African countries colonized by the British should generally be better off than those colonized by the French by virtue of having less institutional disruption, stronger property rights institutions, and less exploitative ongoing economic relations with their former colonies.

Institutional

A country's political and economic institutions can also influence its economic prospects. These institutions do not appear from thin air—they are also related to colonial history. Under colonialism, there was often a local class of people that had disproportionate access to wealth and power: they owned land, were educated, and had higher incomes by virtue of economic favoritism or salaried work with the colonial administrations. As colonialism ended, the local political elite that designed new constitutions for the independent state often came from this privileged class (Ricart-Huguet 2021). These elites often designed the new institutions to reinforce their privileged status through control over local financial markets, business licenses, land, permitting, and other government functions. These exclusionary economic institutions include weak protection of property rights, a biased judicial system, and barriers to land ownership and financial institutions that make it harder for non-elites to build wealth. Such institutions tend to create high levels of inequality, concentrating wealth at the top and inhibiting entrepreneurialism or access to markets at the bottom (Acemoglu, Johnson, and Robinson 2002; Bhattacharyya and Hodler 2014). However, some countries were able to break with their colonial history to design more inclusionary economic institutions with effective private property protections and few barriers to entry. These features reduce transaction costs and create a predictable and stable environment for entrepreneurs, business owners, and investors to grow competitive industries without fear of theft or an arbitrary policy change that might shut down their industry (North 1990). Additionally, as described previously, countries with British (rather than French) colonial history may have adopted British common law systems that include stronger property rights.

Political institutions may also matter, and some argue for a democratic dividend: that democracies are better able to achieve economic development (Acemoglu et al. 2019). In democracies, governments must cater to a larger portion of the population, so they may be less likely to have predatory institutions like those described previously. Democracies may indirectly promote economic growth because they are more likely to invest in resources like education and health and to protect private property rights (Acemoglu and Robinson 2012).

Policy and Government Performance

Others argue that governments can take control over economic growth through policy, noting that governments of poor countries must take a more active role in the economy because of their relative disadvantage in the international market. If a country's economy is oriented around the export of low-value raw materials, it is hard for industrial and manufacturing sectors to flourish because those sectors must compete with established industries in wealthier countries (Chang 2006). Instead, some suggest that the government should engage in directed development of certain sectors that could propel the economy forward (Johnson 1982). This type of policy involves the government identifying and protecting specific industries in which the country could soon create a comparative advantage. "Protection" includes policies like directed government investment, protective tariffs, establishment of special export zones, and government-sponsored workforce training. Ideally, these protective measures are temporary, only lasting until the industry becomes sufficiently competitive, at which point the government may shift these policies to another sector. Proponents of directed development point out that these policies transformed the economies of the so-called East Asian tigers (Haggard 1990; Woo-Cumings 1999).

Regardless of policy, most agree that corruption has the potential to derail economic development, either by undermining business performance or through elite expropriation of national wealth. As noted previously, corruption may be more likely in countries with high-value resources with rents that accrue directly to the government. However, not all corruption is equally damaging: when it is predictable and limited (i.e., not an administration pocketing millions of dollars from the national coffers), corruption may be treated as an informal tax. The issue is not the existence of corruption but its scale and the degree to which it disrupts business (Malesky and Samphantharak 2008).

Sociocultural Explanations

Finally, sociocultural theories examine the impact that deep social divisions may have on economic development. Sociocultural divisions often reflect ethnic diversity but may also involve race, religion, and linguistic divides. While diversity is not inherently bad for economic development, in some cases diversity can transform into social divisions that are highly politically and economically salient (Posner 2004b). Often, diversity becomes divisive when some element of identity—ethnicity, religion, race—becomes important for accessing state resources. For example, when ethnicity determines whether the government invests in infrastructure, schooling, or health in a region, then ethnicity becomes highly politically salient and society becomes divided. These divisions can undermine economic growth in a few ways: they can result in uneven distribution of resources, leaving some areas worse off and undermining national development, and they can also reduce social trust and cohesion (Alesina, Baqir, and Easterly 1999; Alesina and La Ferrara 2005; Robinson 2016).

Table 2.1 presents the hypotheses associated with these ten theories.

Most-Different Case Analysis: Seychelles and Gabon

Seychelles and Gabon differ from each other in many ways, yet both have achieved high levels of economic development in terms of HDI. This most-different case analysis enables an examination of what they have in common that might plausibly explain their shared success. Any factor that differs between the two cannot explain why they have the same outcome and must be ruled out. This section first introduces each case and then examines each theory in turn to determine whether it can explain each country's economic success.

Case Introduction: Seychelles and Gabon

Seychelles is an archipelago made up of 115 islands in the Indian Ocean off Africa's eastern coast. Nearly all Seychellois live on the main island of Mahé. The islands were uninhabited until 1768, when the French claimed the land, established sugar plantations, and imported slaves from elsewhere in Africa. This plantation society persisted until 1814 when the British claimed the colony after their victory in the Napoleonic Wars (Campling, Confiance, and Purvis 2011, 6). Initially, little changed: British administrators ran the island, the French owned the land, and the slaves did all the work. But in 1833, the

Table 2.1 Theories and Hypotheses of Economic Development

Theory	Hypothesis
	Structural/Historical
Geography	Countries with geographical logistical challenges and a topical climate will struggle to achieve economic development.
Resource curse	Countries that become dependent on exporting a single high-value resource will struggle to achieve economic development.
Extractive colonialism	Countries that emerged from colonialism with an economy based on raw material exports and little domestic manufacturing will struggle to achieve economic development.
Identity of colonizer	Countries colonized by countries other than Britain will struggle to achieve economic development.
World economic system	Countries that are still in a dependent economic relationship with their former colonizer will struggle to achieve economic development.
	Institutional
Exclusionary economic institutions	Countries with economic barriers to entry and few property rights protections will struggle to achieve economic development.
Democratic dividend	Nondemocratic countries will struggle to achieve economic development.
	Policy and Performance
Directed development	Countries that pursue directed development through temporary government intervention will be more likely to achieve economic development.
Corruption	Countries with capricious and large-scale corruption will struggle to achieve economic development.
	Sociocultural
Sociocultural divisions	Countries with deep sociocultural divisions will struggle to achieve economic development.

British outlawed slavery in its territories. Once liberated, the former slaves had little interest in performing the same work they had previously been coerced into, and many of them migrated out of Seychelles, prompting a demographic crisis. The French landowners ultimately abandoned sugar—a labor-intensive crop—and shifted to coconuts, which required much less labor to grow. Coconuts became Seychelles's primary export and remained so until the country gained its independence in 1976 (Campling, Confiance, and Purvis 2011, 6–16). From 1976 to 2000, Seychelles transformed from a poor coconut exporter to the wealthiest country in Africa. It did so by successfully transitioning its economy to twin pillars of luxury tourism and tuna fishing and processing. These two industries, plus the subsequent addition of elite banking services, propelled Seychelles's per capita GDP from $814 in 1976 to $16,198 in 2019.[3]

Gabon, a small coastal country in West Africa, was also colonized by the French, though it was inhabited when the French began to officially administer the colony in 1903. This colony's objective was to support private French companies in their endeavor to extract wealth through mining and timber and export those raw materials back to France. In the late 1950s, discoveries of oil deposits off Gabon's coast led to oil dominating the export economy (Edwards 2018). Gabon gained independence in 1960, and within the decade oil became Gabon's largest export and primary source of government revenue (Yates 2014, 167). Foreign companies dominated Gabon's oil industry, creating small enclaves into which they imported skilled workers and developed infrastructure. Communities outside these small enclaves languished, never benefiting from the siloed economic boom. Revenue flowed to the government through rents from the oil industry, creating optimal circumstances for a resource curse. Indeed, Gabon's wealth remained concentrated in the hands of the elite, while the political apparatus remained dominated by President Omar Bongo and his extended family. From its discovery through the early 2000s, oil continued to dominate the economy, GDP skyrocketed while other indicators of development stagnated, and the Bongo family became fabulously wealthy while most other Gabonese struggled to get by.

However, 2009 initiated a sea change in Gabon. Ali Bongo succeeded his father in an election mired by controversy. His governance—while still subject to corruption scandals—has ushered in a period of great policy change. Cognizant that Gabon's oil reserves were dwindling, Bongo initiated an ambitious program to reinvent Gabon's economy by reinvigorating other sectors, including timber, manganese, palm oil, and rubber, and has recently launched a new initiative to invest in forest preservation. Like Seychelles, Gabon's economy has experienced a remarkable transformation: from per capita GDP of $282 at independence in 1960 to $7,767 in 2019.

At independence, both Seychelles and Gabon were poised for economic disaster. Seychelles's economy was based on the export of a minimally processed crop. The discovery of oil in Gabon and the concentration of power in the hands of the elite made it a prime candidate for a resource curse. Yet both countries diversified their economies and have achieved impressive HDI scores. How?

Identifying a Common Factor of Success

Both Gabon and Seychelles have achieved high levels of economic development, but these countries have little in common. Table 2.2 summarizes Seychelles and Gabon's respective status for each hypothesis and indicates

Table 2.2 Theories as Applied to Gabon and Seychelles

Theory	Seychelles	Gabon	Conclusion
		Structural/Historical	
Geography	Unfavorable	Unfavorable	Theory unsupported; predicts both should be poor
Resource curse	No	Yes	Theory unsupported; predicts Gabon should be poor
Extractive colonialism	Raw material export economy	Raw material export economy	Theory unsupported; predicts both should be poor
Identity of colonizer	British	French	Theory unsupported; predicts Gabon should be poor
World economic system	Dependency	Dependency	Theory unsupported; predicts both should be poor
		Institutional	
Exclusionary economic institutions	Better than average	Worse than average	Theory unsupported; predicts Gabon should be poor
Democratic dividend	Democracy post-1993	Nondemocracy	Theory unsupported; predicts Gabon should be poor
		Policy and Performance	
Directed development	Yes	Yes	Theory supported
Corruption	No	Yes	Theory unsupported; predicts Gabon should be poor
		Sociocultural	
Sociocultural divisions	No	Yes	Theory unsupported; predicts Gabon should be poor

whether the case detail supports the theory. As the table illustrates, only one explanation—government policy of directed development—explains both cases.

Beginning with the structural and historical theories, neither country has a particularly favorable geography—Seychelles is a small island nation with the attendant logistical challenges, while Gabon, straddling the equator, is firmly within the tropical latitude that carries a heavy burden of infectious disease (Callander and Topp 2020). Seychelles has avoided the resource curse—its natural resources include coconuts and tuna, neither of which is high value enough to trigger resource curse behavior. However, Gabon does have oil reserves and is often on the list of African countries most profoundly affected by the resource curse (Jensen and Wantchekon 2004; McFerson 2009). Both countries emerged from colonialism exporting raw materials with limited domestic manufacturing, though colonialism in Gabon was more classically extractive than in Seychelles. While Seychelles's experience was closer to settler colonialism, it gained its independence with an economy oriented around raw material export (coconuts, in its case) (Campling, Confiance, and Purvis 2011). Timber was Gabon's primary export for most of its colonial history until the discovery of oil. However, that discovery was not a boon. The French relied on foreign companies to develop the oil resources, creating an enclave of imported workers, shelter, food, and services, and crude oil was exported rather than being processed domestically (Edwards 2018; Yates 2014). In both cases, colonialism created an economy oriented around the export of unprocessed raw materials with limited domestic manufacturing capacity.

Identity of the colonizer and subsequent incorporation into the world economic system cannot explain their success either. Seychelles has a mixed colonial history, first being established as a French settler colony and later administered indirectly as a British colony, while Gabon's colonial history is French. While this history yields mixed predictions for Seychelles, it indicates that Gabon should fare poorly economically. As described previously, the identity of the colonizer is likely to matter through several pathways, including the nature of colonial rule, the legal system that the country adopts after independence, and the nature of its international economic connections.

Seychelles was established as a French settler colony with a slave-based plantation economy but was later administered indirectly by the British. Therefore, one would expect better economic outcomes as a function of the settler population and limited institutional interruption over time (Acemoglu, Johnson, and Robinson 2002). However, as a function of its mixed colonial history, its legal system combines elements of both French civil law and British common law. Importantly, the elements of the law dealing with contracts and torts are French in origin, indicating the Seychelles should have the economic disadvantage of other former French colonies.[4] Furthermore, Seychelles emerged from colonialism in a position of dependency: its weak economy was oriented around coconut export, and its nascent tourism industry had been funded by the British government and was dominated by British companies that repatriated over half of the profits back to Britain (Campling, Confiance, and Purvis 2011, 17).

By contrast, colonialism in Gabon was highly disruptive, as the French destroyed elements of local culture, regrouped villages, and coerced the population into forced labor (Reed 1987, 288–289). Like most other former French colonies, Gabon adopted the French system of civil law and emerged from colonialism in a dependent position. It adopted the CFA franc, pegging its currency to that of France, sent nearly all its raw material exports to France, and imported most processed goods from France. The French government has propped up the Gabonese elite class, ensuring Omar Bongo's long reign and facilitating massive illicit wealth gains for French and Gabonese politicians and businessmen (Reed 1987; Taylor 2019). It exemplifies *francafrique,* with commenters indicating that the relationship of neocolonial dependency between Gabon and France is "an extreme case, verging on caricature" (quoted in Reed 1987, 283), or "perhaps the most perfect example of neocolonialism on the entire continent" (Rich 2007, ix). Neither of these theories drawing on colonialism can therefore explain why both countries subsequently achieved economic success, as both adopted legal systems based on the French civil law and both emerged from colonization in a position of economic dependency.

The exclusionary economic institutions hypothesis also lacks support. Seychelles's economic institutions are less exclusionary than Gabon's, measured in two ways: historical property rights and recent "ease of doing business." According to Variety of Democracy's (V-Dem's) measure of property rights, upon independence Seychelles dramatically improved its private property rights, indicating a quick break from colonial-era property exclusion (on a scale of 0–1, Seychelles scored 0.45 in 1976, compared to the continent's average of 0.38). Gabon's private property protections were dismal in its postindependence years (0.32 in 1976), reflecting the continuation of an exclusionary economic system even after the end of colonialism. In the contemporary period, Seychelles also performs better in terms of economic access, as measured by the World Bank's Ease of Doing Business Index. In 2019, Seychelles scored 61.7 and Gabon scored 45 compared to the continental average of 51.8 (out of 100). Historically and presently, Seychelles has a less exclusionary economic system than Gabon.

There is little evidence of a democratic dividend. Gabon has never been democratic—in fact, it is often held up as a prototypical example of autocratic governance in West Africa (Jensen and Wantchekon 2004). Seychelles became democratic in 1993, after the reintroduction of multiparty elections ended its single-party socialist state. However, Seychelles's economic growth has its roots in its autocratic period—its economic transformation started *before* the country's transition to democracy, so democracy itself cannot explain its economic turnaround.

Turning to policy, there is support for the hypothesis regarding directed development: both countries have pursued some version of directed development, defined as targeted and temporary government intervention to protect and support specific industries. Seychelles has done so three times, intervening to promote industrial tuna fishing, create an elite tourism industry, and cultivate the country as a site for offshore financial services (Charlier 2016). Gabon has undertaken such policies only recently, in a calculated pivot away from reliance on oil (African Development Bank 2016). This factor is examined further in the case analysis. There is little support for the corruption hypothesis. According to V-Dem's control of corruption index (–2 to 2), Seychelles scores much better than the continental average, while Gabon scores worse (in 2019, Seychelles scored 0.97, Gabon scored –0.94, and the continental average was –0.67). Qualitatively, corruption in Seychelles is small-scale and predictable,[5] while in Gabon it is large-scale and capricious.[6]

Finally, there is little support for the sociocultural division hypothesis. According to Posner's (2004a) measure, Seychelles has no significant ethnolinguistic divisions (score of 0), while Gabon does (score of 0.21).[7] Gabon has about thirty different ethnolinguistic groups, but the primary division is between the Fang and all others, as the ruling Bongo family is Fang, and other groups are resentful of their political dominance. In Gabon, 24.2 percent of respondents to the Afrobarometer (Round 7) reported that they had experienced discrimination based on their ethnicity, among the highest in the sample and on par with countries like Kenya and Uganda with deep-seated ethnic divisions. Based on this analysis, the only hypothesis that is plausible for both countries is the government's pursuit of policies of directed development. The following sections investigate how the government pursued this policy in each country.

Seychelles

In Seychelles, the government pursued directed development three times under two phases: the first under the socialist policies of the Second Republic, and the second under the liberal policies of the Third Republic.

As noted previously, Seychelles gained independence in 1976, and in 1977 experienced a coup that installed a socialist one-party state under the leadership of President France-Albert René. This single-party state, which lasted from 1977 to 1991, was known as Seychelles's Second Republic. Shortly after independence, it became clear that revenue from coconut exports would be sorely inadequate to support the national economy, so the government planned selective investments to promote secondary industry through tuna canning and the service sector through the promotion of tourism and hospitality. Given the islands' small size and remote location, the government made the strategic choice to cultivate luxury tourism in order to limit the number of visitors, maximizing revenue per tourist while minimizing the environmental impact (Campling, Confiance, and Purvis 2011, 21). The government regulated hotel standards and nationalized hotels that did not meet those standards, used the state-run airline to increase direct connections to the island, and created tax incentives and managed contracts between government-run hotels and major international chains to improve visibility in the international luxury market (*ibid.*, 22). These supply-side measures transformed Seychelles from a colonial backwater to a luxury tourism destination (Gabbay 1988).

The second pillar of development during the Second Republic was the tuna industry, which the government grew from a small artisanal sector to a major component of national GDP. To cultivate this sector, the government first established an exclusive economic zone extending 200 miles from Seychelles's border and began to sell licenses to foreign vessels fishing within their zone (Nageon de Lestrang 1988). The government subsequently attracted more industrial-scale fishing through massive infrastructure investments, the creation of a parastatal organization to coordinate dock workers, and provisioning of fishing vessels for international fleets operating in the Indian Ocean. The government further bolstered tuna fishing through service provision and licensing fees for European fishing fleets. The final major advancement was the establishment of a cannery that increased the value of the industry. Through the Lomé Conventions (a trade agreement), it also benefited from a trade preference to the European Economic Community (Campling, Confiance, and Purvis 2011, 24–25).

Tourism and tuna became pillars of the Seychellois economy and contributed to rapid growth, but these government-funded investments were costly, and the government took on a great deal of debt. In 1991, the socialist government agreed to reintroduce multiparty elections, and the country transitioned to democracy with its new constitution in 1993, ushering in the Third Republic. Facing a high debt burden and pressure from international financial institutions, Seychelles began to liberalize its economy and remove supports of these industries (Charlier 2016). During this time, the new government also shifted its attention to the development of the service sector through the establishment of Seychelles as a premier overseas financial center (OFC), modeled on the Cayman Islands but catering to African and Arab money (Robinson 2019, 312). The government initially took steps to attract this kind of investment in 1995 with the passage of the Economic Development Act. This initial move took a "buccaneering tone" and encouraged shady financial dealings, but the transparency required in the post-9/11 world led the government to tighten its regulation of money laundering and other criminal activities through a series of acts in the 2000s.

This sector requires the government to walk a fine line between being a reputable, lucrative OFC and becoming a haven for white-collar criminals, requiring careful balance in policy. The possible reputational damage from being perceived as too lax became clear when Seychelles was named the world's fourth biggest tax haven in the 2015 Panama Papers. These reputational risks resurfaced during another episode in 2020, when a Bitcoin trading platform accused of market manipulation taunted American regulators, responding to a request for documents with a meme of one of the company's founders and the text "incorporated in the Seychelles, come at me bro."[8] Nevertheless, this sector is now profitable and growing, providing a third pillar to the Seychellois economy. All three owe their success to government intervention directing and nurturing their growth, and particularly the actions of René, who directed economic planning by naming himself minister of tourism and heading the Seychelles Marketing Board, which oversaw or absorbed most of the country's parastatal organizations (Campling, Confiance, and Purvis 2011, 22–28).

Gabon

Gabon's efforts at directed development concern its pivot from its reliance on oil exports. As noted previously, oil revenue has driven Gabon's economic growth until recently, earning the country a reputation as a resource-cursed state. However, things began to change in 2009, when long-serving president Omar Bongo stepped down and was succeeded by his son, Ali Bongo. Despite being raised in the privileged first family made wealthy by oil, Ali recognized that the country's oil reserves were finite and orchestrated a pivot. In 2009, Bongo initiated the Emerging Gabon plan to increase the revenue potential of Gabon's other resources, including timber, manganese, palm oil, and rubber.[9] Eager to escape the trap of exporting only raw materials, the government banned the export of unprocessed timber to necessitate a local industrialized timber sector, increased industrialization of palm oil and manganese processing to add value to those exports, and established a Special Economic Zone to encourage export-oriented development based on these products. These steps have drawn foreign direct investment from several sources, including the Singaporean Olam Group.[10] While Gabon's oil production is in decline—like other countries in the region—it has been uniquely proactive about directing the shape of economic growth. Market researchers indicate that Gabon has invested significantly more in health and education than its regional neighbors, making it a relatively attractive target for investment in the region.[11] While firms still need to import workers to fill many skilled positions, widespread literacy and "regionally good" health care make the local labor force more capable than in some neighboring countries.

In addition to nurturing these new industrial sectors within Gabon, the government has found a way to raise revenue by protecting rather than exploiting its resources. In 2016, the country implemented a new plan to reduce deforestation through the management of the timber sector and thereby secured payment from the United Nations' Central African Forest Initiative, which provides financial incentives for countries to preserve their forests to reduce global carbon emissions.[12] In the long run, Gabon plans to use its forests to bolster ecotourism and generate carbon credits that companies can buy.[13] While these economic initiatives are new, they have already proven valuable, insulating Gabon's economic performance from the recent volatility of global oil prices.

In both countries, directed development has shaped the direction of economic development: since independence in Seychelles, and over the last decade in Gabon. The counterfactual is that, without such concerted efforts by the government, economic production in Seychelles would have remained oriented around agricultural exports with limited returns, and in Gabon around oil with high volatility (and an expiration date as reserves diminish). Instead, the government in each country made strategic decisions about how to direct state resources into other industries, ultimately leading to greater economic growth and higher levels of human development.

However, the question of where "good policies" come from remains. In both countries, the president was predominantly responsible for their design and implementation. What motivated or enabled such policies? While there are distinct differences in the nature of the economic policies presidents René and Bongo put in place, there are some commonalities in conditions that each leader faced that may explain why they pursued these forms of directed development.

First, both leaders came to power under dubious circumstances, had a precarious hold on power, and faced coup threats. In Seychelles,

René came to power through a coup that ousted the country's first president less than a year after independence. While René's socialist party had the support of nearly half the population prior to the coup, the coup and René's subsequent declaration of a one-party state damaged the government's legitimacy, spurring failed counter coups and antigovernment demonstrations for years (Campling, Confiance, and Purvis 2011, 18–19). In Gabon, the elder Bongo's death triggered a succession crisis marked by the fierce rivalry between Ali and his sister Pascaline.[14] While Ali won the candidacy, it was rumored that he lacked the full backing of his father's political party, and he won the election with only 41.7 percent of the vote. This political insecurity came into sharp focus as he had to blatantly manipulate the 2016 elections to win again, and he then faced a coup attempt in 2019.[15]

As insecure autocrats, both René and Bongo needed to carefully cultivate support to ensure regime survival. René's actions are consistent with an autocrat attempting to make it impossible for an opposition group to hold power: declaring a single-party state, starting a military, and investing full-scale in the popular economic policies he had originally campaigned on, which included expanding local employment opportunities for Seychellois and providing generous social services. In short, his economic approach during the Second Republic was a model of mass patronage (using government resources to provide jobs and welfare to most of the population). While this approach sent the country deep into debt, it successfully bolstered his popularity and political legitimacy (Thompson, Wissink, and Siwisa 2019, 93). While René focused on blocking opposition and cultivating mass support, Bongo's actions are consistent with a need to reorganize an elite patronage network. The elder Bongo's political survival had hinged on using the country's oil money to buy off and otherwise coopt the political opposition (Reed 1987). However, Ali Bongo ascended to the presidency in a much more precarious position at a time when oil production in Gabon was likely to decline quickly. His political survival was contingent on maintaining a patronage network that was funded by a finite and rapidly diminishing resource. For Bongo, diversifying the economy could therefore be helpful in three ways: First, establishing new sources of revenue for the government would extend the time horizon for his ability to maintain elite support. Second, diversifying the source of government revenue would enable him to cultivate a more diverse base of support outside the *francafrique* network of companies and elites oriented around oil. Finally, creating a more complex economic ecosystem could make state capture more challenging, and thus make a coup less lucrative (Dunning 2008).

Finally, both countries shared the ability to attract foreign direct investment to fund directed development, though for different reasons. In Seychelles, René leveraged his country's nonaligned status during the Cold War to extract foreign direct investment (FDI) and grants from a wide variety of wealthy countries, which ultimately kept the economy afloat during its period of intensive spending and helped prevent economic collapse in the face of some of René's unsuccessful parastatal projects (Campling, Confiance, and Purvis 2011, 26). Seychelles's small size also ensured that smaller investments could be highly effective. In Gabon, Bongo has attracted attention for his explicit efforts to diversify the sources of FDI in addition to the nature of economic production, courting and securing loans from Singapore, India, Turkey, and others.[16] This strategy has also involved diversifying Gabon's trade partners to reduce its reliance on France.[17] Gabon's rich natural resources, rather than geopolitics, have enabled it to attract this investment.

In sum, Seychelles and Gabon both achieved economic growth through policies of directed development, implemented by insecure autocrats under pressure to cultivate political support, funded by their ability to attract FDI. For both, these economic policies grew the economy but also bolstered their political support by expanding access to state resources (to the masses in the case of Seychelles, and to a broader group of elites in the case of Gabon).

Most Similar Case Analyses

This most-different case analysis has identified government policy of directed development as the core feature that Seychelles and Gabon share. If this is the definitive factor, then countries similar to Gabon and Seychelles with less economic success should lack this feature. This section presents two brief most-similar case analyses to determine whether this is the case, comparing Seychelles to Sao Tome and Principe (STP) and Gabon to Equatorial Guinea.

Seychelles and Sao Tome and Principe

Like Seychelles, STP is a small island nation off Africa's coast, though it is west rather than east. It was also uninhabited when it was colonized (by the Portuguese) and had a slave-based plantation economy. Like Seychelles, STP gained independence late (in 1975), established a socialist single-party state, and democratized as part of the third wave (in 1991). However, while Seychelles negotiated independence gradually from the British, STP's independence was hard-won from the Portuguese, who were reluctant to relinquish their colonies. At independence, STP inherited an economy oriented around the export of a single agricultural good, in this case cocoa. However, despite their similar prospects, STP's economy all but collapsed by the mid-1980s when international financial institutions enforced economic restructuring to address its debt. The economy continued to stagnate until the discovery of offshore oil reserves in the late 1990s, from which STP began to collect tenuous rents in 2003 (Weszkalnys 2008). While GDP per capita has slowly grown since then, it has not translated to broader economic development—the World Bank estimates two-thirds of the population lives below the poverty line. As of 2016, external debt was more than 74 percent of national GDP (Teixeira and Nascimento 2019, 360). Reflecting this economic weakness, STP performs much worse than Seychelles on the varied components of the HDI. In 2019 in Seychelles, life expectancy was 73.4 years, the average person spent 10 years in school, and gross national income (GNI) per capita was nearly $27,000. In STP, life expectancy was 70.4 years, the average person spent only 6.4 years in school, and GNI per capita was only $3,952.

STP eschewed directed development for a fully communist approach to economic policy postindependence, nationalizing the cocoa sector along with the rest of the economy. Seibert's (2006) detailed political history helps to illuminate why STP took this path. The country's first president, Manuel Pinto da Costa, gained his position as the head of the communist-associated militant organization agitating for independence against Portugal. While he won the presidency with widespread popular support, this support quickly waned as his party split into factions engaged in power struggles, and the population became increasingly agitated about the declining economic conditions. In some ways, Pinto da Costa faced a similar degree of insecurity as René did, experiencing numerous coup attempts himself. However, to garner the favor of the population, he took the radical move of expropriating all the land under cocoa cultivation from private (often Portuguese) ownership, nationalizing all cocoa production, and distributing the land to be managed by Santomeans of the more privileged class. This move—intended to bolster his reputation as a liberator—was economically disastrous, as neither the new plantation managers nor the agricultural ministry now responsible for running the plantations had experience with agricultural production. As a result, cocoa—which comprised 95 percent of STP's exports at the time of independence—collapsed. Despite this magnificent failure, the government proceeded to nationalize the rest of the economy in 1979. In short, the nationalized economy became a way for Pinto da Costa and his party to employ party loyalists and retain their support.

Like René, Pinto da Costa placed himself as a central economic decisionmaker. However, his catastrophic policy choices represent a different political logic. Pinto da Costa used economic policies to buy the loyalty of political elites rather than the broader population, who were systematically shut out of the political networks of goods and services (Seibert 2006, 172). These elites plundered the economy rather than develop it (Frynas, Wood, and Soares de Oliveira 2003). Despite gaining access to large sums of international assistance, government officials made little effort to diversify the economy, instead lining their pockets with foreign aid (Frynas, Wood, and Soares de Oliveira 2003, 56–57). STP's state debt mounted and its utter dependence on aid deepened, but unlike in Seychelles, there were no functioning portions of the economy to pull the country through, leaving it subject to strict economic restrictions led by the International Monetary Fund. STP appeared to be completely economically unviable at the time that oil was discovered offshore, buoying hope of economic recovery (Weszkalnys 2008). However, botched negotiations around oil rents and ongoing political self-dealing have left most Santomeans no better off—like the foreign aid, the oil rents appear to be primarily distributed among the islands' elites and foreign corporations.

In similar positions, both René and Pinto da Costa used state resources to cultivate political support, but in different ways: René pursued mass patronage through state-led directed development, while Pinto da Costa favored elite patronage, rewarding party loyalty through fully communist policies. These different choices relate to the ideology of the movements each led prior to independence. In Seychelles, independence from the British was negotiated and the independence movement was politically moderate. René was thus well-placed to take advantage of nonalignment in the Cold War context, pursuing assistance from both the Soviet Union and the West and crafting middle-of-the-road policies that leveraged state resources without being fully communist. In STP, independence was hard-won from the Portuguese, and the independence movement was by necessity more militant. Its ideology thus reflected a total rejection of imperialism and embrace of communism, leading Pinto da Costa to pursue more revolutionary policies that would reward party loyalists. The different contexts of these independence movements thus led to different political logics shaped by international politics, resulting in different economic policy choices.

Gabon and Equatorial Guinea

Gabon and Equatorial Guinea are also similar: neighboring countries, they share tropical geography and an economy oriented around oil. Both are former colonies that inherited exclusionary economic institutions from their former colonizers (Campos 2003). Both shared early indicators of a resource curse: after the discovery of oil, both experienced rapid increases in GDP alongside sluggish indicators for education and health, indicating that the oil revenue was concentrated in the pockets of the elite. Furthermore, being tied to a single commodity, economic performance was vulnerable to price swings. However, while Gabon recently pivoted to a policy of directed development, Equatorial Guinea has maintained a singular reliance on oil. This divergence is apparent in the components of the HDI for each country. As a result of greater investment in the local labor force, life expectancy in Gabon has risen to 66.5 years, with the average person attaining 8.7 years of schooling. By contrast, in Equatorial Guinea, life expectancy is only 58.7 years, with the average person in school for 5.9 years. According to data from the World Bank, life expectancy in Gabon began increasing at a much faster rate than in Equatorial Guinea around 2008–2009—the same time the government began to pivot its economic policies. According to World Bank measures, GNI per capita (PPP) has increased steadily in Gabon since the mid-2000s, while in Equatorial Guinea—lacking economic diversification—it has been subject to massive annual swings linked to the price of oil. These data suggest that while Gabon and Equatorial Guinea shared similar economic fundamentals in the early 2000s, their fates have since diverged.

Like Gabon, Equatorial Guinea emerged from colonialism with an economy dominated by primary sector exports and quickly adopted an authoritarian political system. At its independence in 1968, well before the discovery of oil, Equatorial Guinea's primary export was cocoa. However, its first dictator, President Francisco Macias Nguema, pursued brutal and disastrous Marxist policies that drove out foreign landowners and contract workers, nationalized all plantations, and forced citizens to work on the state-run plantations (Toto Same 2008, 4–5; Daniele 2011). During this time, the economy contracted by an astounding 40 percent, and about a third of the population left the country or were killed by the regime (Daniele 2011, 562). Nguema was overthrown in a military coup led by his nephew in 1979. The new government, led by President Obiang, was similarly dictatorial but pursued some tepid economic reforms. Despite these reforms, the cocoa industry never recovered (Frynas 2004). Obiang is still in power at the time of writing.

Equatorial Guinea's decimated economy limped along until the discovery of oil in 1992. Oil revenue led the country's GDP to skyrocket, but as Frynas describes, "the staggering increases on paper stand for little in the real world," as the wealth is pocketed by a tiny elite and the capital-intensive industry employs few local people. The oil industry does not stimulate other elements of the local economy either, as employees live in gated compounds that import everything from food to prefabricated buildings (Frynas 2004, 540). By some estimates, the oil boom made quality of life in Equatorial Guinea worse, as Dutch disease caused inflation and altered the exchange rate, making goods in the country more expensive and exports less competitive (Frynas 2004, 542). As in Gabon, the county is likely to exhaust its oil reserves soon. However, the government has made no effort to revitalize other sectors of the economy to account for the transition away from oil.[18]

Why was Gabon able to pivot away from oil, while Equatorial Guinea was not? Two key differences stand out. First, Nguema's dictatorship was far more brutal and economically devastating than anything that Gabon has experienced in its postindependence trajectory, decimating the viability of non-oil sectors (Wood 2004, 553). Second—importantly—the reforms in Gabon started when Ali Bongo succeeded his father and found himself in a politically precarious position. In Equatorial Guinea, Obiang has been president since Nguema's ouster, making him Africa's longest serving leader to date. He has been able to maintain regime survival through the targeted distribution of oil rents to coopt opposition, maintaining an extreme degree of internal regime cohesion (Sa and Sanches 2021; Wood 2004). Oil and other hydrocarbon production is declining, and economic forecasters expect it to run out around 2023–2024.[19] While one might expect this production outlook would spur Obiang to diversify the sources of revenue he can use to maintain political loyalty, there are rumors that his health is failing and he is soon planning to step down (Sa and Sanches 2021, 97). Thus, Obiang's leadership time horizon may be as limited as the country's economic prospects, giving him few incentives to make major changes.

Despite being similarly sized, similarly resourced, and similarly marked by corruption and dynastic politics, the economies of Gabon and Equatorial Guinea are strikingly different. Both countries have suffered at the hands of a ruling class that is quick to pocket national revenues, but in Gabon President Bongo's political precarity may have spurred economic diversification through a policy of directed development, while in Equatorial Guinea, President Obiang's entrenchment and short time horizon may have inhibited the impulse for this policy approach.

While all four countries were functionally dictatorships at the time they crafted their various economic policies, René and Bongo faced different political pressures than did Pinto da Costa and Obiang. Needing to shore up the domestic legitimacy of their newly independent governments, René opted to court the broader population through mass patronage in the form of parastatal organizations offering employment and generous public services, while Pinto da Costa instead cultivated a narrow group of loyalists through elite patronage. These different approaches reflected different party ideologies related to the different contexts of independence in the two countries. Similarly, dwindling oil revenues have worsened Ali Bongo's political precariousness, necessitating economic diversification to expand his network. Meanwhile, Obiang, nearing the natural end of his tenure, has less incentive to do the same despite his country's dwindling oil reserves. René and Bongo both had clear political incentives to use the power of the state to bolster their popularity by expanding economic access, and in both cases, these policies took the form of directed development. Pinto da Costa and Obiang instead opted to maintain economic access for a narrow group of elites, ultimately undermining long-term economic growth.

Conclusion

At independence, many countries in Africa faced significant obstacles to achieving economic development. Yet some have been able to achieve high levels of human development despite this inauspicious start. The case comparisons included in this chapter suggest that governments' policy choices have been a key factor distinguishing the countries that have flourished from those that have floundered. Importantly, those policy choices do not exist in a vacuum, but in all cases discussed in this chapter have a clear relationship to the logic of political survival each leader faced. Despite starting with different resources, backgrounds, and timing, Seychelles and Gabon have used policy to nudge investment toward the "next" sector. They both also had political incentives to diversify and distribute government revenue. Neither approach has been perfect, but they have both consistently outperformed their neighbors and other similarly situated countries in both GDP per capita and quality-of-life indicators.

Of all the hypotheses I consider in this chapter, the policy of directed development leading to economic growth was the only one that found evidence in all four cases. Directed development was evident in three distinct campaigns over the course of Seychelles's postindependence history and is recently observable in Gabon's pivot from oil. While other hypotheses found support in one or two cases—for example, Seychelles lacks sociocultural divisions and large-scale corruption—these hypotheses fell short once applied to other cases. The secondary most-similar comparison provides additional support for good policy as the common denominator between Seychelles and Gabon. The postindependence regimes in STP and Equatorial Guinea were faced with similar economic prospects as their counterparts, yet they pursued tragically terrible policies that crushed local industry; facilitated widespread and damaging corruption, and gutted the institutions that may have been able to reinvest what few resources they had into their countries. In both STP and Equatorial Guinea, the governments claimed ownership over the agricultural sector and proceeded to mismanage it to the point of financial ruin. This comparison offers a cautionary note about the difference between directed development—using government resources to nudge and support promising sectors—and a centrally planned economy, in which the government takes control of a sector in its entirety. Importantly, presidents in both STP and Equatorial Guinea had incentives to cultivate narrow elite patronage networks, while the incentives for presidents in Seychelles and Gabon have favored expanding access.

Seychelles and Gabon are not the only African countries to have achieved high levels of human development as measured by the HDI. Mauritius, South Africa, and Botswana also hold this distinction, and Cabo Verde and Namibia are not far from achieving it. These cases offer the potential for further investigation of directed development policy as a driver for development. Furthermore, examining the success of these countries may enable a deeper examination of the conditions that facilitate some countries to design effective policies while leading others to maintain narrow patronage networks.

Poverty is a persistent problem across the African continent, made more insulting by proclamations that extreme poverty is on the decline everywhere else. It is hard to overstate how essential it is to improve shared economic growth in poor countries, as improving quality of life can literally be an issue of life or death. Yet, for most African countries, it has proved elusive. Centuries of slave trade followed by decades of colonialism set the stage for dictatorship and civil war, and while many African countries house valuable raw materials, they lack the leverage to negotiate good terms of trade or the capital to promote more domestic value-added industry. As a continent, the odds are stacked against African development, a reality that is borne out in stubbornly high rates of poverty. While it is essential to acknowledge these historical challenges, it is also essential not to accept that history is destiny. The cases of Seychelles and Gabon illustrate that, despite these odds, governments can craft policies that yield good economic outcomes. However, it is also important to attend to the political incentives that leaders face to do so.

To say that African governments have the agency to craft prudent policies by no means detracts from the challenging economic circumstances that most of these countries face. There is nothing a contemporary government can do about a history of economic exploitation or a lack of leverage in negotiating terms of trade. The economic hardships that most African countries face are directly related to unchangeable historical factors and international pressures beyond their control. However, in the face of such challenging circumstances, it would be a mistake to dismiss African governments as passive bearers of shoddy luck. The experiences of Seychelles and Gabon indicate that policies make a difference under adverse circumstances. It remains to be seen if the economic reforms each country has undertaken in recent years will be enough to maintain their economic trajectories. At the time of writing, the Covid-19 pandemic continues to generate global economic uncertainty, and it is unclear how well precarious economies will weather this storm. Nevertheless, at this moment, both countries stand out for the policies they have implemented.

Finally, neither country's record is spotless. Some of Seychelles's government-run sectors failed miserably, its redistributive socialist policies were unsustainably expensive, government services continue to be marked by clientelism, and it has suffered reputational damage from some of its attempts to establish financial services. In Gabon, the scale of corruption would be comical if it were not tragic. It is painful to imagine how much better off the country might be had the extended Bongo family not purloined so much of the country's wealth. If the elder Bongo had taken steps toward diversifying the economy earlier, or invested more in social services, the country would be in a much better position today. While Gabon's health and education indicators are much stronger than those of its neighbors, these systems still have a long way to go. The World Bank estimates that about one-third of Gabonese live below the poverty line (which, while better than the continental average, is certainly not great).[20] I highlight these challenges not to cast aspersions on these countries but to underscore that governments do not need to be perfect to implement helpful policy. Directed development is not unattainable, the result of technocratic expertise and an irreproachable civil service. It requires the committed implementation of smart economic policy, the creativity to identify and support emerging sectors, and investment back into the health and education of the population.

Notes

1. Average income measured as GNI per capita (PPP), health as life expectancy in years, and education as years of school.

2. In practice, there was less difference between indirect and direct rule than in theory (Crowder 1982). However, there is mounting evidence that the different conceptual approaches taken by the French and the British produced demonstrably different outcomes in terms of maintenance of precolonial political structures and the nature of the legal system.

3. Data from the World Bank, measured in constant 2020 USD. Like many countries, Seychelles's economy suffered in 2020 due to the Covid-19 pandemic, particularly because of decreased tourism, but it is projected to recover.

4. "Seychelles Legal System," Bar Association of Seychelles, accessed 2022, July 1. https://sites.google.com/site/barassociationsc/seychelles-legal-system

5. Thompson et al. (2019) note Seychelles's state-led development is marked by clientelism and patronage, but these relationships pervade regular citizen interactions with the state, making it a low-level, systematic expectation of state provision rather than large-scale, capricious corruption. Robinson (2019, 311) describes it as "illegal favours" and the need to look the other way when officials encounter "kinfolk doing the wrong thing."

6. See, for example, Al Jazeera. 2019, November 29. "Eight Detained in Gabon Anti-corruption Crackdown"; Reuters. 2019, November 30. "Gabon's President's Spokesman Detained in Anti-corruption Crackdown"; France24. 2019, July 7. "Gabon's Timber Industry Reeling After Corruption Scandal."

7. According to Posner (2004), Seychelles scores 0 on ethnolinguistic fractionalization, while Gabon scores 0.21. Seychelles's score is 0 because the islands were uninhabited when originally colonized by the French, who then brought labor in the form of slaves. Creole emerged as the dominant language over time, and while there are class distinctions, these distinctions do not reflect sociocultural divisions (Houbert 2002).

8. Zephyr Net. 2020, June 10. "BitMEX Taunts Plaintiff: Incorporated in Seychelles, Come at Me Bro," Zephyr Net.

9. Fitch Solutions. "Q1 2020 Report: Congo-Brazzaville & Gabon Country Risk Report."

10. *African Business*. 2017, October 18. "Olam's Port Ambitions." *African Business*. https://african.business/2017/10/energy-resources/olams-port-ambitions/

11. BMI Research. "Q1 2018 Gabon Operational Risk Report," p. 5. *BMI Research*.

12. BBC. 2021, June 22. "Gabon Is First African Country Paid to Protect Rainforest." *BBC*. https://www.bbc.com/news/world-africa-57567829

13. Squazzin, Antony and Akshat Rathi. 2021, June 23. "Gabon Pitches New Funding Model to Protect Africa's Amazon." *Bloomberg*. https://www.bloomberg.com/news/articles/2021-06-23/gabon-pitches-new-funding-model-to-protect-africa-s-amazon

14. BBC. 2009, July 16. "Bongo Son Set for Gabon Candidacy." http://news.bbc.co.uk/2/hi/africa/8153318.stm

15. MacLean, Ruth. 2016, August 31. "Violence Erupts After Gabon Election as Incumbent Ali Bongo Named Victor." *The Guardian*. https://www.theguardian.com/world/2016/aug/31/gabon-election-results-disputed-incumbent-ali-bongo-victor-jean-ping

16. Botsford, Polly. n.d. "New Start Leads to Exciting Times for Gabon." *FDI Intelligence.* https://www.fdiintelligence.com/content/feature/new-start-leads-to-exciting-times-for-gabon-29017

17. The Observatory of Economic Complexity (oec.world) now estimates that China is Gabon's largest trading partner, and trade flows between Gabon and countries in Asia and the Middle East now rival its French and other European flows.

18. Fitch Solutions. 2019. "Equatorial Guinea Country Risk Report."

19. Fitch Solutions, 2019. "Equatorial Guinea Country Risk Report."

20. World Bank. 2019. "Public Expenditure Review: Gabon." https://openknowledge.worldbank.org/handle/10986/31785

3

Achieving Good Governance

Living in a country with good governance is a fundamental desire for most people. This concept has been promoted by myriad actors, from civil society groups to donor governments to international organizations. However, good governance is hard to define, taking on different meanings for different people. Unlike democracy, which focuses on the process through which a government is formed, good governance focuses on outcomes: how government performs. The term is so capacious that by 2002 the United Nations' *World Development Report* included 116 characteristics of good governance (Grindle 2004, 527–528). In addition to being broad, it is also subjective and can therefore take on contradictory meanings. For example, some might consider a good government to be one that protects equality by ensuring that all citizens are treated in the same way. However, in a society where certain groups have been historically marginalized, others might consider a good government to be one that promotes equity: giving disadvantaged groups additional assistance to achieve equal outcomes. Over time, the concept of good governance became a "hitching post" for all the good things one might hope to see in a country (Grindle 2017, 17).

While the concept of good governance has taken on multiple meanings, the World Bank has developed a governance indicator that captures its core features. It includes six composite indicators of good governance: voice and accountability (measured by freedom of expression, media, and participation in selecting government); political stability (absence of political violence, coup threats, and terrorism); government effectiveness (quality and implementation of policies); regulatory quality (formulation and implementation of regulations for sound economic function); rule of law (contract enforcement, independent function of courts and the police system, and crime rates); and control of corruption (use of public power for private gain, elite capture of the state to pursue private interests). To score each country, the creators of this dataset use surveys and interviews with country experts recruited from international organizations, nongovernmental organizations, and the private sector. The final score is the result of their perceptions and experiences.[1]

These indicators each capture a different component of governance, but they are closely correlated. African countries score poorly across the board. Most score in the bottom half globally in each category, with many in the bottom quartile. However, there is a lot of variation in performance, overall as well as within indicators. As Figure 3.1 illustrates, two countries that stand out for their excellent performance are Mauritius and Botswana.

Relative to other African countries, Mauritius performs particularly well in terms of political stability, government effectiveness, and regulatory quality, while Botswana excels on political stability and control of corruption. Other countries with strong scores include Cape Verde, Seychelles, Namibia, South Africa, Ghana, and Rwanda, but while these countries tend to perform well in one or two areas, Botswana and Mauritius have by far the strongest scores overall. Averaging the six indicators, which run from –2.5 (worst) to 2.5 (best), Mauritius scores 0.76 and Botswana scores 0.58, against a regional mean of –0.68.

The primary analysis of this chapter is a most-different case comparison of Mauritius and Botswana, with a focus on understanding how these very different countries achieved such strong governance. Most-similar case comparisons then compare Mauritius to Comoros and Botswana to Uganda. Comoros (–0.88) and Uganda (–0.59) each score near the middle of Africa's range of governance—they are far from the worst performers. However, they share important similarities with Mauritius and Botswana that make comparison useful. Additional detail on case selection is available in the appendix.

Theoretical Approaches to Explaining Good Governance

Numerous theories address why some countries have better governance than others. In this chapter I consider eight theories grouped in three categories: institutions, demography, and agency.

Institutions

Some of the most prominent explanations for good governance focus on the nature of a country's institutions. In this context, *institutions* refer to the collection of laws and rules that shape how the government functions:

Figure 3.1 African Countries as Scored by the World Governance Indicator, 2019

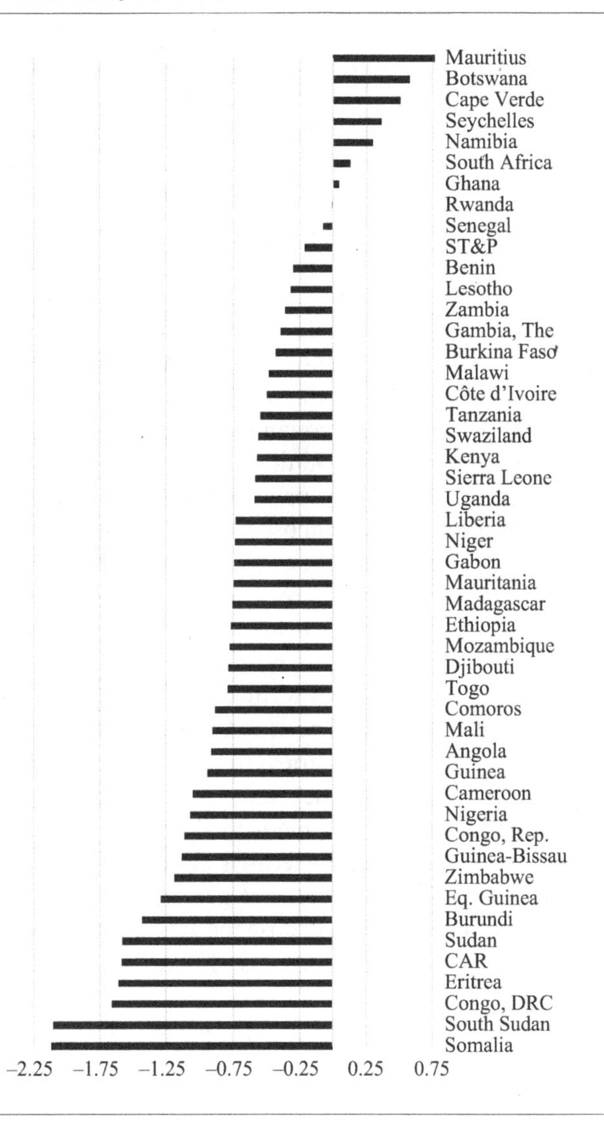

the constitution, the organization of the executive branch, the legislature, and the judiciary. The first set of theories has to do with the origin of a government's institutions, while the second has to do with the way revenue shapes them. Both approaches take a long historical view of institutional development over time.

The first set of theories examines whether institutions are endogenous (originating from within) or exogenous (originating externally). Endogenous institutions develop organically in response to the specific social, cultural, and economic make-up of a society. Daron Acemoglu and James Robinson's (2012) description of institutional development in the thirteen American colonies captures this process. In their retelling, colonial settlers found themselves in a challenging position with small populations to perform the work necessary for survival. Early leaders in the colonies found that if they excluded the settlers from local decisionmaking, the settlers could easily move to a different colony. To maintain a local population, these local leaders needed to form egalitarian institutions in which everyone (which at the time meant landowning white men) had a say in local affairs. These types of egalitarian institutions, which formed in response to local conditions, shaped American political culture and later formed the basis of American democracy. Importantly, endogenous institutions emerge and evolve in response to local conditions; they both shape and reflect local political culture and therefore are appropriate for a certain time and place.

Exogenous institutions are imposed by or adopted from an external source. In the African case, this source was almost always a country's former colonizer. At independence, most countries rapidly adopted constitutions that closely resembled those of their former colonizers: Westminster-style parliamentary democracy in the case of former British colonies, and semi-presidential systems in the case of former French colonies (Young 2012, 115).[2] These institutions—endogenous to Great Britain and France—were exogenous to their new host countries. In most cases, these constitutions did not last long, but Africa's independent institutions continued to borrow features from European and American electoral regimes. While some new governments were able to make their governance more endogenous by incorporating features of precolonial governing institutions, in other countries that proved impossible because those precolonial institutions had been warped or destroyed by the process of colonization (Chanock 1985; Mamdani 1996).

One theory advanced by political scientists is that endogenous institutions are more likely to yield good governance (Englebert 2002). Because they emerged in response to local problems and are thus suited to local conditions, they are more likely to be locally appropriate. While endogenous institutions are not always good and exogenous institutions are not always bad, the theory holds that endogenous institutions are more likely to be effective because they should reinforce locally legitimate norms of governance rather than working against the grain (Kelsall 2008). At the least, endogenous institutions are more likely to be aligned with informal norms of political culture, generating greater institutional stability (Helmke and Levitsky 2004).

A second institutional approach examines how a country's economic structure influences the accountability of political institutions. This approach focuses on how a government earns its revenue: through rents or taxes. All governments need revenue to function, but they may have different options for how to collect that money. Rents, on the one hand, are the revenue that accrues directly to the government from land or resources that the government itself owns, such as by leasing government-owned land or from government-run industry (like oil extraction). Taxes, on the other hand, are the portion of the earnings that individuals or businesses make that must be paid to the government. Whether a government gets its revenue primarily from rents or taxes has implications for whether it develops avenues for political accountability.

Taxes are generally unpopular—people do not enjoy giving a portion of their earnings to the government. While tax payment can legally be enforced, in practice it requires voluntary compliance: it is prohibitively expensive to audit all taxpayers. Voluntary compliance is more likely when the population trusts that the government will use tax money to produce public goods—like roads and schools—and distribute them fairly (Ali, Fjeldstad, and Sjursen 2014). This relationship is a fiscal contract: the population voluntarily gives the government some of its money and expects that the government will do the right thing with it (Levi 2020). People typically do not trust governments blindly, however. They often demand some kind of oversight or accountability to ensure that the government is not misusing those resources (Levi 2020; North and Weingast 1989). Therefore, when the government must rely on taxes for its revenue, it must also design institutions that enable some kind of transparency, oversight, and accountability—all components of good governance. Accountability in the modern world generally means that citizens have regular opportunities to voice their opinions and to remove officials from office if they are poor stewards of public revenue.

Alternatively, when a government can rely on rents, it has no need to design such institutions: it does not rely on the population's voluntary compliance for its revenue (Ross 2015). Such rents, often from high-value resources controlled by the government, generate the political side of the resource curse described in Chapter 2. The resource curse can influence the quality of governance in two ways. First, by generating nontax revenue, it can insulate authoritarian leaders from the demands of the population and help them remain in office longer (Brautigam, Fjeldstad, and Moore 2008; Ombga 2009). Second, because it makes governing a country potentially quite lucrative, resource rents can lead to a great deal of corruption (Vicente 2010). However, as Dunning (2008) points out, the authoritarian impact of resource rents can sometimes be dampened if it means that a democratic government can avoid taxing the private wealth of elites. In that way, resources might be a governance curse when they are discovered in an authoritarian country, but a boon when they are discovered in a democracy. The implication is that governments that rely on rents for revenue *before* they develop accountability-oriented institutions associated with good governance are unlikely to ever develop them, while governments that rely on taxes for their revenue will.

Demography and Social Characteristics

Other theories focus on the internal characteristics of a society, considering how these factors might influence government performance. One set of theories examines the impact of sociocultural divisions, and another focuses on the concept of social capital. Both approaches assume that good governance requires people within a society to work together to solve basic problems of resource distribution and to hold leaders accountable for their performance. Good governance can therefore break down if too many people free-ride or cheat by not contributing taxes, not paying attention to political decisions, or not taking action to hold leaders accountable. It can also break down if society is too deeply divided to agree upon how resources should be distributed.

Beginning with the latter, many researchers have pointed out that governance is more challenging in diverse societies. Typically, the forms of diversity they highlight include race, ethnicity, religion, and language, all of which might overlap and confer some degree of cultural diversity within a country. In Africa, many analyses focus on ethnic diversity as the most politically salient (Adida et al. 2017; Elischer 2013; Gadjanova 2017; Posner 2004a). Diversity may undermine governance for several reasons: people from different groups might prioritize different things, they might have trouble communicating well with each other, and distrust between communities might undermine cooperation (Habyarimana et al. 2007). There are plenty of examples of countries in which ethnic or other cultural identities form important political divisions, rendering politics a (sometimes violent) competition between groups rather than a venue for agreeing upon common goals (Klaus and Mitchell 2015; Thaut Vinson 2020). However, diversity does not inevitably lead to such intractable political problems. It is important to consider how the condition of diversity interacts with other factors listed here—specifically, institutions and leadership—to understand how they may ameliorate or exacerbate the challenges associated with diversity

(Horowitz 1993; Horowitz and Klaus 2020; Lijphart 2004; Posner 2004a; Reilly 2001).

Others subscribe to the idea that social capital is key for achieving good governance. Gabriel Almond and Sidney Verba (1963) developed the idea that local civic culture could influence citizens' political behavior and their ability to hold government accountable. Robert Putnam (1993) applied this idea in his study of Italy, in which he observed that localities in the north had more effective governments than those of the south. He postulated that the difference was in the social capital that these communities enjoyed. Social capital—defined as social trust and expectations of reciprocity—is built through repeated interactions with friends, neighborhoods, and civic associations. These interactions generate a collective identity, improve information flows, and—importantly—lead to more successful collective endeavors. Putnam argued that governance is better in northern Italy because communities with more social capital were able to organize themselves to hold local government officials accountable for their performance. In southern Italy, which was more atomistic, people who were dissatisfied with government performance lacked the social resources to organize their communities, so local governments became increasingly inept and corrupt. Therefore, we would expect that countries with higher levels of social capital have better governance.

Another version of this theory highlights the importance of a strong civil society for holding governments accountable. Civil society refers to a specific form of organizing around issues of public interest. A strong, autonomous civil society can draw attention to important issues and put public pressure on governments to address them, improving governance (Bernhard, Fernandes, and Branco 2017). Many commentators have lamented that civil society across Africa is weak, causing problems for governance (Gyimah-Boadi 1996). Others have noted that predatory governments can capture civil society, leading it to entrench rather than ameliorate poor governance (Fatton 1995). However, other studies indicate that strong civil society movements do result in governance improvements, such as the role of women's civil society organizations in improving women's representation in legislatures (Tripp 2016). Therefore, we should expect that civil society can improve governance when it is strong and independent of the government.

Agency

The last theoretical category focuses on individual agency: perhaps countries with better governance just have particularly good leaders. As Nicholas Cheeseman (2015, 5) notes, facing pressures to liberalize their governments,

"African leaders demonstrated very different capacities to put the national interest first." While Cheeseman focuses on structural characteristics that influenced leaders' choices, he also identifies variation in the quality of leadership and proclivities for self-serving behavior. In the African context, one feature of leadership appears to be particularly important for governance: the leader's choice of a political strategy based on unity rather than courting an ethnic or regional base. For example, Tanzania's first president, Julius Nyerere, overcame the challenges of ethnic diversity by selecting Swahili, a neutral trading language, to be the country's national language and orchestrating a coordinated nationalistic curriculum to overcome social division (Miguel 2004). Similarly, while sometimes criticized for heavy-handedness, Rwanda's postgenocide president Paul Kagame has played a key role in stabilizing the country by outlawing divisive talk of ethnic identity and prioritizing a discourse of national unity (though he has also used this power to silence critics) (Adamczyk 2011; Wrong 2021). Contrarily, Cameroon's Paul Biya made ethnicity highly politically salient by encouraging separate "hometown associations" for all of the country's more than 200 ethnic groups in an effort to divide his opposition (Albaugh 2011). This leadership choice is particularly important immediately postindependence, as these leaders influence institutional design and set the precedent for postindependence politics (Riedl 2018).

Case analysis carried out by teams of researchers at the Uongozi Institute indicate that some elements of good leadership are intrinsic (and therefore hard to measure before the fact), while external factors are also important (Perera et al. 2018). While some leaders may be predisposed to select unifying versus divisive strategies, certain conditions may strengthen the incentives for a unity-based approach. First is the existing degree of politicization of identities within the country. In some colonies, colonizers created and stoked ethnic divisions as part of a divide-and-conquer strategy (Strauss 2006, 20–21). In these cases, new leaders may inherit a political system in which identity is already deeply politicized. In such cases, new leaders in a strong position (representing a large group) may have incentives to further stoke divisions to divide the opposition. Alternatively, new leaders in a weak position, representing a smaller group, may have incentives to pursue a unifying agenda oriented around coopting potential adversaries into the government (Arriola, Devaro, and Meng 2021). However, cooptation can also produce "exclusive elite bargains" that pit one set of groups against others (Lindemann 2010). Therefore, it is likely that leaders' choices will interact with the politization of identities at the time of independence.

These theories and their related hypotheses are summarized in Table 3.1.

Table 3.1 Theories Explaining Good Governance

Theory	Hypothesis
	Institutions
Endogenous vs. exogenous	Countries with exogenous institutions will struggle to achieve good governance.
Rents vs. taxes	Countries that rely on rents more than taxes will struggle to achieve good governance.
	Sociocultural Factors
Sociocultural diversity	Countries with a high degree of ethnic (or other) diversity will struggle to achieve good governance.
Social capital	Countries with low levels of social capital will struggle to achieve good governance.
Civil society	Countries with weak civil society will struggle to achieve good governance.
	Agency
Political leadership	Countries with leaders that emphasize division rather than unity will struggle to achieve good governance.

Most-Different Case Analysis: Mauritius and Botswana

Which of these theories can best explain good governance? In this chapter, I examine two countries, Mauritius and Botswana, to determine which of these theories most convincingly explains why they both score so well on indicators of governance.

Case Introduction: Mauritius and Botswana

Mauritius, an island in the Indian Ocean off Africa's eastern coast, was uninhabited until the colonial era. Originally settled and then abandoned by the Dutch, the island became permanently populated in 1721 with the arrival of the French. As in Seychelles (see Chapter 2), the French established sugar plantations using Africans as slave labor, and then lost the island to the British in 1814 after the Napoleonic Wars (Frankel 2016, 301). The British administration remained hands-off, leaving the island as the domain of the landowning Franco-Mauricien elite. The abolition of slavery in 1833 generated a labor shortage on the island, so from 1849 to 1923, the British brought a steady stream of indentured workers from India (Lange 2009, 73). By the late nineteenth century, the island was a diverse and hierarchical society of British administrators, wealthy Franco-Mauricien landowners, Creole descendants of former slaves, and Hindus and Muslims of Indian origin. Mauritius gained its independence in 1968 with a democratic constitution, and with the exception of one political crisis shortly after independence, has had stable democratic elections ever since, with government characterized by a merit-based, competent bureaucracy administering popular social programs. A robust civil society is an effective government watchdog (Carroll and Carroll 1997).

Botswana, a landlocked country just north of South Africa, had a very different political trajectory. The region has been inhabited for thousands of years, originally by the Basarwa,[3] and subsequently by various Bantu populations. By the mid-1800s, the area was dominated by five main Tswana chiefdoms (Lange 2009, 142). The region came under British colonial administration in 1885 as the Bechuanaland Protectorate. The British intervened little in Tswana chiefly politics and generally had a cooperative understanding with the chiefs. Botswana gained independence in 1966, and its new constitution established a democracy but retained the role of the chiefs. Despite the discovery of diamonds shortly after independence and fears that diamond rents would corrupt the government, Botswana has retained stable governance with a competent bureaucracy that has managed to channel diamond revenue into schools, health care, and infrastructure (Acemoglu, Johnson, and Robinson 2002).

Mauritius and Botswana: Identifying a Common Factor of Success

Mauritius and Botswana have different histories, geographies, and demographies. Yet both emerged from colonialism impoverished and built legitimate, respected governing institutions that led to bureaucratic effectiveness, economic growth, poverty reduction, control of corruption, and political stability. What can explain how they both achieved such success? The theories as applied to these two countries are summarized in Table 3.2. As the table demonstrates, these countries have two things in common: there is some degree of endogeneity in their institutions, and they both had postindependence leaders who pursued a political strategy of unity.

Starting with institutional theories: While Mauritius and Botswana were both colonized, they had unusual colonial experiences and emerged at independence with institutions that included endogenous components. There is therefore some support for the hypothesis that endogenous institutions produce good governance, explored in more detail in the following case analysis. The next theory examines how the government's source of revenue influences accountability in governing institutions. According to the Organization for Economic Cooperation and Development's public

Table 3.2 Theories as Applied to Mauritius and Botswana

Theory	Mauritius	Botswana	Explanation
		Institutions	
Endogenous vs. exogenous	Endogenous	Endogenous	Theory supported
Rents vs. taxes	Taxes	Rents	Theory unsupported; predicts Botswana should have poor governance
		Sociocultural Factors	
Sociocultural diversity	High	Low	Theory unsupported; predicts Mauritius should have poor governance
Social capital	Better than average	Worse than average	Theory unsupported; predicts Botswana should have poor governance
Civil society	Strong	Weak	Theory unsupported; predicts Botswana should have poor governance
		Agency	
Political leadership	Unifying first prime minister	Unifying first president	Theory supported

revenues database, most of Mauritius's revenue comes from taxation, while most of Botswana's comes from diamond rents.[4] In Mauritius, from 1990 to 2018 (the period for which there is data), taxes contributed 84–94 percent of all government revenue, largely from a flat rate value-added tax on goods and services that applies to the entire population. As Mauritian elections regularly result in the incumbent party losing power, there is evidence that Mauritius's electoral system facilitates accountability.

By contrast, in Botswana from 2004 to 2018 (dates for which data exist), rents exceed tax revenue every year, making up 55–66 percent of total government revenue. The largest contributor to Botswana's nontax revenue is mineral rents and royalties. Alongside its reliance on rents, avenues for government accountability are limited in Botswana. Despite having a democratic constitution, the ruling Botswana Democratic Party

(BDP) has never lost office, and critics indicate that the ruling party faces little real accountability for its actions, as the opposition party has little influence in parliament and there are few checks on presidential power (Ghebremusse 2018; Good 1999). Additionally, the government has effectively muzzled the media from criticizing it (Sebudubudu and Osei-Hwedie 2006; Taylor 2003). Botswana has achieved a high score on governance despite these challenges, undermining the hypothesis that reliance on rents instead of taxes leads to poor governance.

Mauritius and Botswana differ in terms of their sociocultural characteristics: by Posner's (2004a) measure, ranging from 0 to 1, Mauritian society is ethnically and racially diverse (score of 0.6), while Botswana's is not (score of 0). In Mauritius, group boundaries around race and religion are socially and politically important: People tend to live in homogenous communities, and intermarriage is rare (Ramtohul 2020). During the period immediately preceding independence, communal violence led some to believe that Mauritian society would implode (Frankel 2016, 303). Yet the political institutions Mauritius put in place upon independence had a remarkable impact depoliticizing these social identities. The structure of the institutions, which requires parties to work in coalitions and build consensus, has encouraged moderation and cooperation (Brautigam 1997, 53). By contrast, in Botswana, identity distinctions between the various Tswana groups have never been politicized (Lange 2009, 142), though the country rightly attracts criticism for its inhumane treatment of the minority Basarwa (Nthomang 2004). Mauritius provides evidence against the hypothesis that diversity leads to poor governance, demonstrating that the challenges posed by diversity can be overcome by institutional design.

The next theories examining the countries' social context focus on social capital and the role of civil society, with the hypotheses that countries with more social capital or strong civil societies experience better governance. Neither hypothesis finds support. Social capital is significantly higher in Mauritius than Botswana: according to the Legatum Institute's ranking of 167 countries by social capital, Mauritius ranked 38th (score of 58.7) while Botswana ranked 103rd (score of 50). Similarly, while Mauritius has a rich and effective civil society dating back to the colonial era, civil society in Botswana is weak. Quantitatively, Varieties of Democracy (V-Dem) has scored civil society activity in Mauritius at about 2.6 out of 3 since independence, indicating that there is a diverse array of civil society organization with broad popular involvement. Botswana's score has hovered closer to 2, indicating that organizations exist but tend to have limited popular involvement. Qualitatively, in Mauritius, civic organizing began during the colonial era in the form of agricultural cooperatives and has extended to the present with "civic networks" and "ethnic associations" that create a liaison between society and the government (Carroll and Carroll 1997, 481–482; Lange 2009, 74–75; Sandbrook 2007, 211). In Botswana, however, civil society participation has been limited by the degree of bureaucratization of the state (Good 1999, 21; de Jager and Sebudubudu 2017, 21; Taylor 2003, 216). Botswana thus provides evidence against both these hypotheses.

The final theory explaining good governance focuses on agency: specifically, the role of individual leaders in eschewing divisive political strategies. In both countries, many credit the first head of state—Prime Minister Ramgoolam in Mauritius and President Khama in Botswana—with unifying leadership (Carroll and Carroll 1997, 470). In both countries, social unification has persisted: both score far better than the African average (and have since independence) on V-Dem's measure of exclusion by social group, which estimates how frequently people lose access to public services or spaces on the basis of their social group identity. Botswana and Mauritius each score around 0.2, while the African average is about 0.5 on a scale of 0–1, where 1 indicates widespread social exclusion. This hypothesis finds some support and is explored in the following analysis alongside the endogenous development of institutions in both countries.

Mauritius

In Mauritius, the political institutions have endogenous characteristics, and the redesign of the political institutions upon independence reflects that the first prime minister, Seewoosagur Ramgoolam, was committed to pursuing a political strategy of unity rather than divide-and-conquer. Because Mauritius was uninhabited at colonization, it had no precolonial institutions. However, as a settler community, the colonial and then independent governing institutions adapted to local circumstances over time. While colonial Mauritius was hardly democratic, the administration began to slowly extend participation in governance (Frankel 2016; Lange 2009). In 1886, the administration allowed landholders with a certain income to vote, enabling the Creole elite to join the white Franco-Mauritians in the island's elected administration. By 1948, a new constitution allowed all literate adults to vote, resulting in a massive expansion of the franchise among the Indo-Mauricien population, and the 1959 legislative elections were held with universal franchise (Frankel 2016, 302). Independence was a slow, negotiated process, and the political institutions that emerged were the result of compromise between the (noncolonial) political elites during a series of election commissions that took place prior to independence (Brautigam 1997, 53).

Members of the commission were wary of triggering violence between the Franco-Mauritian economic elite, the Hindu majority, and the Muslim minority by creating an electoral system that concentrated too much power in one group. Therefore, they structured the parliament to have three members each from twenty districts, plus two from the island of Rodriguez. This structure encouraged parties to run in coalitions to pick up as many seats as possible in each district. They also created the "best loser" system: eight additional seats can be added to parliament if there is underrepresentation of any of the island's registered ethnic minorities. For example, if no Creoles are elected, the losing Creole candidate with the most votes would receive one of the special seats. This provision also encourages parties to run a diverse slate of candidates to increase their odds of picking up a "best loser" seat (Brautigam 1997, 53). While Mauritius "imported" a British Westminster-style parliament, broad swaths of the population had direct experience participating in it for forty years prior to independence, enabling the election commissions to alter the boilerplate parliamentary system to suit the specific needs of the island.

Mauritius's first prime minister was Seewoosagur Ramgoolam. As a member of the majority Hindu community, he could have attempted to manipulate the political institutions to entrench the Hindu majority in power. Just before independence, the census indicated that Hindus of Indian origin comprised half the population, the other half divided between Muslims, Creoles, Franco-Mauritians, and Chinese (de Smith 1968). Pitting minority groups against each other to prevent an opposition party from coalescing was a tactic that was popular across many newly independent countries at the time, but he instead rejected communalism and pursued a coalition-building, issue-oriented approach (Sandbrook 2007, 209–210). The electoral institutions that Mauritius adopted can help explain this restraint.

In the Westminster-style parliamentary system that Mauritians agreed to adopt, the prime minister is selected by the party with the majority in the legislature. If no party has an outright majority—more than 50 percent of the seats—they must form a coalition with another party to form a majority. During the transitional period prior to independence, while the parties were still negotiating the finer details of the constitution, there were a number of elections held within Mauritius. While Ramgoolam's Labor Party was the most popular, in the 1963 elections it failed to win an outright majority. Ramgoolam knew that his party's ability to govern therefore depended on its ability to form a coalition with other parties, such as those appealing primarily to the Muslim or Franco-Mauritian population. Ultimately, during the inaugural elections, his Labor Party formed a coalition with the Muslim

Committee for Action and the Independence Forward parties, which together won 54.5 percent of the vote and the legislative majority (de Smith 1968).

The institutional configuration and distribution of parties at independence incentivized Ramgoolam to pursue a unifying approach, as appealing to Hindus only would have been a losing proposition. However, he continued to promote unification and moderation even in the face of political crisis. Shortly after independence, the radical party *Mouvement Militant Mauricien* (MMM) won a shocking victory in a by-election, prompting the government to declare a state of emergency and postpone the 1972 elections (Brautigam 1997, 49–50). While other African heads of state in similar positions ultimately declared single-party states and consolidated power around their base, Ramgoolam did not (Young 2012, chap. 4). The general election of 1976 went forward, and while the MMM won some seats, the structure of the electoral institutions rewarded more moderate parties that worked in coalition. The crisis passed, and extremist parties found little political success. Ultimately, Mauritius's endogenous political institutions encouraged coalition-building, and Ramgoolam bolstered the strength of these institutions by eschewing divisive political strategies.

Botswana

Botswana, too, emerged from colonialism with some endogeneity in its institutions. Prior to colonialism, the Tswana chieftaincies had a great deal of power but were held in check by the *kgotla*: regular meetings between the chief and subjects in which (male) subjects were able to air their opinions and grievances, and the chief would summarize these opinions to build consensus around governance decisions (Pitcher, Moran, and Johnston 2009, 146). While these meetings were not necessarily democratic, they did provide an element of participation and accountability, as chiefs perceived to flout public consensus might face desertion or even murder (Lange 2009, 142–143).

Unlike in other parts of colonial Africa, the Tswana chiefs requested British intervention to protect them from the Boers, the Dutch-descended South Africans who were beginning to encroach upon their territory (Lange 2009, 144). The British administered Botswana as a protectorate and largely left the precolonial political institutions of the chieftaincy intact. Colonialism did alter the power of the chieftaincy in some ways, as the British provided material backing for the chiefs and directed some of their decisions, in several circumstances removing chiefs who disagreed with them (Lange 2009, 148–150). However, the structure and importance of these institutions endured. Upon independence, while Botswana adopted a parliamentary system from the British, it also retained the chieftaincy and *kgotlas* as institutions of local governance (Pitcher, Moran, and Johnston 2009). Indeed, the first president—Seretse Khama—was previously a chief, and his party, the BDP, actively incorporated chiefs into its base and used *kgotlas* to communicate to the population (*ibid.*, 147). These institutions have maintained their relevance and connect the population to national political institutions (Hope 2000, 524–525).

The chieftaincies and the *kgotlas* retained their importance as political institutions in independent Botswana in part due to the actions of Seretse Khama, Botswana's first president. Founder of the BDP and a former chief himself, Khama built a political base by drawing village chiefs into his party's ranks through promotion of pan-Tswana nationalism: uniting the various Tswana tribes under the banner of a modern state (Robinson and Parsons 2006, 147). His close work with both traditional authorities and the colonial administration smoothed the transition to independence and bolstered the legitimacy of the newly independent government (Lange 2009, 155). His political leadership had two important impacts: First, it guaranteed the persistence of Botswana's endogenous political institutions (the chieftaincies) in the new independent state. Second, rather than appealing to his own former chieftaincy as a base, he followed the unifying political strategy of pan-Tswana nationalism, uniting the various Tswana groups under a single political banner.

Though holding the title of president, the chief executive in Botswana is selected through a Westminster-style electoral system: citizens vote for legislative representatives, and a candidate put forth by the majority party in the legislature becomes the president. This means that the president must have the support of the majority of the legislature to gain and hold onto this position. Needing a legislative majority, it was clearly politically expedient for Khama to appeal to Tswana nationalism. Appealing only to his own chieftaincy as a base would have been a losing proposition numerically, and while there are differences between the Tswana chieftaincies, there was no recent history of grievances or politicized identity that he could have manipulated to his advantage if he had been so inclined. In the 1965 and 1969 elections prior to independence, Khama's party won 90 percent and 77 percent of the legislative seats, respectively. Given that his strategy so effectively delivered an overwhelming majority, there were no incentives to deviate from his unifying strategy.

These cases indicate that Mauritius and Botswana have two important features in common that have contributed to good governance. First, they both developed modern political institutions that were at least partially endogenous. This occurred differently in each country. Mauritius, which was uninhabited upon colonization, developed political institutions that changed slowly over time to accommodate increasing portions of the citizenry. In Botswana, precolonial institutions were largely unaltered by colonialism and then incorporated into the new constitution, enabling continuity and legitimacy for the new government. In both cases, these political institutions were well-suited to the context. Additionally, both countries had leadership that pursued a political strategy of unity, setting a precedent for the way political institutions would function. In Mauritius, Prime Minister Ramgoolam took steps to depoliticize racial and ethnic identity that had threatened to destabilize the country. This strategy enabled him to build a winning legislative coalition that would have been impossible with a party appealing primarily to Hindus. In Botswana, President Seretse Khama ensured the integration of national and traditional political structures through pan-Tswana nationalism, which enabled him to retain a legislative majority. In these countries, endogenous institutions and unifying leadership set the stage for good governance over time.

Most-Similar Case Analyses

This most-different case analysis identified (partially) endogenous institutions and unifying leadership as essential for establishing good governance in Mauritius and Botswana. If these factors are indeed definitive, then countries similar to Mauritius and Botswana that experience worse governance should lack these features. This section compares Mauritius to Comoros and Botswana to Uganda to evaluate support for these hypotheses.

Mauritius and the Comoros

Like Mauritius, Comoros is an island nation off Africa's east coast. Its colonial history began similarly, with brief stops by Arab traders and the Portuguese before the four main islands were colonized by the French. Unlike in Mauritius, the French retained the islands after the Napoleonic Wars, and they remained under French control until 1975. After independence, the first president was ousted in a coup less than a month into his term. The country subsequently suffered at least nineteen coups and coup attempts between 1975 and 2000 and a decade-long secession crisis that was only resolved in 2007 with the help of African Union troops (Baker 2009). The government remains plagued by corruption and dysfunction (Poupko 2017, 334). Despite similar beginnings, Comoros has had much worse governance, most recently scoring –0.88 on the World Governance Index compared to Mauritius's 0.76.

Political institutions in Mauritius and Comoros have very different origins. While Mauritius's political institutions developed slowly over time in response to the local social context, Comoros has suffered a confusion of imported and pseudo-traditional institutions. At the time of colonization, the Comoro islands were ruled as distinct sultanates. When the French officially incorporated the four islands as a colony in 1915, they disempowered the sultans and replaced the existing political structures with administrative units based on the French system (Walker 2007, 592–594). However, they provided no monetary support for these institutions, leaving the islands largely without any functioning government. France was reluctant to relinquish these colonies, but finally three of the four islands unilaterally declared independence in 1975.[5] The political situation at independence was bleak, as the islands had an amalgamation of French institutions and colonial institutional inventions: an "irrelevant state managed by a handful of French-educated elite Comorians . . . [that was] a distant reality, foreign and incomprehensible, centralized, costly and run by unqualified personnel" (Walker 2007, 595–596). The first president, Ahmed Abdallah, was ousted in a coup less than a month into his term (Poupko 2017, 333–334). His successor, Ali Soilih, attempted a massive revolution to remove French influence from Comoro governance. However, his fervor resulted in his ouster in a coup as well. Ahmed Abdallah was reinstated and promptly reimposed French administrative structures (Baker 2009, 221).

As this sequence of events demonstrates, an additional key difference between Mauritius and Comoros is the action of early independence leaders. Unlike the unifying leadership provided by Ramgoolam and his party in Mauritius, politics in Comoros was rocked by instability and nearly annual coups or coup attempts—many of which have involved French influence (Hassan 2009, 229). Prior to independence, Comorian political parties were incoherent and reflected inter-island rivalry more than anything else (Ostheimer 1973). After independence, ongoing instability and coup attempts stemmed from the intense rivalry between the islands and the tendency for national leaders to use centralized financial resources only for their own island (Hassan 2009, 231–232). Governance declined so precipitously during this time that Nzwani (one of the three islands) attempted to secede in 1997, sparking recurrent violence until the African Union stepped in in 2007 (Baker 2009, 215–217). Indeed, the Comoros have scored much worse than Mauritius on V-Dem's measure of exclusion by social group since each country's independence (most recently, in 2019, 0.49 in Comoros compared to 0.14 in Mauritius).

The trends of poorly adapted institutions and divisive leadership have persisted over time. Following the period of routine coups, the islands adopted a new constitution that would grant each island some autonomy and rotate the presidency between them. Each island, in its turn, would be able to hold a primary to determine the top three candidates from that island, followed by a general election involving all three islands (Poupko 2017, 334). While this structure is a nod to local circumstances and the need to balance the political influence of each island, it also inherently removes the democratic accountability mechanism: fear of losing an election. Each president serves only one term before the presidency rotates to the next island. Power is highly centralized in the presidency, rendering the legislative assembly weak (*ibid.*). Therefore, presidents have no incentive to rule well—rather, they have the incentive to use the power of the presidency to accumulate as much wealth as possible before they must turn it over. One critic has alleged that political organizations in Comoros are "nothing but fronts set up by the local elite . . . for amassing fortune and power" (Hassan 2009, 231).

The comparison between these two island nations indicates that the different quality of governance they experience stems from different histories of institutional development and the quality of leadership postindependence. While Mauritius had endogenous institutional development with thoughtful adaptation to local circumstances, captained by a leader with incentives to promote unity, Comoros had its endogenous institutions destroyed by colonialism and a postindependence period marked by leaders succumbing to persistent regional rivalry. Notably, the incentives for divisive leadership in the Comoros were intensified by the nature of French rule during colonialism and ongoing French political meddling after independence.

Botswana and Uganda

Botswana and Uganda are not ideal most-similar cases. While located in different regions (Southern and East Africa, respectively) and with some key sociodemographic differences, the two countries are as similar as possible and share key characteristics that make comparison fruitful (see the appendix for rationale of case selection). Like Botswana, Uganda was a British protectorate and therefore had a less intense colonial experience with more local political autonomy than many other African colonies. During the nineteenth century, Uganda was ravaged by the slave trade and incursions from Egypt; British presence in the area was initially welcomed in service of abolishing the slave trade and quelling the associated violence (Amone and Muura 2014, 247). Uganda negotiated its independence from Britain in 1963 and initially had a multiparty democracy modeled on the British Westminster system. However, unlike in Botswana, governance in Uganda quickly unraveled. The first prime minister, Milton Obote, performed poorly, stoked ethnic tensions, and was ousted in a coup in 1971.

He was succeeded by the brutal dictator Idi Amin, whose reign of terror lasted until 1979 (Kanyeihamba 2010, Chapters 4–7). When Amin was finally deposed, Obote took the presidency again and presided over another five years of misrule before being ousted by Yoweri Museveni's National Resistance Movement. Museveni's rule began in 1986 and continues at the time of writing. Initially lauded as a new African democrat, it quickly became clear that Museveni was intolerant of dissent and instead augured a new, softer form of authoritarianism. While Uganda has enjoyed stability since 1986, Museveni's regime performs poorly on most indicators of good governance, scoring –0.59 on the World Governance Index, compared to Botswana's 0.58.

The first important difference between Botswana and Uganda is that, while the region that became Botswana mostly "made sense" as a country (in that the chiefdoms comprising it had shared history and cultural features), Uganda did not. Prior to colonialism, the area that became Uganda was populated by several unrelated kingdoms alongside other acephalous communities (Amone and Muura 2014; Kasozi 1994). Thus, the Uganda that the British carved out on a map did not match the political reality on the ground (Kabwegyere 1974). During colonialism, the British exhibited a clear preference for the Baganda, the largest centrally organized ethnic group, and as a result they became increasingly politically and economically important—generating resentment among other groups (Mawby 2020, 21; Mazrui 2019). The colonial experience varied for groups within Uganda; while some (like the Baganda) retained some political autonomy, others, like the Acholi, experienced extensive, often violent intervention (Amone and Muura 2014).

Creating a national government out of the patchwork of precolonial polities and assorted colonial agreements with different groups proved exceptionally challenging. As the colonial era ended, British administrators and Ugandan elites worked to produce political institutions to govern the independent state. The result was an unworkable amalgam in which a Westminster-style parliamentary system was layered on top of an ad hoc hodgepodge of subnational units, each with different degrees of autonomy and an unclear relationship to the central government (Kanyeihamba 2010; Mawby 2020, 33). Some of these subnational units, like Buganda, retained some precolonial institutions, but others had been acephalous and were now folded into larger invented administrative units. Unlike in Botswana, where precolonial institutions were left intact and had a coherent relationship to the postcolonial state, in Uganda the exogenous British-style institutions were dominant and subsumed what endogenous political institutions remained.

Another key difference between the two countries was the persistence of interethnic rivalry, which was ultimately reflected in the divisive leadership strategy that Obote followed. Leading up to independence, Ugandan society was deeply divided along ethnic and religious lines. There was no inherent sense of pan-Ugandan nationalism that Obote could have drawn on (Lindemann 2010, 12). Rather, colonial meddling had led to resentments and rivalries, particularly directed toward the Baganda, which had been heavily favored by the colonial administration. Initially, Obote, from the relatively small Langi group, attempted a strategy of power sharing in his government. His Ugandan People's Congress (UPC) party formed a coalition with the Bagandan Kabaka Yekka (KY) party to win the country's first election, and he made an effort to achieve ethnic balance in the ministers appointed to the government (Lindemann 2010, 13). However, this initial attempt at balancing soon gave way to factional infighting and increasing resentment of the Baganda's overrepresentation in the government. The Baganda's numerical majority, political experience, and economic clout made the UPC–KY coalition an effective way to gain a parliamentary majority, but those same features made the KY party the biggest threat to Obote's ongoing leadership (Mawby 2020, 34).

The UPC–KY coalition fell apart in 1964, and Obote became more vocal about correcting the historical marginalization of the tribes to the north and the east (Glentworth and Hancock 1973, 239–240). The Baganda had been promised special semiautonomous status upon independence, along with the promise that their leader, the Kabaka, would be the country's first president, serving alongside Obote as prime minister. In 1966, Prime Minister Obote reneged on that promise when he annulled the constitution, unceremoniously removed the Kabaka, appointed himself as president, and created a new institutional arrangement that dramatically reduced local autonomy, folding local territories under the power of the central government (Leonard Boyle 2017, 599; Lindemann 2010, 22; Mawby 2020, 35). This move deepened the country's factional rifts. Simultaneously, Obote had stacked the military with northerners, creating a great imbalance that ultimately led to his ouster in a coup in 1971, led by Idi Amin, a military officer who felt himself being edged out on the basis of his ethnicity (Omara-Otunnu 1987, chap. 6).

Amin's ascendance to the presidency represented a shift in the ethnic balance of power rather than a repudiation of divisive politics. His brutal dictatorship marked a deepening of identity-based division, this time accompanied by expelling all people of Asian descent from the country, packing the military and government with ethnic allies, and presiding over a murderous (and often capricious) reign of terror across the country

(Leonard Boyle 2017). When Amin was finally deposed in 1979, Milton Obote became president again and employed the same tactics as he had in his first presidency. Finally, he was ousted by Yoweri Museveni after a five-year civil war. Museveni, who took office in 1986, has been president ever since. Museveni took the opportunity to remake the country's institutions to purge ethnic favoritism and divisiveness from politics. Instead, he swung hard in the opposite direction, declaring a "no party" democracy because of the history of ethnic violence associated with party politics (Carbone 2001). While opposition parties are now legal in Uganda, elections are far from fair, and opposition party members are routinely harassed, jailed, and injured.[6]

In sum, Uganda's national government was ultimately exogenous—divorced from the various systems governing its many precolonial polities, and clearly ill-suited to the conditions in independent Uganda. While he initially attempted a strategy of ethnic balancing, Obote ultimately found it more politically expedient to build political coalitions based on ethnoregional identity. Obote's leadership entrenched sociocultural division as the organizing principle of Ugandan politics, leading to decades of violence and instability. It is important to note that Botswana was a more logical national political unit at independence than was Uganda, deepening the challenge of creating suitable institutions and overcoming sociocultural rifts. Nevertheless, leaders in other countries—like Tanzania's Julius Nyerere—indicate that such a feat was certainly possible, if challenging.

Ultimately, the major difference between Mauritius and Botswana, on the one hand, and Comoros and Uganda, on the other hand, is whether the country's history, sociodemographic landscape, and institutional design favored what Reilly (2001) refers to as centripetal (center-loving) or centrifugal (center-fearing) politics. In Botswana and Mauritius, the political institutions favored centripetal politics: the first leaders had to appeal to the country's "center" and build majority coalitions to be politically successful. In the Comoros and Uganda, the deep social divisions wrought by colonialism and the incoherence of the political institutions fostered centrifugal leadership: leaders cultivating narrow, identity-based interests rather than building majority coalitions. While these different circumstances favored different outcomes, individual leadership decisions are still important. Faced with political crisis and identity-based social divides, Prime Minister Ramgoolam in Mauritius could have dissolved the constitution like many other African leaders (including Obote in Uganda) did at the time. Instead, he chose to promote unification and maintain Mauritian institutions' centripetal design, enabling stability for years to come.

Conclusion

The quality of a country's governance has enormous implications for the quality of life of most people who live there. If the government is inefficient, nonfunctional, wracked with violence and corruption, or neglects its basic functions, these failures can ripple outward and pervade people's lives. Countries with poor governance struggle to provide public goods like infrastructure, education, or health care; they may be unable to support private industry, enforce contracts, or protect property rights; and they may lack a fair and effective legal system. All these things that a government is supposed to produce are linked to the quality of the government in question. Good governance is challenging to achieve, and failure to do so has many consequences.

As in other postcolonial regions, governance in Africa is complicated because colonialism represented a massive rupture between the endogenous preexisting political institutions and the contemporary state. However, a history of colonialism does not mean that African countries are doomed to bad governance. Numerous African countries have achieved good governance despite colonial history. The case comparisons I've presented in this chapter offer suggestions as to why. Both Mauritius and Botswana emerged from colonialism with some degree of endogeneity in their institutions. In Mauritius, the political institutions of the settler colony developed slowly and became inclusive over time, while in Botswana, key components of precolonial political institutions were left intact under a less intense form of colonialism than what many other African countries experienced. Upon independence, the first leaders (Prime Minister Ramgoolam in Mauritius and President Khama in Botswana) rejected divisive politics and instead took actions to ensure unity and a national identity. In Mauritius, this meant altering the parliamentary system to ensure ethnoreligious balance in democratic representation. In Botswana, this meant integrating the structure of the chieftaincy into the new democratic constitution. The first leaders' unifying actions set a precedent for politics moving forward.

Importantly, for both Khama and Ramgoolam, the political incentive structure favored the creation of what Lindemann (2010) called an "inclusive elite bargain" and what Reilly (2001) calls "centripetal politics." Botswana at independence had a coherent national identity, and Khama's political success had been built upon courting chiefs through a platform of pan-Tswana nationalism and maintaining chiefs' political power in the new independent government. In Mauritius, where there were deeper identity-based social rifts, Ramgoolam would have been unable to win by appealing to his own group. As a Hindu, he was from the largest group, but it was not large enough to win a legislative majority, so he had to pursue a strategy of coalition-building. Mauritius's constitutional design ensured that the elites from all major social groups had a pathway for representation and a stake in the survival of the government. Such inclusive elite bargains failed to materialize in Uganda and the Comoros. In Uganda, Obote initially appeared to attempt unifying leadership. Like Ramgoolam, he needed to court support outside his own group to remain politically viable. However, unlike Ramgoolam, Obote was in a much weaker position. His ethnic ties were to a group and region that did not have the plurality, and he therefore pursued a coalition of convenience with the numerically powerful but deeply resented Baganda. Ultimately, the power of this group within his coalition threatened his position, leading him to abandon his attempts at an inclusive bargain and instead entrench his power through an exclusionary elite bargain that explicitly sidelined the Baganda. In Comoros, the divisive rivalries dating back to colonialism and ongoing intervention by the French eliminated any incentives for an inclusionary bargain. In both the Comoros and Uganda, without inclusionary bargains, centrifugal politics followed. An important lesson to draw from the experiences of these countries is that sociocultural divisions do not necessarily mean a country will suffer poor governance, but that institutions in such countries must be designed in such a way as to incentivize leaders to form broad coalitions across groups.

While colonial history has an outsized relationship to governance today, it is important to also acknowledge that things within people's control—like the design of inclusive institutions that tap into local legitimate practices—can augur a brighter future. It was not inevitable that Botswana would adopt a constitution that incorporated the chieftaincy, or that Mauritius would come up with creative amendments to the parliamentary system. It was not inevitable that Uganda's constitutional design would reinforce social divisions, or that Comoros would design a power-sharing system that allowed presidents to act with impunity. At the same time, designing functional institutions is a heavier lift in countries where colonial rule was more intrusive or created a less coherent state.

Mauritius and Botswana are not the only examples of good governance on the continent—Cape Verde, Seychelles, Namibia, South Africa, Ghana, and Rwanda also have positive scores on the world governance indicator. These countries—spanning multiple regions and with varied colonial histories—offer ample opportunity to evaluate how explanatory endogenous political institutions and unifying leadership are in generating good governance elsewhere.

As with the other countries that I highlight in this book as successes, Mauritius and Botswana are not perfect. After decades of strong democratic performance, Mauritius has experienced recent and worrying declines.[7] The ruling party in Botswana has never lost an election, restrictions on people's ability to dissent are concerning, and its treatment of the Basarwa is troubling. Nevertheless, both countries have produced impressive track records of government performance. Similarly, Comoros and Uganda are not beyond hope. Both have experienced progress in recent years. All four cases highlight that governance is not static—its quality can change over time. Understanding the factors that help produce good governance can help generate improvements everywhere.

Notes

1. For more detail on the construction of these indicators, see Kaufmann, Kraay, and Mastruzzi (2010).

2. The small number of colonies held by other European powers—Italians, Spanish, and Portuguese—are more of a mixed bag and tended to have protracted wars for independence rather than the negotiated transitions of the British and the French, and therefore had different experiences of constitutional development.

3. Basarwa is their preferred term; they are also known as the San or Bushmen.

4. Author's calculations from "Details of Public Revenues" at https://stats.oecd.org/

5. The fourth island, Mayotte, opted to remain part of France.

6. For example, Dahir, Abdi Latif. 2020, November 27. "Jailed, Exiled and Silenced: Smothering East Africa's Political Opposition," *New York Times.* https://www.nytimes.com/2020/11/27/world/africa/Africa-leaders-suppression.html

7. Darga, Louis Amédée and Suhaylah Peeraullee. 2021, June 25. "Can Mauritians Save a Democracy in Trouble?" *Washington Post.* https://www.washingtonpost.com/politics/2021/06/25/can-mauritians-save-democracy-trouble/

4

Public Health Responses to Malaria

In the public imagination, Africa is wracked with terrible disease. In 2014, the Ebola epidemic centered in West Africa triggered extraordinary fear. Some universities prohibited the return of students from the entire African continent—despite the fact that students from Cape Town, South Africa, for example, lived further away from the disease epicenter than those in Paris, France.[1] As Laura Seay and Kim Yi Dionne cogently explained, the global response to the Ebola outbreak reflected "a long and ugly tradition of treating Africans as savage animals and the African continent as a dirty, diseased place to be feared," a tradition rooted in racism, colonial history, and ongoing media depictions of the continent.[2] These narratives obscure the reality that, in many African countries, public health conditions have dramatically improved over the past thirty years. According to the World Bank, infant mortality has dropped by 47 percent and life expectancy has increased by 23 percent since 1990.[3] These improved statistics are directly related to improved public health, with endemic diseases like malaria decreasing by 37% and epidemic-scale diseases like HIV/AIDS decreasing by 71 percent over 2000–2019.[4]

In general, public health across sub-Saharan Africa is improving, and there is reason to be optimistic that these trends will continue. Nevertheless, it is also important to remain clear-eyed about the public health challenges that continue to face the continent. The Covid-19 pandemic, ongoing at the time of writing, has laid bare the challenges of implementing emergency public health procedures in low-income countries without a robust social safety net (Kavanagh and Singh 2020). While the continent's rate of malaria incidence has dramatically decreased, it still accounts for 94 percent of global cases (World Health Organization 2020). Moreover, as wealth increases and lifestyles change, many countries find themselves facing public health challenges associated with poverty, like waterborne illness, alongside those associated with wealth, like diabetes and heart disease. In this context, it is essential to understand why some countries have been particularly effective at improving public health conditions.

Comparing public health responses across such a vast continent is challenging because different countries face different public health threats that require different types of intervention. The African continent spans many climatic zones, so diseases have a higher natural prevalence in different areas. These varying disease burdens matter because vector-borne diseases like malaria or sleeping sickness require different types of interventions than waterborne illnesses like typhoid, parasitic illnesses like schistosomiasis, or sexually transmitted diseases like HIV. A country's public health infrastructure might be excellent at mosquito abatement to control malaria, for example, but not as good at the contact tracing required for sexually transmitted diseases.

Acknowledging these differences, in this chapter I focus on malaria. This focus reflects malaria's danger: as of 2019, it was responsible for an astonishing 386,000 deaths annually in Africa—mostly in children under five (World Health Organization 2020, 22). Malaria is a vector-borne disease transmitted by mosquitos, so the conclusions I draw in this chapter are not necessarily relevant for other public health challenges such as waterborne diseases. However, it provides insight into how public health systems deal with long-running, persistent threats. To evaluate which countries have been particularly successful at addressing this public health challenge, I examine disease incidence from 2000 to 2018 using the World Bank's estimates.[5] Because malaria prevalence is much higher in countries with tropical climates, African countries had a wide variety of baseline rates in 2000. The different baseline levels of risk make it challenging to determine what "success" is. Therefore, I focus on countries with higher baseline risk: eighteen countries that had malaria incidence exceeding 400 per 1,000 people in 2000. Figure 4.1 illustrates the annual malaria incidence for each of these countries alongside the percent decrease over the period 2000–2018.

Of these countries, Guinea-Bissau and Malawi had the largest percent reduction in incidence. Guinea-Bissau reduced its malaria incidence from 474.5 to 123.3 per 1,000, a reduction of 74 percent. Malawi reduced its malaria incidence from 436.5 to 213.6 per 1,000, a reduction of 50 percent. These countries have different geographies, histories, and political systems. However, they both managed impressive anti-malaria efforts. Sierra Leone and Mozambique serve as the shadow cases for Guinea-Bissau and Malawi, respectively. In 2000, Sierra Leone's estimated malaria incidence was 465.7 per year, just slightly lower than in Guinea-Bissau, but by 2018 it was only able to reduce this burden by 31 percent, to 320.4. Mozambique's estimated malaria incidence was 492.5 in 2000, and it managed a

Figure 4.1 Malaria Incidence and Percent Reduction, 2000–2018

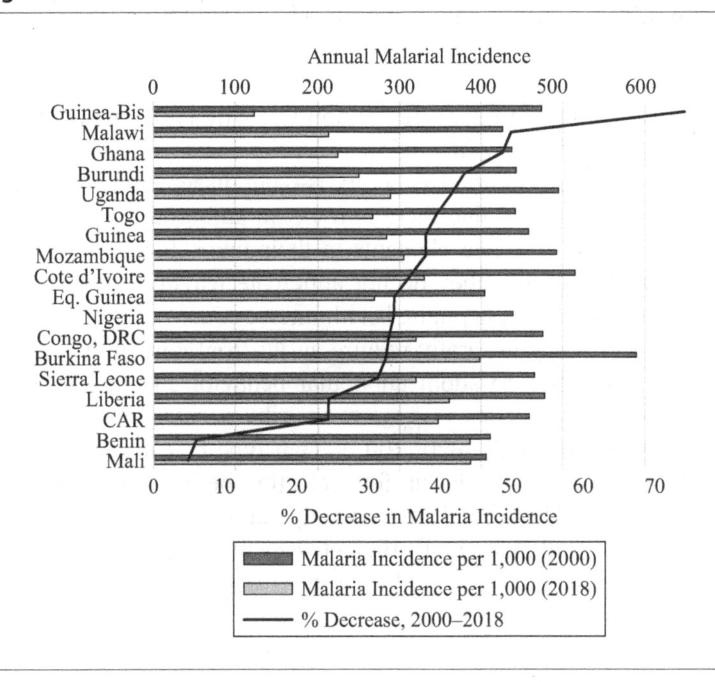

38 percent reduction to 305.3 in 2018. While Sierra Leone and Mozambique are not the worst performers, they are the most suitable comparison cases: their locations and climates mean the mosquito population in each of these comparison cases is similar to the main case, allowing for more direct comparison of public health interventions. Why were Guinea-Bissau and Malawi able to achieve such impressive reductions in malaria incidence, while Sierra Leone and Mozambique had more modest reductions? The following section describes theories of public health success that may help explain these differences.

Theories of Public Health Success

Why are some countries better than others at addressing threats to public health? Part of the challenge in improving public health is that many elements must align to achieve an outcome. Once effective interventions are available, the government must have sufficient political will to implement policies at a national level; the country must have enough internal capacity or external support to deliver the intervention; finally, the population must be willing and able to adopt the intervention and/or undertake behavior change. Failure at any of these levels could derail public health interventions. Theories of when public health interventions are likely to be more successful are related to this interrelated set of challenges.

Institutions

Institutions may influence the degree of political will a government has to face a health crisis. Existing institutional theories focus on regime type—how democratic or authoritarian a country is—but disagree on why it matters. Some writers suggest that there may be an authoritarian advantage. Authoritarian rulers have two elements in their favor. First, they have a long time horizon because they do not anticipate leaving office. A long time horizon matters because public health interventions are often not successful overnight—they generally require an up-front cost or attempts to convince the population to adopt unpopular behavior change, while the potential payoff only becomes apparent months or years later (Dionne 2011; Kavanagh and Singh 2020, 1002). That type of calculation might look bad to a democratic leader up for reelection before the intervention would show results. The second advantage that authoritarian governments may have is the combination of efficient decisionmaking and coercive capacity (Greer et al. 2021, 13). Authoritarian rulers do not need to negotiate with opposition parties to determine a course of action, so they may be able to make fast, effective decisions in the face of a public health threat. Similarly, if authoritarians have a strong coercive capacity, they may be able to quickly implement unpopular policies. Such capacity is particularly important when the public may not agree with the best practices set out by the international scientific community (Fox 2014). However, because the authoritarian advantage depends on the government's ability to coerce, it is only theoretically possible in a state with strong, centralized power.

Alternatively, there may be a democratic dividend. Democratic leaders inevitably must worry about reelection, which theoretically incentivizes them to be responsive to public demands. If the public is concerned about a public health issue, then a democratically elected government must address it or risk being voted out office (Gerring, Thacker, and Alfaro 2012; Wigley and Akkoyunlu-Wigley 2017). Therefore, democratic governments may be better at addressing public health challenges when there is both public demand for action and the possibility that the ruling party could be voted out of office.

Sociocultural Factors

For public health interventions to be effective, the public must comply with guidelines. In countries with deep identity-based social divisions—like those in which communities are divided according to ethnicity, religion, race, or other characteristics—it may be harder to generate compliance.

When deep boundaries between groups generate an "us vs. them" mentality, it can alter people's perceptions of risk, resulting in attribution of diseases to a "dirty, dangerous other" rather than understanding that diseases do not observe social boundaries (Lieberman 2009). Such divisions in society can also degrade social trust, which is essential for the will to undertake painful or costly behavior changes (Arakelyan et al. 2021). Therefore, public health interventions may be more effective in societies without deep social divisions or in places with greater social trust.

Local Actors

The final theories relate to the actors carrying out public health interventions. In many African countries, major public health initiatives are carried out as joint projects between governments, international funders, and nongovernmental organizations (NGOs). This collection of actors can create a complicated landscape with many possible ways things can go wrong. Donors often have incentives that are misaligned with the needs of local populations, and global health initiatives can sometimes import one-size-fits-all technical solutions that do not make sense given the local context in a country (Dionne 2018). It is therefore important for international organizations to form meaningful partnerships with the local agencies implementing interventions on the ground. Local implementing actors may be the government, local civil society organizations, or local NGOs. However, these organizations also vary in their capacity and performance (McDonnell 2020; Seay 2013). Theoretically, it is essential that they have two characteristics: First, they must have the trust of the community: numerous studies have shown that if people do not trust an institution or organization, they are unlikely to follow advice or accept medical interventions from actors associated with it (Blair, Morse, and Tsai 2017; Kohler et al. 2022; Vinck et al. 2019). Second, the actors implementing the intervention must have national reach to effectively cover the relevant population. National reach is related to two factors: capacity and will. Local actors must have the logistical capacity to work in hard-to-reach areas, but they must also have the will to do so. Some actors may fail to achieve national reach because they simply lack capacity, while others fail because of a lack of will to serve groups based on politics or other identity divisions.

Additionally, for local implementing actors to be effective, the government must prioritize the particular area of intervention. Though the government may rely on external funding or various NGOs to implement public health services, it must at least make space for those actors. If the government is not really committed to public health goals, then local actors may undermine rather than bolster internationally coordinated public health efforts

(Bor 2007; Fox 2014). For example, the response to the HIV/AIDS crisis in South Africa was derailed when President Thabo Mbeki publicly questioned whether HIV caused AIDS and refused to deliver life-saving antiretroviral medications (Dionne 2018, 23). Government commitment is therefore likely to be important, regardless of which actors implement the program.

External Support

Finally, for countries with limited fiscal capacity, external support from international donors and public health agencies is important to expand

Table 4.1 Theories of Public Health Success

Theory	Implication
	Institutions
Authoritarian advantage	Authoritarian governments with strong centralization and coercive capacity are better able to address public health challenges.
Democratic dividend	Democratic governments facing public demand and possibility of election loss are better able to address public health challenges.
	Sociocultural Factors
Social divisions	Countries without deep social divisions are better able to address public health challenges.
Social trust	Countries with higher levels of social trust are better able to address public health challenges.
	Local Actors
Trust	Countries in which interventions partner with local actors that the community trusts are better able to address public health challenges.
Reach	Countries in which interventions partner with local actors that have national reach are better able to address public health challenges.
Government commitment	Countries are better able to address public health challenges when the government is committed to it.
	External Support
Donor support	Countries with higher levels of donor support are better able to address public health challenges.

implementation capacity. Countries that struggle to attract donor support—due to conflict, perceptions of corruption, or other factors—may struggle to produce the resources necessary to procure medical equipment and implement public health protocols.

Most-Different Case Analysis: Guinea-Bissau and Malawi

Among the poorest countries in Africa, Guinea-Bissau and Malawi are unlikely cases to highlight as public health success stories. Located in West Africa, where the tropical climate contributes to the high malaria burden, Guinea-Bissau had one of the continent's highest rates of malaria incidence when the World Health Organization (WHO) started recording it in 2000. Unfortunately, Guinea-Bissau has also faced grave governance challenges, marked by coups and civil conflict (Embalo 2012). With the exception of its lucrative and illicit drug trafficking activity—which has primarily benefited the network of elites who control it—the economy has struggled (Shaw 2015). The World Bank estimates that about 48 percent of the population live below the poverty line.[6] In this context, the country's dramatic malaria reduction is striking.

Malawi, in southern Africa, is in a region with generally lower levels of malaria. It is one of only two countries in the region that began 2000 with a malaria incidence over 400 per 1,000 people. While Malawi has suffered much less political violence and instability than Guinea-Bissau, it has struggled with corruption crises and grinding poverty (over half the population lives below the national poverty line[7]) (Dulani and Dionne 2014). Despite these challenges around fiscal capacity, Malawi has also experienced an impressive reduction in malaria. What do Malawi and Guinea-Bissau have in common that can explain their shared success?

Guinea-Bissau and Malawi: Identifying a Common Factor of Success

As Table 4.2 illustrates, six hypotheses find support in both Guinea-Bissau and Malawi: both countries lack deep social divisions, have high levels of social trust, and had malaria programs carried out by local actors with national reach and the trust of the population. Both also enjoyed government commitment and donor support.

There is no evidence to support the two hypotheses on regime type. The authoritarian advantage explains neither case. Using Polity V's threshold for democracy (score of 6 or higher on a 10-point scale), Guinea-Bissau was authoritarian for most of 2000–2018, except a brief

Table 4.2 Theories as Applied to Guinea-Bissau and Malawi

Theory	Guinea-Bissau	Malawi	Explanation
	Institutions		
Authoritarian advantage	No	No	Theory unsupported; predicts neither
Democratic dividend	No	No	Theory unsupported; predicts neither
	Sociocultural Factors		
Social divisions	No	No	Supports theory
Social trust	Higher than average	Higher than average	Supports theory
	Local Actors		
Reach	National	National	Supports theory
Trust	High	High	Supports theory
Government commitment	Present	Present	Supports theory
	External Support		
Donor support	High	High	Supports theory

democratic interlude from 2006 to 2012. However, it lacked the necessary capacity for authoritarianism to confer any advantage. Using Hanson and Sigman's (2021) measure of state capacity, which accounts for coercive capacity (military and police), extractive capacity (revenue), and administrative capacity (ability to carry out state functions), Guinea-Bissau performs poorly compared to the rest of sub-Saharan Africa. For the period 2000–2015 for which data are available, Guinea-Bissau's average score is –0.809 on the index, which ranges from –3 to 3. This score places Guinea-Bissau just above the bottom quartile for sub-Saharan Africa. Qualitatively, Guinea-Bissau's authoritarianism has been chaotic rather than effective. Since its independence from Portugal in 1974, a series of political crises, coups, and civil conflicts have undermined governance (Embalo 2012). For the military and politicians alike, control over the government is an opportunity for personal enrichment, while ordinary people see almost no evidence of a functioning state (Shaw 2015, 343–344). In 2018, the first nationally representative public opinion survey carried out in Guinea-Bissau revealed that "the majority of the citizens had no contact" with the courts, police, service agencies, or school staff, and "64% of the population said they felt abandoned by the state" (Carter 2018, 2). Drawing from the theory, Guinea-Bissau's authoritarianism conferred no advantage during this period due its lack of central capacity and dereliction of duty.

Conversely, by Polity V's measure, Malawi was democratic for most of that period, except for a brief authoritarian setback from 2001 to 2005. The authoritarian advantage therefore cannot explain its success. However, the democratic dividend is an unsatisfactory explanation as well. The implication of this theory is that democratic governments are more likely to act if there is high public demand and they fear losing office through elections. However, the incumbent party in Malawi never lost an election from the reintroduction of party politics in 1994 until Joyce Banda was voted out of office in 2014.[8] During the 2000–2018 period, health was not the most salient demand of Malawi's population. Responding to the Afrobarometer's question of "what is the most important problem facing your country," challenges associated with health are eclipsed by those of food shortages and economic management. From 2002 to 2015, the percentage of Malawians who list "health" as one of their top three concerns ranges from only 16.1 percent to a high of 36.4 percent (in 2015). By contrast, about 70 percent of the population lists "food shortage" as one of their top concerns over this same period.

Qualitative evidence additionally suggests that Malawian presidents during this time were more interested in extraconstitutional methods for holding onto power than pleasing their constituents. Malawian presidents have regularly attempted to subvert the country's democracy, from Bakili Muzuli (1994–2004) attempting to eliminate the constitutional provision limiting presidents to two terms, to Bingu wa Mutharika (2005–2012) attempting to install his brother as his successor, to Joyce Banda's (2012–2014) implication in a massive corruption scheme (Dionne and Dulani 2013; Dulani and Dionne 2014). President Mutharika also presided over numerous attempts to shut down political opposition, including harassing and arresting critics, reducing the power of the courts, and controlling the media (Dionne and Dulani 2013, 114). Considering that the democratic dividend for public health relies on politicians listening to their constituents' demands to earn reelection, there is little evidence that either the demand or the fear of losing elections could have driven public health outcomes in this case. As Guinea-Bissau was not a democracy for most of the period under investigation, this theory cannot explain its performance either.

The other six hypotheses do have some support. Both Guinea-Bissau and Malawi have low levels of interethnic animosity, indicating that a lack of social divisions may have been helpful for each. In surveys asking how people would feel about having someone from a different ethnicity for a neighbor, 76 percent of respondents in Guinea-Bissau and 85.8 percent Malawi said they would like it, compared to 54.4 percent on average across sub-Saharan Africa.[9] While there has been conflict in Guinea-Bissau and ethnoregional electoral politics in Malawi, neither has contributed to animus between groups. In Guinea-Bissau, elite infighting rather than identity-based division has driven political instability (Vigh 2009). While ethnic identity emerges from time to time as an element of political conflict, qualitative analyses indicate that it does not drive this conflict, which is concentrated at the elite level rather than spread throughout society (Embalo 2012). In Malawi, ethnic divisions can be politically salient because of the way that ethnic groups are concentrated in regions and associated with ethnoregional political parties (Posner 2004b). However, these divisions are not hardened or immutable—the elections of 2009 disrupted the pattern of ethnic voting (Ferree and Horowitz 2010). Furthermore, high rates of ethnic intermarriage in Malawi have diluted older patterns of ethnic politics in recent years (Dulani et al. 2021).

Social trust is also higher than average in both countries. In a survey question asking about how much people trust their neighbors, 68 percent of Bissau-Guineans and 84.6 percent of Malawians indicated they trust their neighbors "somewhat" or "a lot," compared to 61.7 percent on average across sub-Saharan Africa.[10] Similarly, the Legatum Institute estimates that both countries have higher than average interpersonal trust, ranking Guinea-Bissau 47th (score of 44.2) and Malawi 64th (score of 40) out of 167 countries.

The next group of theories examines the characteristics of the local actors who partner with international donors and organizations to carry out the public health interventions. To determine who the relevant actors were in each country, I analyzed peer-reviewed medical and public health publications that discussed malaria interventions in each respective country for information about which actors carried out health interventions, and I corroborated these publications with reports from the Global Fund—the major funder for malaria interventions in all four cases in this chapter. As the following cases illustrate, the medical literature on Guinea-Bissau largely references voluntary community organizations and NGOs,[11] while the literature on Malawi references the Ministry of Health (e.g., Rodríguez, Banda, and Namakhoma 2015).

In both countries, these organizations garnered public trust during key implementation periods. In Guinea-Bissau, trust in community organizations and civil society is high, with only 23 percent and 24 percent of survey respondents indicating that they distrust these groups, respectively.

By contrast, lack of trust in governing institutions is much higher, ranging from 41 percent to 46 percent for the legislature, ruling party, and other elements of administration (Carter 2018, 2). In Malawi, pluralities of respondents report the highest level of trust in the president, the legislature, and government institutions across multiple rounds of the Afrobarometer survey. For example, in 2011, only 14.6 percent and 13.5 percent expressed distrust of the president and the ruling party, respectively. Trust in the presidency declined precipitously in 2014, as the survey came on the tails of the "Cashgate" scandal that implicated then-president Joyce Banda (Dulani and Dionne 2014). Trust in the presidency and other government institutions like the national legislature continued to decline under Banda's successor, Peter Mutharika (the brother of the previous president, Bingu wa Mutharika). However, by the time institutional trust declined, Malawi's malaria reduction program had already shown great signs of success, and the following qualitative accounts indicate that behavior change (i.e., using bed nets) occurred during the period of high institutional trust. In both countries, populations indicate relatively high levels of trust in the actors that carried out the public health programs. Meta-analysis of medical publications indicate that the respective service providers in each country managed national reach as well (discussed later in the chapter).

Next, I determine government commitment by looking at two factors: first, whether the government has an official agency or program dedicated to malaria specifically, and second, whether this agency and government statements about malaria generally follow internationally accepted best practices. This is a low bar, but it indicates whether the government considers malaria important and is unlikely to interfere with the best practices of public health practitioners. Guinea-Bissau has a National Malaria Control Program that has been engaged in some activities since 2000 (Ursing et al. 2014). Malawi's National Malaria Control Programme has been operational since 1984, and by all accounts the country has been an early adopter of evidence-based malaria interventions (Mwendera et al. 2019). There is no evidence in either county that these programs or government officials have made public statements advocating against standard practices of malaria control. While Malawi's program appears to be much more active than Guinea-Bissau's, the governments of both countries have been committed enough to at least stay out of the way of local actors engaged in malaria control work, though Malawi's government has been far more proactive than Guinea-Bissau's.

Finally, to determine donor support, I examine funding for malaria through the Institute for Health Metrics and Evaluation, which compiles data on donor contributions earmarked for malaria and other diseases.[12] This dataset includes malaria funding from all major bilateral and multilateral donors. Over 2000–2017, the eighteen counties I considered in this chapter received a cumulative total of $27 per capita on average, ranging from a low of $11.73 per capita in Nigeria to a high of $66.39 per capita in Liberia. Guinea-Bissau and Malawi are both in the top third of recipients, receiving $33.68 and $36.04 per capita, respectively. It is therefore plausible that a high level of donor funding has contributed to the success of each of their programs.

The following case analysis examines the role of the six factors that Guinea-Bissau and Malawi share—lack of social division, high social trust, and the reach and trust in local actors, government commitment, and donor support.

Guinea-Bissau

In 2000, the WHO estimated that 47.5 percent of the population of Guinea-Bissau contracted malaria every year. This gave Guinea-Bissau the unfortunate status of being one of the most malaria-prone countries on the most malaria-prone continent. As such, it became a target country for the United Nations Development Program's (UNDP's) Global Fund to Fight AIDS, Tuberculosis, and Malaria (hereafter, the Global Fund). The Global Fund's primary initial contribution was the distribution of bed nets. Because the mosquitos that transmit malaria are active at night, sleeping under a bed net—particularly one that has been treated with insecticides—is one of the most effective interventions. Initially, this campaign targeted children under the age of five and pregnant women, the populations most at risk of severe complications and death due to malaria. Financed by the Global Fund, this campaign was purportedly organized by the Ministry of Health but was carried out by volunteer community health workers. Ultimately, it resulted in a massive decline in malaria incidence (Hutchins et al. 2020; Rodrigues et al. 2008). This campaign coincided with the overuse of chloroquine, a drug used to treat malaria. Medical researchers found that doctors prescribed chloroquine to nearly every child who came to a health center, regardless of a malaria diagnosis (Ursing et al. 2009). However, while generally used to treat malaria, chloroquine can also prevent infection and likely offered additional protection to this age group. Unfortunately, the overwhelming success of this initial campaign contributed to a malaria resurgence from 2010 to 2012, as children aged out of the target group lacking the immunity they would have acquired had they been infected earlier (Ursing et al. 2014). The World Bank estimated that malaria incidence bounced back from a low of 72 cases per 1,000 people in 2007 to 140 in 2011. Response was rapid, with the bed-net distribution program expanded to target the entire population in 2011. As a result, malaria incidence declined to 71 cases per 1,000 people by 2016.

The peer-reviewed medical and public health literature from Guinea-Bissau indicate that the government has limited involvement in malaria initiatives, which are primarily funded internationally and carried out through private labs or community volunteer groups. Of the twelve articles reviewed, only one directly referenced a government campaign: the attempt at universal insecticide treatment of bed nets, which resulted in coverage of only 3 percent of the population (Rodrigues et al. 2008). The Global Fund indicates it had an explicit policy of avoiding working through the government, instead directing its resources through the UNDP, which worked directly with community volunteers.[13] Most of the international medical interventions have been tested only through the Bandim Health Project, a Danish-affiliated health center based in the capital (Kofoed et al. 2007; Ursing et al. 2007). Yet, despite the limited reach of these interventions, public health experts suggest that Guinea-Bissau's malaria reduction is most likely due to mass compliance with bed net use (Ursing et al. 2014). In 2018, a survey of residents of a remote archipelago in Guinea-Bissau found that *every* household surveyed had at least one bed net, and 89 percent of the population slept under a net, despite their inconvenience and the other possible household uses of netting (Hutchins et al. 2020). This high uptake rate is likely because the nets were being distributed by local health workers to their own communities; these volunteer health workers also instructed their neighbors on proper use and described why they are important to prevent malaria (Hutchins et al. 2020, 2). Distribution and education by trusted members of the community was essential for creating a "culture of net use," in which sleeping under a bed net is "a socially accepted norm and habitual behavior" (Berthe et al. 2014, 2).[14]

The medical literature agrees that the effective bed-net distribution campaign has been the primary driver of malaria reduction in Guinea-Bissau. The relevant intervention was carried out by community volunteers—who Bissau-Guineans are much more likely to trust than the government. Their efforts also gave this particular campaign national reach. It is difficult to assess the role of social trust and the lack of social divisions, as the public health literature did not address either issue directly. However, one can infer from the absence of their mention these factors did not pose a prominent obstacle in Guinea-Bissau. Finally, while government commitment did not enable this campaign—the UNDP avoided working with government agencies—it did not thwart it either.

Malawi

In 2000 the WHO estimated that 43.7 percent of Malawians contracted malaria each year. That number declined from 2001 to 2005, rebounded from 2006 to 2009, and then saw a steady decline from 2009 through 2016, when the WHO estimated that 21.1 percent of Malawians contracted the disease each year. This incidence rate has held steady for the past few years. Malawi's malaria control campaign is complicated by the mosquitos in the region, which have developed insecticide resistance and which are active earlier in the evening, making insecticide-treated bed nets insufficient as a single intervention (Zgambo, Mbakaya, and Kalembo 2017). These complications make it even more impressive that Malawi was able to halve its malaria burden over this period.

Malawi's national efforts at malaria control date back to 1984, though early interventions were limited due to lack of resources (Hershey et al. 2017, 76; Mwendera et al. 2019, 2). While it historically relied heavily on NGOs, the national malaria program pivoted after about 2005 to be carried out primarily by the Ministry of Health. Earlier interventions were more limited in scope, focusing on the Blantrye district (where the capital is located) or a small pilot area, but later scaled up to be nationally representative. These two shifts—toward implementation by the central government and nationalization of the programs—are evident in the shifting focus of the medical literature over this time. Of a sample of twelve peer-reviewed medical and public health articles about Malawi's malaria program from 2002 to 2019, only two (published in 2002 and 2005) note that NGOs were the primary implementing partners (Holtz et al. 2002; Mathanga et al. 2005). These both discuss the first mass campaign to distribute bed nets, which began in 1998. Unfortunately, because of the financial and capacity constraints of the Malawian state, the initial bed nets were "socially marketed" by the NGO Population Services International: they were sold at a subsidized price rather than distributed free of cost (Holtz et al. 2002; Mathanga et al. 2005). Bed net use was limited during this time, especially in rural areas, because most people could not afford to purchase them even at the subsidized price (Holtz et al. 2002; Mathanga and Bowie 2007). Later programs after around 2002 were carried out in collaboration with the government. Reports from the Global Fund during this time indicate that all funding went directly to the Ministry of Health.[15]

In 2005, the Malawian government established the National Malaria Control Program alongside a comprehensive five-year plan to coordinate three interventions: expanding access to treatment, preventive treatment for pregnant women, and indoor spraying of pesticides. Like in Guinea-Bissau, much of the funding for these initiatives came from the

Global Fund and the US President's Malaria Initiative, but in the case of Malawi, the government was much more involved in the implementation of the program (Mathanga et al. 2012; Mwendera et al. 2019; Rodríguez, Banda, and Namakhoma 2015). After 2005, all the medical publications reviewed name the central government and the Ministry of Health as the primary local actors responsible for these interventions.[16] Initial progress was slow because of the limited reach of the program. Early intervention efforts were concentrated in areas of greater wealth (Mathanga and Bowie 2007), with uneven distribution across the country (Mathanga et al. 2012). These initial challenges in achieving national reach were largely due to capacity rather than will, and publications after 2012 note considerable scaling up of these programs, ultimately achieving national reach (Bennett et al. 2013; Hershey et al. 2017; Wondji et al. 2012). As in Guinea-Bissau, this reach has been achieved partially through the use of community-based health surveillance assistants, who helped reach rural locations with a lower density of health clinics (Rodríguez, Banda, and Namakhoma 2015). Reliance on these community workers scaled up in 2008, the timing of which coincides with the decline in malaria cases from 2009.

After 2005, Malawi's malaria program was carried out by an actor that most of the population trusts (the central government), and while initial implementation was scattered, the government was able to achieve national scaling by 2011 with the Global Fund's support. As noted previously, trust in the central government declined after 2014, but trust in community workers—the primary point of contact with the health system for many people—has remained high (Kok et al. 2017, 1410). Assessing the role of social trust and the lack of social divisions in the program's relative success is more challenging; comparatively, social trust is high in Malawi and social divisions generate little animosity (and are becoming less pronounced over time). None of the public health analyses credit either of these features for the success of these programs, but neither are they identified as challenges. The studies that focus on challenges to Malawi's malaria programs tend to identify technical issues, such as the mosquitos' development of insecticide resistance (Zgambo, Mbakaya, and Kalembo 2017). A recent assessment of challenges to Malawi's program indicates that aside from resources, the biggest issue is top-down program design, reflecting the role of the central government. This assessment indicated a need for community outreach but noted that the primary need for such outreach was improved education rather than a lack of trust or social division (Mwendera et al. 2019). While the data available to assess these factors is limited, it appears that in Malawi neither social divisions nor trust posed barriers to the malaria program.

Most-Similar Case Analyses

The most-different case analysis indicated six things that Guinea-Bissau and Malawi have in common: high levels of social trust, low levels of social division, and local program implementers that had the trust of the population and national reach, government commitment, and donor support. This section presents two most-similar case analyses to determine whether these factors were present in Sierra Leone and Mozambique, where malaria reduction was less successful than in Guinea-Bissau and Malawi, respectively.

Guinea Bissau and Sierra Leone

While Guinea-Bissau saw a tremendous reduction in its malaria burden between 2000 and 2018, malaria incidence in Sierra Leone has been stubbornly persistent, despite the countries' outward similarities. Both are small countries in West Africa, on either side of Guinea, with similar climates and malaria case characteristics. Both have histories of civil conflict, though Sierra Leone's eleven-year civil war was more extensive and brutal than Guinea-Bissau's. As in Guinea-Bissau, Sierra Leone's history of instability decimated its public health infrastructure, and its transition to postconflict democracy has been marred by charges of corruption and repression of opposition parties. Yet, facing similarly challenging circumstances, Sierra Leone has made much less progress than Guinea-Bissau. Sierra Leone had an estimated annual malaria rate of 46.5 percent in 2000 and experienced a decline to 32 percent in 2018 (a 31 percent reduction). In brief, the following evidence suggests that the two countries differ little in terms of social divisions, trust, or government commitment, but did have very different experiences in the way that donors engaged local actors.

Both Sierra Leone and Guinea-Bissau have little interethnic animosity. When asked how they would feel about having a neighbor of a different ethnicity, 87 percent of Sierra Leoneans said they would like it (compared to 76 percent of Bissau-Guineans and 54.4 percent on average across sub-Saharan Africa).[17] Like in Guinea-Bissau, Sierra Leone's civil war was not driven by social identity but rather poverty, economic inequality, and the politicization of the chieftaincy (Fanthorpe 2006). While there is some history of competition between the two largest ethnic groups, the Mande and the Temne, this competition has not become politicized (Kandeh 2008). There is thus little evidence that identity-based divisions thwarted Sierra Leone's malaria efforts.

Comparing social trust between Sierra Leone and Guinea Bissau, the evidence is mixed. In Sierra Leone, only 50.8 percent of people say they trust their neighbors "somewhat" or "a lot," compared to 68 percent in Guinea-Bissau and 61.7 percent on average across sub-Saharan Africa.[18] However, other accounts of social trust in Sierra Leone indicate that it is relatively high: the Legatum Institute ranks Sierra Leone 23rd of 167 countries (score of 50.7) on interpersonal trust, compared to Guinea-Bissau's ranking of 47 (score of 44.2). Qualitatively, one recent study found high levels of social trust in Sierra Leone specifically around medical issues, with people indicating they regularly conferred with other community members about health issues (Arakelyan et al. 2021). Social trust is not a compelling difference between Sierra Leone and Guinea Bissau, though trust in health institutions is; this issue is addressed subsequently.

Next is the involvement of local actors, which has been minimal until recently in Sierra Leone. Nearly all programs have been carried out by international NGOs, and the involvement of Sierra Leonean actors is unclear. Of nine peer-reviewed public health articles, ranging from 2010 to 2021, references to partnership with the central government only appear in programs that commenced after 2014. Prior to that, nearly all malaria projects carried out in Sierra Leone reference work completed by Médecins sans Frontières (MSF) or private research groups, concentrated almost entirely in the two districts of Bo and Pujehun (Gerstl et al. 2010; Nnedu et al. 2010; Tayler-Smith et al. 2011; Thomson et al. 2011). Similarly, the Global Fund reports that its malaria funding was all distributed to the international NGO Catholic Relief Services, and it notes that few donor organizations in the country coordinate with each other or report their activities to the Ministry of Health.[19] Programs were typically confined to small areas. For example, MSF reported good results for a mass bed-net distribution program that employed community members to distribute and educate their neighbors about the nets, similar to Guinea-Bissau's successful program (Gerstl et al. 2010). However, the program was only deployed in their catchment area, covering two districts. At the end of the study period, they reported a bed net use rate of 77 percent for children under 5, while the rate outside the area was 5 percent (Gerstl et al. 2010, 485–486). Until 2014, malaria prevention efforts were ad hoc, uncoordinated, and without national reach.[20] While the government was ostensibly committed to malaria prevention—the National Malaria Control program dates back to 1994 and its list of activities is consistent with best practices[21]—the government's weakness during this period meant that it was only minimally involved.

An important contextual factor in Sierra Leone is the general mistrust in the medical system (Enria et al. 2021). Sierra Leone's health system was decimated by its civil war, and its postwar reconstitution was badly mismanaged. While the health care system is supposed to provide many services for free, health workers regularly illegally charge patients, and Sierra Leoneans view the system as corrupt and untrustworthy (Pieterse and Lodge 2015). This mistrust extends to international organizations and "outsiders," who are associated with everything from the slave trade and natural resource exploitation to heavy-handed and poorly explained Ebola containment protocols (Enria et al. 2021; Wilkinson and Fairhead 2017). Additionally, Sierra Leone received only about half the donor support that Guinea-Bissau did for malaria: $18.98 per capita over 2000–2017 (placing it in the bottom third of recipients considered). Of the six hypotheses indicated previously, three are consistent with this case: lack of trust in and national reach of public health actors and low levels of donor support.

Things began to change in 2014. The central government became more involved in malaria prevention, staging a vast scale-up of bed-net distribution based on a house-to-house registration campaign, which resulted in 62 percent of households owning at least one bed net (Aregawi et al. 2016, 2). Almost immediately on the heels of this campaign, a massive Ebola epidemic swept through West Africa. While the epidemic itself was catastrophic, one consequence was the rapid scale-up of Sierra Leone's public health infrastructure, including a major push for the distribution of at-home malaria treatments to reduce the burden on the medical system to reserve those resources for Ebola patients (Aregawi et al. 2016). This program involved a coalition between Sierra Leone's Ministry of Health and Sanitation (MoHS), MSF, the United Nations International Children's Emergency Fund (UNICEF), the Global Fund, and the WHO and involved collaborating with local authorities (chiefs and local councilors) to make use of the bed-net registration campaign to distribute medication to all households in affected areas. Over eight days in December 2014 and January 2015, 8,330 health staff and community health workers distributed at-home malaria care to over 90 percent of the population in the Ebola-affected area. Importantly, the ultimate effectiveness of this campaign is attributable to reliance on chiefs to access all households and monitor compliance—inserting locally trusted actors into the health initiative (Wilkinson and Fairhead 2017).

Despite the health care disruption caused by the Ebola epidemic, this massive mobilization has coincided with a decline in malaria incidence in Sierra Leone post-2015. There is evidence that this scale-up has been effective in other ways as well. The central government undertook another centralized distribution of bed nets in 2017 (McCoy et al. 2021, 4), and a recent survey shows high levels of knowledge about malaria prevention and demand for bed nets, though there is a persistent net shortage (Wang et al. 2021). Post-Ebola, international funders appear more willing to work with Sierra Leone's central government. For example, the US President's Malaria Initiative began working with the government in 2017, resulting in a large scale-up of national efforts. The new National Malaria Control Program of 2016–2020 has contributed to broader malaria interventions—even in the face of Covid-19—and Sierra Leone has even become the first country to nationally scale a program for intermittent preventive treatment for infants.[22] While Sierra Leone's malaria prevalence is still high, it is now trending downward. Sierra Leone's malaria program has faced significant challenges; namely, low funding, lack of trust in the medical system, and the lack of partnership with local actors at a national scale until recently. However, recent initiatives in this direction and a corresponding decline in malaria incidence augurs well for the future.

Malawi and Mozambique

As Malawi halved its malaria burden, Mozambique reduced its malaria prevalence by 38 percent. As the following analysis will make clear, Mozambique is not an ideal most-similar comparison to Malawi—they differ in many important ways. However, as the only two countries in southern Africa with a malaria incidence over 400 per 1,000 people in 2000, this structured comparison can still help illuminate why Mozambique struggled more. Sharing a border, Mozambique and Malawi also share certain elements of malaria pathology that make treating it particularly difficult: mosquitoes in this region have developed resistance to some common insecticides, and they bite earlier in the evening, so bed nets are insufficient to stop malaria's spread. These factors make malaria reduction more complicated, but as described previously, Malawi coped with its challenges better than Mozambique. In brief, the hypotheses about social divisions and the national reach of the malaria program hold some explanatory power.

First, social divisions are deeper in Mozambique than in Malawi. In Mozambique, only 48.8 percent of respondents to the Afrobarometer said they would like to have someone of a different ethnicity as a neighbor, compared to 85.8 percent in Malawi (and 54.4 percent on average across sub-Saharan Africa). In Mozambique, ethnicity coincides somewhat with region and party affiliation. While many countries have ethnoregional politics without deep social divisions (Malawi, for example), in Mozambique partisanship is deeply polarizing. Mozambique descended into civil war almost immediately after it won its independence from Portugal in 1975. This conflict can be crudely summarized as a Cold War proxy war between the communist Frelimo and the capitalist Renamo, but the ideological split between the two also coincided with region and ethnicity (Funada-Classen 2013). The horrific war atrocities seeded deep animosities between the two groups of combatants. The war ended in a ceasefire in 1992 with no clear victor and no process of national reconciliation. Instead, the peace agreement established multiparty democracy with Frelimo and Renamo as the two primary parties (Pitcher 2021). Frelimo, with its base in the south around the capital of Maputo, has been politically dominant ever since. Renamo, with its base in the country's center, has triggered sporadic anti-state violence and has been shut out of state resources (Pitcher 2021).

Social trust is also much greater in Malawi than Mozambique. In Mozambique, only 59.5 percent of the population told the Afrobarometer they trusted their neighbors "somewhat" or "a lot," compared to 84.6 percent in Malawi (and 61.7 percent on average across sub-Saharan Africa). Similarly, the Legatum Institute ranks Mozambique 138th of 167 countries (score of 30.8) on interpersonal trust, compared to Malawi's ranking of 64 (score of 40). Theoretically, lack of trust may impede public health interventions if it affects the population's willingness to undertake behavior change. However, available qualitative evidence does not support this idea: a recent study indicated that community-based efforts to improve malaria knowledge and encourage behavior change in Mozambique were broadly effective (de Sousa Pinto da Fonseca et al. 2021). While social trust in Mozambique is low, there is no evidence that it has hampered malaria-related behavior change.

Malaria control efforts in Mozambique are carried out through the central government's National Malaria Control Program. Indicative of government commitment, this program has been active since 1982 and has a history of following best practices.[23] Of twelve peer-reviewed public health publications from 2007 to 2021, all mention the government as the primary implementing partner. Most funding for malaria programs comes from the Global Fund, 75 percent of which goes directly to the Ministry of Health.[24] Trust in the central government (as measured by trust in the president and parliament) is relatively high (and similar to Malawi), with only 10.7 percent and 12.4 percent expressing distrust in the president and the legislature, respectively, during the middle of the implementation period in 2012. Additionally, the government relies on community health workers (CHWs) for some malaria treatment and prevention activities, like providing intermittent preventive treatment to pregnant women. Qualitative evidence indicates that these CHWs, who are selected by their communities, are generally well-trusted (Enguita-Fernàndez et al. 2021; Kok et al. 2017). While trust in the government and CHWs is relatively high, there is considerable evidence that the government concentrates resources (including malaria interventions) in the region around the capital, indicating that it lacks the will to achieve national reach (Sumich 2010).

Most analyses of malaria prevention initiatives in Mozambique note that they are concentrated in the southern province, especially around Maputo, where malaria prevalence is the lowest but Frelimo support is strongest (Aide et al. 2019; Dos Anjos Luis and Cabral 2016; Carlucci et al. 2017; Casimiro et al. 2007; Cirera et al. 2020; Coleman et al. 2008; Montgomery, Munguambe, and Pool 2010). Mozambique's earliest comprehensive program on malaria control was the Lubombo Spatial Development Initiative, a joint program between the governments of Mozambique, eSwatini, and South Africa. Its goal was to entirely eliminate malaria in South Africa and eSwatini by targeting malaria transmission in southern Mozambique, the source of most malaria infections in the other two countries (Aide et al. 2019). It included annual rounds of indoor pesticide spraying, distribution of insecticide-treated bed nets, and intensified efforts at providing children and pregnant women with effective malaria treatments (Aide et al. 2019, 3). This integrated set of interventions was highly effective. Central and northern Mozambique, the areas with the highest burden (and greater support for Renamo), were not part of this intensive program.

Efforts to scale indoor residual spraying and bed-net distribution have been slow. By 2014, only eleven of seventeen districts in Zambezia Province—an area of central Mozambique with high malaria prevalence—had been served by the bed-net distribution program, and net usage in some areas was still only 38 percent due a lack of access (Carlucci et al. 2017). Access to health resources in Mozambique is closely correlated with income and related to Frelimo support, with the poorest provinces with the greatest need receiving the fewest interventions (Arroz 2017; Llop-Girones and Jones 2021). Emblematic of this inequality, there are ongoing malaria eradication projects in the south, where the malaria burden is extremely low, while at the same time rates of childhood malaria in Zambezia province have remained steady for the past decade (Cirera et al. 2020; de Sousa Pinto da Fonseca et al. 2021). This inequality cannot be attributed to inadequate donor support: Mozambique received nearly the same amount of donor funding as Malawi over 2000–2017 ($34.72 per capita), placing it in the top third of recipients as well.

Mozambique differs from Malawi in social division and the national reach of the program, and indeed, they are interrelated. Mozambique's social divisions, resulting from its civil war, have manifested in part through concentration of malaria resources in the country's south, where malaria rates are (and have historically been) the lowest. Persistence of malaria in the country's most heavily affected regions has been exacerbated by this uneven distribution of resources.

The only hypothesis that finds support across all four cases is the national reach of the implementing actor. In both Sierra Leone and Mozambique, recent histories of civil war hampered national efforts at malaria control, but in different ways. In Sierra Leone, the civil war decimated the government's health infrastructure, leading to widespread corruption in the health sector and deep mistrust in the health system generally. The result was that the international NGOs engaged in malaria control avoided working through the government, resulting in an ad hoc collection of programs with patchy coverage. Malaria rates have begun to decline since the post-Ebola pivot to partnering with the government and using chiefs as trusted intermediaries to achieve national reach. In Mozambique, the social divisions wrought by the country's lengthy civil war are now expressed through an uneven distribution of national resources. In this case, the lack of national reach appears related to will rather than trust or capacity.

Conclusion

Malaria has long been one of the biggest and most persistent threats to public health in sub-Saharan Africa. While malaria incidence has declined precipitously other regions, reduction efforts have stagnated across much of Africa. Yet some countries have achieved relative success in reducing their malaria burdens. The cases presented here indicate that the most important factor distinguishing the most successful countries from those with more modest improvements was that donors were able to partner with a local implementing actor with national reach. However, different contributing factors inhibited national reach in Sierra Leone and Mozambique.

All four countries in this chapter have limited fiscal and logistical capacities, and therefore their malaria reduction programs were conducted through the support of international donors. The way these international actors created partnerships with local actors was critical for the success of these programs, and the way they approached it required flexibility. In Malawi, donors were thus able to effectively engage with the central government, creating programming through the Ministry of Health that could be implemented nationally. While the program faced challenges, the government made a good partner due to the high levels of institutional trust. Ethnoregional political divisions were not deep enough to derail the program, particularly since the party in power changed multiple times over the implementation period. In Guinea-Bissau, it was clear that the government would not make an effective partner due to its history of instability, lack of public service delivery, and lack of institutional trust held by Bissau-Guineans. Instead, donors and international organizations were able to partner with community groups that people did trust and were able to dispatch these volunteers nationally. The fact that malaria in Guinea-Bissau is well controlled with bed nets certainly helped these efforts as well.

In Sierra Leone and Mozambique, engagement of local actors was less effective, but for different reasons. In Sierra Leone, donor agencies did not systematically work with a local actor—in this case the government—until the Ebola epidemic. During most of the period under consideration, nearly all malaria efforts in the country were carried out by international NGOs without national reach. Post-Ebola, as the donor community has begun to engage the government and chiefs as local intermediaries, malaria prevention has finally scaled nationally, and incidence rates are declining. In Mozambique, donor agencies have worked with the government throughout this period. However, the government has concentrated resources in the south until recently, neglecting regions of the country with the highest rates of malaria. This regional concentration is likely related to Mozambique's deep and highly politicized social divisions.

Taken together, these cases illustrate that public health successes are eminently possible in countries with lower financial and logistical capacity. However, success requires effective engagement of local actors, and context determines which actors are likely to be the most effective partners. In the countries where national-level malaria reduction was more successful, it was because donors engaged local partners with the ability and will to implement the interventions nationally. While social divisions themselves did not impede malaria intervention, they did lead to the regional concentration of resources in Mozambique.

Malawi and Guinea-Bissau are not the only countries that have seen significant malaria reduction: Ghana, Burundi, and Uganda have also experienced declines in incidence over 40 percent. It would be fruitful to examine whether the nature of engagement with local actors led to strong national programs there as well, especially given Burundi's recent history of civil war and Uganda's long-running social divisions. Additionally, malaria is not the only significant public health concern on the continent. Tuberculosis and HIV/AIDS continue to pose challenges as well, and some countries have done better than others at addressing these issues. It would be further worth examining whether public health success in one area, like malaria reduction, indicates success in addressing other public health challenges.

While the barriers to achieving malaria reduction in countries like Sierra Leone and Mozambique are frustrating, successes in Guinea-Bissau and Malawi highlight important lessons. Public health improvements can be achieved even in challenging circumstances, with adequate attention to the context and the actors that are best situated to reach the most people. At the time of writing, a malaria vaccine was finally approved by the WHO, bringing renewed hope of limiting the effect of this disease even in places where the mosquitos that carry it have developed insecticide resistance and are active early in the evening.[25] Rolling out this vaccine to those in affected areas will be a massive feat—one that will require careful engagement of local actors.

Notes

1. Cripps, Karla. 2014, October 21. "Ebola Fears Crippling Africa's Safari Industry," *CNN*. October 21, 2014. https://www.cnn.com/travel/article/africa-safaris-ebola/index.html

2. Seay, Laura and Kim Yi Dionne, "The Long and Ugly Tradition of Treating Africa as a Dirty, Diseased Place," *Washington Post: Monkey* Cage, August 25, 2014. https://www.washingtonpost.com/news/monkey-cage/wp/2014/08/25/othering-ebola-and-the-history-and-politics-of-pointing-at-immigrants-as-potential-disease-vectors/

3. Infant mortality (per 1,000 live births): 106.6 (1990) to 51.7 (2019); life expectancy: 50.2 (1990) to 61.6 (2019).

4. Incidence of malaria (per 1,000 population): 349.7 (2000) to 219.1 (2019); incidence of HIV (per 1,000 uninfected population): 3.16 (2000) to 0.93 (2019).

5. For malaria, the World Bank reports the number of new cases of malaria per year per 1,000 people "at risk," meaning people living in places where malaria transmission occurs. These numbers are estimates based on a combination of confirmed cases, extent of health service use, and likelihood of underreporting. More information is available at https://www.who.int/data/gho/indicator-metadata-registry/imr-details/4670

6. Poverty headcount ratio at national poverty lines (% of population) estimated at 48.7% in 2010; 47.7% in 2018.

7. Poverty headcount ratio at national poverty lines (% of population) estimated at 50.7% in 2010 and 2019.

8. While the party affiliation of the president changed during this time, it was due to internal party splits rather than voters electing a new party. The United Democratic Front was the party in power from 1994 to 2004, when incumbent president Mutharika split with the party and started the Democratic Progressive Party, under which he was reelected in 2009. He died in office and was succeeded by his vice president, Joyce Banda, who herself had split with the party and started the People's Party. However, her succession was a matter of constitutional order rather than reelection. She was the first incumbent to be unseated through an election, in 2014.

9. Guinea-Bissau data from the 2018 Voices of the People survey, which is modeled on the Afrobarometer but not administered by the same organization. Data for Malawi and the comparison sample from Afrobarometer Round 7.

10. Guinea-Bissau data from the 2018 Voices of the People survey, Malawi from Round 5 of the Afrobarometer (the relevant question was not asked in more recent years).

11. E.g., UNDP. 2019, April 24. "Can Data Save Lives?" https://stories.undp.org/is-the-digital-divide-hampering-the-malaria-response-in-africa

12. Data accessed through https://ghdx.healthdata.org/series/financing-global-health-fgh

13. The Global Fund. 2014. "Global Fund Grants to Guinea-Bissau." www.theglobalfund.org/media/2607/oig_gf-oig-14-014_report_en.pdf

14. Sadly, malaria incidence has been on the rise in Guinea-Bissau since 2017. It is possible that this perceived increase is a result of better reporting, as the Global Fund began working with health centers to put a digitized reporting system into place: https://www.undp.org/blogs/digital-divide-hampering-malaria-response-africa

15. Another round of funding from 2018 to 2020, after the implementation period examined in this chapter, allocated significant funding to the international NGO World Vision.

16. Bennett et al. 2013; Van Den Berg et al. 2018; Hershey et al. 2017; Mathanga et al. 2012; Mathanga and Bowie 2007; Mwendera et al. 2019; Roca-Feltrer et al. 2012; Rodríguez, Banda, and Namakhoma 2015; Wondji et al. 2012; Zgambo, Mbakaya, and Kalembo 2017.

17. Data from Round 7 of the Afrobarometer for Sierra Leone; 2018 Voices of the People survey for Guinea-Bissau.

18. Data from Round 5 of the Afrobarometer for Sierra Leone; 2018 Voices of the People survey for Guinea-Bissau.

19. Global Fund. 2019. "Global Fund Grants to the Republic of Sierra Leone." https://www.theglobalfund.org/media/8204/oig_gf-oig-19-001_report_en.pdf

20. It is possible that focus on malaria was delayed by a disproportionate focus on HIV/AIDS in the 2000s. In the wake of Sierra Leone's brutal civil war, international public health workers were concerned that the country exhibited many risk factors of an HIV/AIDS epidemic. As a result, a great deal of the external public health assistance for the country was earmarked for HIV/AIDS, by one account "cannibalizing" the ability of the meager public health infrastructure to handle other ailments (Benton 2015, 14). Focus on preventing HIV may have crowded out resources for malaria (Benton and Dionne 2015, 227).

21. Government of Sierra Leone Ministry of Health and Sanitation. 2015. "National Malaria Control Strategic Plan, 2016–2020." p. 38. https://www.afro.who.int/publications/sierra-leone-malaria-control-strategic-plan-2016-2020

22. ICAP Global Health. 2019, April 25. "ICAP Supports Sierra Leone to Become First Country with National Coverage of Infant Malaria Prevention." https://icap.columbia.edu/news-events/icap-supports-sierra-leone-to-become-first-country-with-national-coverage-of-infant-malaria-prevention/

23. National Malaria Control Programme. 2006. "Strategic Plan for Malaria Control in Mozambique." https://www.afro.who.int/sites/default/files/2017-06/Strategic%20plan%20for%20malaria%20control%20in%20Mozambique.pdf

24. The remaining 25% goes to the international NGO World Vision. The Global Fund. 2022. "Global Fund Grants in the Republic of Mozambique."

25. World Health Organization. 2021, October 6. "WHO Recommends Groundbreaking Malaria Vaccine for Children at Risk."https://www.who.int/news/item/06-10-2021-who-recommends-groundbreaking-malaria-vaccine-for-children-at-risk

5

City Planning for Climate Adaptation

Climate change is one of the most pernicious challenges that African countries face. It threatens progress in nearly all the other areas discussed in this book. Changing weather patterns, including more frequent and extreme instances of drought and flooding, can undermine agriculture and cause disasters in cities, which in turn threaten economic development and produce crises of internally displaced persons. A rapidly changing environment can also intensify public health challenges, expanding the range of disease vectors like mosquitos and (in the case of flooding) increasing incidence of waterborne illnesses (Kareem et al. 2020). In addition to posing both urgent and long-term challenges, it is an issue of social justice: African countries have contributed the least to global climate change, but are among those projected to be most affected by it (Morgan et al. 2019). Far from being hypothetical or distant, residents of major cities in southern Africa report that climate change is already affecting their lives and livelihoods (Steynor et al. 2020). Given these realities, African countries must urgently take steps to adapt to a changing climate.

Since addressing climate change became an important part of the international agenda, most treaties, protocols, and action plans have focused on mitigation (reducing greenhouse gas, or GHG, emissions) on the part of wealthy industrialized countries with the aim of limiting overall warming to 1.5–2.0 degrees Celsius. Indeed, the wealthiest countries continue to be the biggest producers of GHG emissions and are also less likely to experience the worst effects of climate change (Althor, Watson, and Fuller 2016). Poor and middle-income countries, however, produce significantly less per capita and are more likely to experience the worst effects of climate change. In terms of GHG emissions per capita, the World Bank estimates that African countries are at the bottom of the global list (excepting South Africa, which is 37th). Yet, they top the list of countries likely to be most heavily affected by climate change (Morgan et al. 2019). Therefore, when discussing climate action in African countries, it is important to focus on adaptation (improving resilience to climate-related challenges) in addition to mitigation.

There is a great deal being done across African countries to adapt to changing climate realities: climate-smart agriculture, architecture meant to reduce indoor temperatures, diversifying household assets to overcome food insecurity, and adoption of drought-resistant crops (see, for example, the *African Handbook of Climate Change Adaptation*, 2021). It is challenging to systematically analyze these adaptations and interventions because they are largely ad hoc. While some countries have climate action plans, none of them integrate all these interventions and adaptations. Many of them are carried out by local communities, nongovernmental organizations, civil society organizations, or local government. Some are implemented with national or international support; others are fully local and independent.

While a vibrant network of community groups and organizations is conducting research and implementing all manner of programs to promote adaptation (Kareem et al. 2020), national and local governments are not excused from taking action. Some interventions, like those involving infrastructure and markets, can only occur at the level of government. National action is essential for countries that need to engage in climate mitigation, but interventions at the level of local government may be more appropriate for climate adaptation. Because countries are made up of numerous microclimates, with each region facing a different set of challenges and opportunities, local governments are better equipped to assess the specific issues that climate change poses. National frameworks for climate action are still important, but cities and municipal governments are often in a better position to determine the most important climate adaptations (Reckien et al. 2018).

There has been a global surge in cities taking action on both climate mitigation and adaptation. Major international networks, like C40 Cities and the Global Covenant of Mayors, have emerged to support action at the city level. These networks encourage knowledge-sharing, experience, and resources, including financial assistance and capacity-building for cities in poorer countries. Membership in these networks is a boon for cities engaged in climate adaptation, as they provide international recognition and access to financial resources to undertake adaptation efforts that benefit the city both immediately and in the long run. However, only some African cities have joined these networks, and far fewer have designed or implemented the climate action plans that such networks support. Why are some cities so much more successful at systematically acting in support of climate adaptation?

To answer this question, in this chapter, I focus on membership and action in one such international network: the Global Covenant of Mayors (GCoM). This group began in 2008 to help municipalities in the European Union meet regional climate targets. While initially focused on mitigation efforts, it expanded in 2015 to incorporate adaptation and merged with another global initiative to expand its reach beyond Europe (Palermo et al. 2020). Joining the GCoM confers resources and enables action in cities that may have struggled financially to make change, and tracks cities' actions through a series of badges for making and then implementing plans for mitigation and adaptation (Pasquini 2020). Cities can earn up to nine badges in three areas: mitigation (reducing GHG emissions), adaptation (improving resilience to climate-related challenges), and extending access to renewable energy. In each area, cities earn a badge for undertaking an assessment of current challenges and needs, setting targets and goals, and producing comprehensive planning documents. Furthermore, cities must demonstrate annual progress to be designated "compliant." This tracking thus provides a way to see which cities are being most proactive (Hughes 2017; Sharp, Daley, and Lynch 2011).

At the time of writing, 257 African cities have joined the GCoM, but only 29 have earned badges (see Figure 5.1). In this chapter I proceed with two of the highest achieving cities, Durban, South Africa (6 badges) and Lagos, Nigeria (4 badges), and compare them to other cities in the same country that joined the GCoM but have not achieved any badges: Bloemfontein (South Africa) and Abuja (Nigeria). Why have Durban and Lagos been more successful than Bloemfontein and Abuja? The following section presents theories of cities' willingness to address climate change.

Theoretical Approaches to Explaining Climate Action

Most scholarship that examines cities' climate action focuses on cities in wealthy, industrialized countries that produce large amounts of GHG emissions, so the pressure to act involves mitigation in addition to adaptation. Most African cities have a lower financial capacity and more pressure to adapt than to mitigate, so the factors involved in their decisionmaking

Figure 5.1 African Cities with GCoM Badges

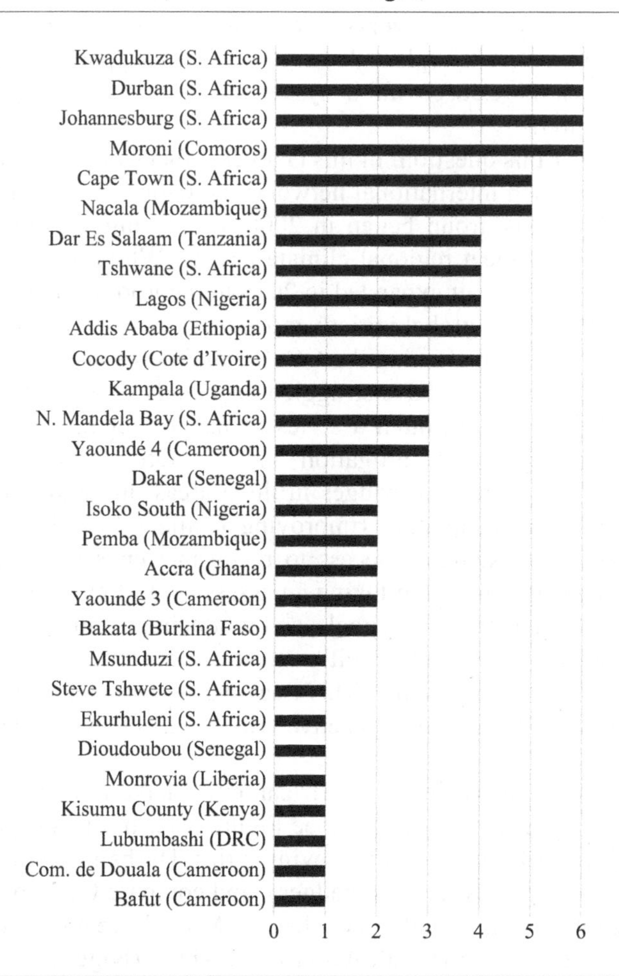

may differ. Nevertheless, theories provide a baseline for understanding why some African cities have been more proactive.

Structure

The first set of theories examine structural characteristics. Research on industrialized cities in wealthy countries notes that fiscal capacity influences whether these cities implement climate action plans, finding that wealthier cities are more likely to act (Reckien et al. 2018; Yeganeh, McCoy, and

Schenk 2020). This finding reflects that climate action in industrialized cities often involves costly mitigation measures that may temporarily impact economic production. However, there are two reasons that fiscal capacity may operate differently in African cities. First, these cities are more likely to consider adaptation than mitigation measures, which are less likely to threaten industrial economic activities. Second, for cities from poorer or middle-income countries, joining international networks like GCoM comes with resources and financial support for climate action (Wijaya et al. 2020). Therefore, in this context, one might expect more action in middle-income cities: those that are wealthy enough to have the bureaucratic and fiscal capacity to undertake climate action, but not so wealthy that they face pressure from advanced industrial interests. These cities would have the most to gain from joining international networks. An additional structural theory to consider is a city's degree of international connectivity. Because climate change is a global issue, and membership in the GCoM reflects membership in an international network, it follows that cities with a greater degree of international connectivity may have greater exposure and access to the international communities that would facilitate joining and making progress through a program like this.

Existing research also highlights structural factors related to a city's exposure to weather events. Climate risk is the likelihood that a city will face significant disasters as a direct result of climate change, such as sea level rise, drought, or severe storms. The greater the climate risk a city faces, the more salient the problem, and therefore the more likely the city will take action (Sharp, Daley, and Lynch 2011). Not all climate risk has the same political impact, however. Some forms produce problems slowly over time, such as incremental changes in rainfall. In other cases, major disasters can be focus events that create a window of political opportunity for drastic action, as the problem of climate change is suddenly and clearly related to immediate problems (Uittenbroek, Janssen-Jansen, and Runhaar 2016). Emission reliance refers to a city's economic reliance on polluting industries that contribute to climate change (Sharp, Daley, and Lynch 2011). If a city's economy hinges on industries that produce a great deal of GHG emissions, then it has an incentive to avoid mitigation measures and downplay the severity of climate change, possibly also damaging the likelihood of adaptation measures (Yeganeh, McCoy, and Schenk 2020). Even when adaptation measures do not directly affect a polluting industry, denial of climate change as a problem may be so deeply rooted that it makes adaptation politically untenable (Foss 2018).

Agency and Institutions

Political leadership is also important. As evidenced by its name, the GCoM is premised on the political agency of mayors, who may act as a local champion and propel a city toward action (Uittenbroek, Janssen-Jansen, and Runhaar 2016). A mayor's ability to act, however, is influenced by the institutions in place in city government. A mayor may be able to sign onto the GCoM, but other city agencies might be responsible for drafting or implementing an action plan (Hughes 2017). If leaders within those departments are unmotivated, a mayor may sign onto the GCoM and then be unable to spur other city agencies to act. Therefore, an activist mayor may be better able to steer a climate adaptation agenda in city governments that are more centralized and under the control of the mayor's office (Foss 2018; Sharp, Daley, and Lynch 2011).

Civil Society

Finally, existing research demonstrates that public support for climate action is the strongest predictor of whether governments (in democracies) undertake it (Yeganeh, McCoy, and Schenk 2020). The public's awareness and knowledge of climate change are important for propelling local governments to act (Pasquini 2020). Additionally, active environmentalist organizations can put pressure on governments and help build capacity to find appropriate adaptation measures (Sharp, Daley, and Lynch 2011). At the same time, public pressure is a double-edged sword: vocal opposition to climate adaptation can derail the process of forming and implementing adaption plans (Foss 2018). Table 5.1 summarizes these theories and their related hypotheses.

Most-Different Case Analysis: Lagos (Nigeria) and Durban (South Africa)

Which of these theories can best explain why some African cities have been more proactive in pursuing climate adaptation policies? In this chapter, I examine Lagos, Nigeria and Durban, South Africa as two very different cities that have taken climate adaptation action.

Case Introduction: Lagos and Durban

With an estimated population of 20 million, Lagos is one of the world's largest megacities (Cheeseman and de Gramont 2017, 458). An economic powerhouse, it is also marked by a high degree of inequality and environmental precarity. While there are many environmental problems associated with such a rapidly growing urban area, climate change has dramatically

Table 5.1 Theories of Climate Adaptation Action

Theory	Hypothesis
	Structure
Wealth	Middle-income cities will undertake climate adaptation action through GCoM.
International connectivity	Cities with greater international connectivity will undertake climate adaptation through GCoM.
Climate risk	Cities at greater risk of climate-related challenges will undertake climate adaptation action through GCoM.
Focus event	Cities that experience a dramatic climate-related disaster will undertake climate adaptation action through GCoM.
Emission reliance	Cities that rely less on GHG-emitting industries will undertake climate adaptation action through GCoM.
	Agency and Institutions
Local champions	Cities with a strong activist in government will undertake climate adaptation efforts through the GCoM.
City governance	Cities with activist mayors and centralized governance will undertake climate adaptation efforts through the GCoM.
	Civil Society
Awareness	Cities where the public has greater knowledge of climate change will undertake climate adaptation efforts through the GCoM.
Environmental activists	Cities with strong and active environmentalist organizations will undertake climate adaptation efforts through the GCoM.
Vocal opposition	Cities without vocal public opposition will undertake climate adaptation efforts through the GCoM.

intensified at least two issues facing the city. First, as a coastal city built onto low-lying islands, Lagos faces an existential threat from sea level rise.[1] Seasonal flooding has become progressively worse and threatens to render parts of the city unlivable. Additionally, the massive city generates an urban heat island, amplifying the impact of the warming climate and increasing the number of dangerously hot days annually.[2] Recognizing these challenges, Lagos joined the GCoM in 2015 and has earned four badges: all three for adaptation exercises and one for undertaking a mitigation inventory.

Durban is much smaller than Lagos, with about 3.7 million residents. Situated on South Africa's east coast, it is marked by both affluence and inequality. While its current level of climate-related risk is moderate, it stands to face serious challenges in the coming decades because of increased intensity of storms, flooding of low-lying coastal areas, and drought in the higher elevations that may affect its water supply.[3] Durban also joined the GCoM in 2015 and has earned six badges: all three for each of mitigation and adaptation.

Both cities are within larger administrative units that were responsible for joining the GCoM: Lagos city is in Lagos State and is administered by the Lagos state government rather than having an independent mayor. Durban is within and administered by the eThekwini municipality, which includes rural areas surrounding the city.

Lagos and Durban: Identifying a Common Factor of Success

Lagos and Durban both have a reputation as early adopters of climate adaptation. This section considers what these cities have in common that might be able to explain their shared success. The theories as applied to these two countries are summarized in Table 5.2. As the table illustrates, these cities have five things in common: upper-middle income status, international connectivity, one or more focus events, a local champion that spearheaded the climate adaption efforts, and no vocal opposition.

Beginning with structural features, Lagos and Durban are upper-middle income cities.[4] While both cities have high inequality, average annual income in Lagos is about $6,476[5] and in Durban is about $8,460.[6] Directly comparing the fiscal capacity of the two municipal areas is challenging, as they have dramatically different needs and budgets. Lagos state government, responsible for the sprawling megacity, is wealthy by African standards, generating between $44 and $62 per capita in revenue and operating a $2.2 billion annual budget.[7] Durban's municipal revenue is more modest, at around $0.73 per capita, but its operating revenue exceeds its budget of $2.7 million.[8] Lagos state's revenue per capita and budget are an order of magnitude higher than Durban's, indicating a greater degree of fiscal capacity. Nevertheless, as upper-middle income cities, both cities generate enough wealth per capita to support climate adaptation exercises but would also benefit from membership in international networks.

Additionally, both cities have some degree of international connectivity as measured through international airline connections. Because airlines

Table 5.2 Theories as Applied to Lagos and Durban

Theory	Lagos	Durban	Conclusion
		Structure	
Wealth	Upper-middle income	Upper-middle income	Supports theory
International connectivity	Connected	Connected	Supports theory
Climate risk	High	Medium/low	Theory unsupported; predicts Durban would struggle
Focus events	Yes	Yes	Supports theory
Emission reliance	Low	High	Theory unsupported; predicts Durban would struggle
		Agency and Institutions	
Local champion	Yes	Yes	Supports theory
City governance	Centralized	Fragmented	Theory unsupported; predicts Durban would struggle
		Civil Society	
Awareness	Low	Low	Theory unsupported; predicts both would struggle
Environmental activists	Yes	No	Theory unsupported; predicts Durban would struggle
Vocal opposition	Low	Low	Supports theory

have the capacity and incentive to react rapidly to demand, this measure is a common way to assess the "international character" of a city (Otiso et al. 2011, 610). The travel company Rome to Rio created the Global Connectivity Ranking, which includes all 1,212 cities globally with international airports.[9] In 2014, the year prior to signing onto the GCoM, Durban ranked 639th (of 1,212) with seven international connections, while Lagos ranked 172nd with twenty-nine international connections. While Lagos has a higher degree of connectivity than Durban, both cities have international airports and rank in the top half of this list for connectivity.

However, Lagos faces a much greater degree of climate risk than Durban does (according to assessment by Verisk Maplecroft 2021).

Because Lagos is built across a series of low-lying islands, it faces an existential threat from sea level rise and already experiences regular massive flooding events[10]—a particular problem for the half of the city's residents who live in informal housing.[11] These floods also affect affluent areas and have drawn international attention as repeated focus events. While Durban also faces threats from increasing storm intensity, flooding, and drought, these climate-related challenges are currently less intense than those faced by Lagos. However, Durban experienced a series of unusual focus events from 2007 to 2009, including major flooding and tornadoes.[12] While Lagos has a much higher degree of climate risk than Durban, both have experienced focus events.

Similarly, Lagos and Durban face different levels of emission reliance (the degree to which the local economy depends on polluting industries). Emission reliance in Lagos is relatively low. While Nigeria is known for being a major oil producer, that oil comes from the states around the Niger Delta—not Lagos State. Most of the emissions that the Lagosian economy produces are from electricity generation: the grid, which is powered by gas and hydropower, and diesel generators used to support industry, office parks, and private homes when the grid does not function.[13] Within electricity generation, about 62 percent of those emissions are linked to manufacturing and commercial buildings. Additional emissions come from traffic congestion and the poor waste management system in the city. However, improving the functioning and efficiency of these systems does not pose a threat to Lagosian industry, as the emissions are linked to the form of energy generation rather than manufacturing or industrial processes. Both mitigation (through diversifying and improving the grid, reducing traffic, and improving waste management) and adaptation (through improving flood resilience) are likely to bolster rather than dampen economic production—particularly if grid improvements can reduce reliance on diesel-fueled generators. Emission reliance in Durban is higher for two reasons. First, a greater share of emissions (30 percent compared to 20 percent) is related to transport and is hard to change, as Durban's economy relies on high volumes of diesel-fueled freight traffic at its port. Second, South Africa's national grid is fueled by coal. Forty-one percent of the city's emissions can be attributed to its manufacturing sector's energy use, but because of the grid's reliance on coal, there are few steps the city could take to reduce emissions in this sector beyond reducing overall use.[14] Therefore, while there are numerous areas for efficiency gains to reduce emissions in Lagos without dampening economic production, in Durban the emissions are related to freight and industrial electricity use with fewer avenues for emissions reductions. Durban's own climate action plan states that "a large portion of Durban's [emissions] reductions will be from electricity and requires decarbonization of the grid, which largely depends on the national government."[15]

The next set of theories considers agency and institutions. First, there is evidence of the importance of a local champion promoting climate action in both cities. Babatunde Fashola in Lagos and Debra Roberts in Durban each emerge as key figures advancing climate change adaptation as a key issue in their respective cities. Fashola, the governor of Lagos State from 2007 to 2015, heavily emphasized conservationism and the need to address climate change throughout his tenure (Adedara 2020). He established the annual Lagos State Climate Change Summit, alongside numerous other organizations and initiatives to push climate adaptation in the city.[16] While his successor, Akinwunmi Ambode, was the governor who signed onto the Global Covenant of Mayors, Fashola laid the groundwork and established Lagos's reputation as a city taking climate adaptation seriously. The accompanying theory in this section is that the structure of city governance is likely to affect the impact a local champion can make—in cities with centralized control, an activist mayor might have more of an impact. This was certainly the case in Lagos: Lagos State has a governor with broad powers, while Lagos City has no city government (it is instead made up of numerous local government administrations with mostly administrative functions).[17] This structure is why Ambode, the governor of the state, could sign onto the GCoM as Lagos City's de facto mayor. The broad powers of the governorship enabled Fashola to take many direct actions in the pursuit of climate adaptation and facilitated Ambode to continue his legacy.

In Durban, Debra Roberts—a civil servant—has been the principal driver of climate action (Carmin, Anguelovski, and Roberts 2012). As the head of Durban's Environmental Management Department in 2004, she commissioned an assessment of the climate change impacts that Durban would likely face, the results of which prompted her to take action by leading the development of an adaptation plan. However, because the city's government is so fragmented, this plan was dormant until 2008, when Roberts worked with each municipal department to create an individual adaptation plan. Like in Lagos, Roberts acted as a local champion who pushed climate adaptation onto the agenda. However, because the structure of eThekwini municipality is far more decentralized than Lagos State, she had to broach it in a different manner.

The final set of theories examines the impact of civil society. The first issue to consider is awareness, with the expectation that a population with greater awareness of climate change would put more pressure on the government to take adaptation measures. However, awareness in Lagos and

Durban is low: according to Round 7 of the Afrobarometer, only 44 percent and 36 percent of residents of Lagos State and eThekwini municipality, respectively, have heard of climate change.[18] Awareness in these cities is lower than the average of the thirty-four countries included in the Afrobarometer (56.5 percent). While Lagos and Durban have low levels of awareness in common, this commonality runs counter to the hypothesis.

The next issue to consider is the activity of activist groups that might pressure the government. While both Nigeria and South Africa have recent histories of large-scale protest movements, these movements have tended to focus on social grievances and the ability of the government to provide basic services rather than the environment (Ojedokun, Ogunleye, and Aderinto 2021; Simon 2016). While there have not been equivalent large-scale environmental movements in either country, in Lagos, there is evidence that local environmental groups were active in the development of the climate action plan: civil society was included in the process, and a number of Nigerian environmentalist organizations signed off on the city's final Climate Action Plan (Lagos State Government 2019). There is little evidence of such involvement in the case of Durban, however. While the city's Climate Action Plan lists "civil society" as an actor responsible for carrying out some elements of the plan, no groups are ever named and none appear to have been involved in drafting the plan (eThekwini Municipality 2019). In 2009, the city held its first climate summit in an explicit attempt to engage civil society, but the participants almost immediately became inactive due to lack of cohesion, leadership, and funding (Roberts and O'Donoghue 2013, 313). While South Africa's civil society has been active on issues of social justice and service delivery, many people view environmental issues to be secondary to immediate challenges of poverty and access to services.[19] Planning and implementation of climate adaptation have been technocratic and initiated within city government rather than resulting from external pressure (Roberts and O'Donoghue 2013).

The last factor to consider is the existence of a vocal opposition that might stymie climate action. There is no evidence of vocal opposition in either city. In Lagos, awareness of climate change is generally low, but among those who do have a good awareness of climate change, most respond to it with "indifference" (Oluwafemi 2019). Awareness is higher and concern is greater among the highly educated corporate class, where many link flooding to climate change and perceive it as a risk. Among this more influential class, there is little evidence of opposition to climate adaptation—it simply isn't as pressing of a concern as other challenges like crime and traffic (Asiyanbi 2015). In Durban, skeptics in city government initially balked at using scarce resources for climate adaptation but quickly became convinced that improving the city's resilience to weather events was beneficial after the 2007 flooding event (Carmin, Anguelovski, and Roberts 2012). As in Lagos, public awareness of climate change is low, and there is no evidence of backlash against the city's plan.

What Lagos and Durban have in common is being upper-middle income, having international connectivity, experiencing several focus events, having a local champion, and the lack of a vocal opposition. The following cases analyze how these factors may have contributed to the cities' shared success.

Lagos

Lagos joined the GCoM in 2015 after years of environmental actions and reforms. Under Nigeria's federal structure, Lagos the city is administered by the governor of Lagos State. Since Nigeria's return to multiparty democracy in 1999, Lagos State has often elected a governor from the opposition party and has attracted attention for unusually strong local governance, particularly considering that Lagos is a sprawling, unwieldy megacity (Cheeseman and de Gramont 2017, 458). The first two governors of Lagos State since 1999, Bola Tinubu (1999–2007) and Babatunde Fashola (2007–2015), developed reputations for taking the city's environmental challenges seriously (Adedara 2020; Ajibade et al. 2016, 11–12). While Tinubu's tenure was focused primarily on strengthening the local tax system, Fashola inherited a stable government with a good fiscal capacity that enabled him to pursue climate adaptation and other environmentally oriented policies (Cheeseman and de Gramont 2017). These included broad-based strategies of expanding green spaces and improving infrastructure (Ajibade et al. 2016, 11–13).

The greening strategy included planting over five million trees and establishing nearly two hundred parks, while infrastructure projects included improvements to the drainage systems and early warning systems for flooding (Ajibade et al. 2016, 11–13). These policies, designed to align with the United Nation's Sustainable Development Goals, drew international praise. The government pursued innovative policies of climate adaptation as well, such as experimenting with floating, flood-proof architecture and using land reclamation technology to build climate-proof housing in the highly anticipated Eko Atlantic city.[20] This particular innovation was a direct response to major flooding events. While Fashola's public addresses indicated a broad interest in environmental preservation, he also recognized the necessity of taking such steps to make Lagos more livable and protect the functioning of its economy (Adedara 2020).

These policies were precursors to stronger international engagement in climate adaptation programs. Fashola institutionalized climate adaptation into state government, establishing a dedicated climate change unit and producing the Lagos State Climate Policy and the Lagos State Climate Change Adaptation Policy in 2012 (Ajibade et al. 2016, 14). He also established the annual Lagos International Climate Change Summit in 2009, inserting Lagos into international networks of local governments and international organizations focused on environmental sustainability. Involvement in these networks, such as the International Council for Local Environmental Initiatives (ICLEI) and the C40 Cities Climate Leadership Group, paved the way for Lagos to sign onto the GCoM, under which Lagos garnered additional support for producing its Climate Action Plan.[21] These networks additionally reflect how international connectivity supported Lagos's climate actions. The governors succeeding Fashola have carried on the elements of these plans, including implementing measures like flood early warning systems, building sea walls, experimenting with ferry transport, and improving the city's drainage systems to help abate flooding.[22]

Fashola's dramatic impact on Lagos's climate action was possible because of the centralization of power in the Lagos state government. The sweeping powers of the governor's office enabled Fashola to pursue policies toward achieving his high-modernist vision of Lagos as a modern, clean, climate-ready city (Cheeseman and de Gramont 2017, 470). While the concentrated power of the governorship allowed for decisive action, it has also brought criticism that these measures disproportionately protect the wealthy and middle class at the expense of the poor—particularly after actions like forced resettlement of slum-dwellers in flood-prone areas and disproportionate investment in infrastructure in wealthier areas (Adama 2018; Ajibade et al. 2016). Nevertheless, Fashola acted as a local champion to put climate change and other environmental challenges at the top of the agenda in Lagos. The city's middle-income status enabled it to take initial steps toward climate adaptation and insert itself into international networks, while focus events like major flooding directly inspired some of the projects, like the flood warning system and floodproof architecture. The public has broadly supported these efforts, and concern largely relates to insufficient protection of the poor rather than climate skepticism.

Durban

Like Lagos, Durban joined the GCoM in 2015 after over a decade of preparatory work. While the city had previously engaged in some international climate initiatives, like ICLEI–Local Governments for Sustainability, these efforts tended to be short-lived and contingent on international funding (Carmin, Anguelovski, and Roberts 2012, 22). Sustained efforts at climate adaption began in 2004 with the efforts of Debra Roberts, the head of the municipal Environmental Management Department, who commissioned a climate impact assessment and initiated the Municipal Climate Protection Program within her department (Roberts and O'Donoghue 2013, 306). This assessment indicated that Durban would likely face a slew of threats, from flooding and increased storm intensity to food insecurity and disease (Carmin, Anguelovski, and Roberts 2012, 21). These findings led Roberts to launch an integrated strategy of climate assessment across the entire municipal government. Unfortunately, this initiative got little traction: it was funded through her department's biodiversity budget, which meant that the only real action taken was around biodiversity (Roberts and O'Donoghue 2013, 306). Additionally, local government structure slowed uptake of the initiative. The city of Durban is managed by the larger municipality of eThekwini, which has a mayor, an executive committee, and 205 councilors. A city manager oversees operations divided across seven siloed areas, each with its own deputy city manager (Carmin, Anguelovski, and Roberts 2012, 20–21). These separate operational areas had no reason to integrate climate adaptation into their already stretched budgets, particularly as other things were deemed more urgent than a distant threat from climate change (Roberts and O'Donoghue 2013).

In 2008, after it became clear that this initial strategy was ineffective, Roberts pursued a new tactic. Rather than an integrated, city-wide action plan, she initiated work with two operational departments (health and water) to develop specific climate adaptation goals that aligned with the departments' existing budgets (Roberts 2015, 539). This sectoral approach hinged on Roberts identifying champions in each department who would spearhead the sectoral approach to climate adaptation, determine how to make it fit into the department's existing plans, and recruit colleagues to take climate change more seriously (Roberts and O'Donoghue 2013, 307). The timing of this new initiative auspiciously aligned with unusually bad flooding in 2007 and damaging tornadoes in 2008–2009, which acted as focus events, convincing more civil servants that adaptation needed to be built into their departments' plans (Carmin, Anguelovski, and Roberts 2012, 23).

These actions gained momentum in 2010, when the Municipal Climate Protection Program finally got its own funding and Durban won the bid to host the United Nations Framework Convention on Climate Change

(UNFCCC) conference. Roberts considers the conference to be a major turning point for climate action in the city. The outcome of the conference, the Durban Adaptation Charter, put Durban and city-level adaptation programs on the international stage, and encouraged Durban's mayor, James Mxumalo, to become a champion of climate initiatives himself—reflecting the role of international connectivity in shining a spotlight on climate issues (Roberts and O'Donoghue 2013, 313). Additionally, in 2012 eThekwini Municipality appointed a new municipal manager who wanted to build upon the conference's legacy by pursuing more comprehensive climate action (Roberts and O'Donoghue 2013, 313). By 2014 Durban had produced a municipal-level climate change strategy in preparation for joining the GCoM in 2015.[23] This strategy included both adaptation measures to be spearheaded by the newly renamed Environmental Planning and Climate Protection Department as well as mitigation measures to be carried out by the Energy Office. This planning enabled Durban to earn all six GCoM adaptation and mitigation badges.

Durban's ultimate success in addressing climate insecurity through city governance is largely the result of the work of Debra Roberts and other champions working within city government, insisting that climate adaptation not fall by the wayside. The focus events of natural disasters during 2007–2009 and the attention brought by the UNFCCC conference helped to center climate change on the city's agenda. The city's middle-income status enabled early climate work to fit within existing departments' budgets and made the city an appealing site for the UNFCCC conference, while budget limitations made international support imperative. Because this process was largely internal to the municipal government, there was little risk of drawing a vocal opposition—particularly since the early climate adaptation efforts were worked into the existing plans of the operational departments.

In both Lagos and Durban, individual actors played an outsized role in placing climate adaptation on the city's agenda—though the institutional arrangements of each city meant they went about it in different ways. In Lagos, the governor's sweeping and centralized powers meant that Governor Fashola could take decisive action with relative ease. In Durban, decentralized governance meant that Debra Roberts had to work slowly to recruit ever more climate champions in each department. While neither Lagos nor Durban have an excess of funding, both cities were on strong enough financial ground to fund at least some of their initiatives, and both had their actions bolstered through attention from international conferences. Furthermore, focus events generated a sense of urgency around action. Finally, in both cities, the process of incorporating climate adaptation policy did not face the backlash of a vocal public opposition, though for different reasons. In Lagos, the power of the governor's office insulated its decision-making from public backlash, had there been any.[24] In Durban, the process was firmly bureaucratic and internal to local government offices, drawing little public attention. The cities' finances, international connections, focus events, and lack of opposition were enabling conditions that allowed a local champion to ensure climate adaptation would be integral to public policy.

Most-Similar Cases: Abuja, Nigeria, and Bloemfontein, South Africa

Lagos and Durban each evidenced a history of climate action before joining the GCoM, and they subsequently made quick progress earning badges. However, other cities in these two countries—Abuja in Nigeria and Bloemfontein in South Africa—joined the GCoM but failed to make discernable progress. Neither has achieved any badges, and both have fallen out of compliance, indicating that they have not submitted annual reports documenting progress. Like Lagos and Durban, Abuja and Bloemfontein are sizable urban municipalities with a large government presence. This set of case analyses examines whether the hypotheses regarding wealth, international connections, focus events, local champions, or vocal opposition explain these cities' lack of action.

Abuja and Lagos, Nigeria

Abuja, located in Nigeria's interior, is the country's capital city. The government moved the capital from Lagos to Abuja in 1991 as part of a post-colonial project to balance the country's distribution of power between the geographically concentrated religious and ethnic groups. Abuja was planned from the ground up, following a modernist vision of a new, clean, efficient city. However, Abuja's population growth has outstripped its plan, leading to striking disparities between the carefully designed urban center and the sprawling informal settlements around the periphery. While there are multiple reasons for this in-migration, including deteriorating security in Nigeria's north, one source is internal displacement as changing climatic patterns have created major challenges for small farmers.[25] Despite the challenges caused by climate change, Abuja's municipal government has done little to adapt. The city only joined the GCoM in January 2021. Unlike Lagos, which engaged in a decade of climate planning and action prior to signing onto the covenant and moved quickly through the program's benchmarks, Abuja has no history of climate action and has yet to make progress on these benchmarks.

Abuja does differ from Lagos in important ways that may have affected its orientation toward climate adaptation. First, Abuja is poorer, falling into the lower-middle income category, and it only has the fiscal capacity to raise revenue to cover 25 percent of its budget.[26] It is therefore possible that Abuja lacks the fiscal capacity to undertake major adaptation planning. It also lacks the dramatic focus events that Lagos has had. Near the Sahel, it is in a region that is projected to experience a major strain on farming due to changes in rainfall (Morgan et al. 2019). However, drought and inconsistent rainfall are creeping, slow problems and do not constitute the same type of focus event that major flooding or dramatic, damaging storms do. Abuja thus lacks two of the enabling conditions present in Lagos. Notably, however, Abuja does have a strong degree of international connectivity: its airport boasts fifteen international connections, even more than Durban.

While Abuja has a centralized governance structure, like Lagos, there has been a conspicuous absence of local climate champions within the government. The Abuja Environmental Protection Board, the government agency that should have jurisdiction over climate-related issues, has a reputation primarily for harassing the city's urban poor (Adama 2018).[27] Rather than considering systemic issues like climate change, the agency focuses on removing visible threats to the city's cleanliness, such as street vendors, shared taxis, and the informal settlements where most of the city's poor live. There is no evidence that it considers issues of climate change. While there has also been a lack of vocal opposition in Abuja, there has been little for them to oppose: there are no publicly available strategy documents or commissioned reports around climate change. Indicative of climate apathy within the local government, the University of Abuja recently launched a campaign to improve awareness around climate-related issues and decided to work with a prominent international NGO rather than the local government on the campaign.[28]

Three hypotheses thus explain outcomes in both Lagos and Abuja: Abuja is poorer, has not experienced focus events, and lacks a local champion.

Durban (eThekwini Municipality) and Bloemfontein (Mangaung Municipality), South Africa

Bloemfontein is the major city within Mangaung Municipality in Free State, South Africa. It is adjacent to Kwa-Zulu Natal, where Durban is located, though Free State is landlocked. Bloemfontein serves as the center of the judicial system for the national government, and the city's economy is primarily oriented around services and finance, though the municipality includes some rural areas engaged in agriculture. Like Durban,

Bloemfontein signed onto the GCoM in 2015, but has made no progress and has fallen out of compliance.

Wealth cannot explain Bloemfontein's struggles. Per capita GDP in Bloemfontein is $7,839.87, just slightly lower than in Durban and well within the upper-middle income category.[29] Bloemfontein is a smaller city with a smaller budget than Durban, but its budget was nearly balanced in 2019 (it had approximately a $700 shortfall).[30] However, it has no international connections (its airport is only domestic), and it has not experienced focus events the way Durban has. While the two provinces are adjacent, Durban's focus events were related to its coastline. Because Bloemfontein is further inland and in a semiarid environment, changing rainfall associated with climate change is likely to have a significant impact on agriculture, with unpredictable periods of drought. Additionally, Bloemfontein is at greater risk for extreme temperatures, heat waves, and elevated fire danger (Mbileni 2015). However, these problems are gradual and have not generated focus events as in Durban.

There is no evidence of a local champion taking on climate change as an issue in the Mangaung municipal government. Rather, the evidence suggests that, after 2016, the municipal government became disinterested in climate change. In 2015, under the mayorship of Thabo Manyoni, the municipal government commissioned an environmental consulting firm to draft a local climate strategy (Mbileni 2015). Manyoni was an outspoken and well-known local government advocate, earning a nomination as a World Mayor in 2014.[31] However, he was ousted as mayor due to factional infighting within his party, the African National Congress, mid-2016.[32] After his exit, local government efforts at planning for climate adaptation petered out.

There is no evidence that this false start was due to vocal opposition in Bloemfontein. Rather, evidence points to an apathetic government. Environmental activists have complained that the government does not pay attention to their attempts to engage the government in policy change (Geymonat 2019). Anita Venter, a researcher at the University of the Free State and founder of the Start Living Green initiative, states that even where environmental groups *do* try to work with the local government, rapid turnover of civil service positions makes it a challenge to even know who to lobby.[33] There is little evidence that a vocal opposition has the blocked climate action that began in 2015. Rather, it is simply no longer on the agenda.

The evidence suggests that, had he remained in office, Thabo Manyoni may have been a local champion for climate change in Bloemfontein. However, his ouster left a vacuum, as indicated by the municipal documents related to climate and city planning. The author of the 2015 climate strategy noted two major challenges in its development: First, it was difficult to establish a baseline for climate mitigation efforts because the municipality had never undertaken an emissions inventory to understand which of its industries might be producing greenhouse gases. Second, the consulting firm organized stakeholder workshops to include municipal officials and the broader community in the process of creating the climate strategy (Mbileni 2015, 19–20). However, the report's author noted that these workshops were poorly attended by municipal officials, indicating a lack of buy-in to the process. The Environment Impact Management Plan created for the municipality the following year indicates repeatedly that the local government had not yet planned any implementation of the climate strategy.[34] Mayor Manyoni's initiation of these actions—signing onto the GCoM and commissioning a climate strategy—indicates that he had an interest in climate adaptation and could possibly have acted as a local climate champion. However, the rest of the municipal government did not share his enthusiasm. After his ouster, initiatives to address climate change all but disappeared, and unlike in Durban, there were no international conferences to shine a spotlight on climate change and propel the process forward.

In the 2019–2020 municipal annual report, the word "climate" appears only twice, when climate change is identified as a risk (by contrast, it appears 76 times in eThekwini's annual report). In the 265-page report, the section on environmental protection spans less than half a page and only discusses water pollution and monitoring air quality to prevent sulfur dioxide emissions.[35] Additionally, the report notes that fewer than half of the posts in the Environmental Health Department are filled.[36] At the time of writing, the Manguang Municipality Environmental Management website only mentions climate change once, stating their plan to "monitor air quality and develop approaches to reduce contribution to climate change."[37] These documents together indicate that the municipality never developed an adaptation plan based on the strategy it commissioned in 2015 and suggest that climate change is not a priority for the Environmental Management Department (or the municipal government as a whole).

The comparison of Durban to Bloemfontein and Lagos to Abuja affirms that the combination of focus events and the actions of a local champion appear to be most important for precipitating city-level climate action. While international connections facilitated the process in Lagos and Durban, Abuja's connections did not help the process there. While Abuja's poverty may have contributed to its lack of action, income cannot explain why Bloemfontein was so much less active than Durban. In both Durban and Lagos, the local champion who put climate change on the agenda was active within government for a long period of time, which allowed these policies to be enduring. By contrast, in Bloemfontein, the mayor who initiated climate actions was voted out of office the following year, and the churn of local civil servants precluded anyone being left in government who could pursue those initial actions. In Abuja, there is no evidence of such a champion in the government, and the few environmental initiatives work around rather than with the government. Additionally, both Durban and Lagos experience climate change through dramatic weather events characterized by flooding in areas that affect relatively affluent neighborhoods and impact business and tourism. By contrast, in Abuja and Bloemfontein, climate change is marked by increasing heat and long-term changes to rain patterns that threaten farming and food security. While these types of climate threat are just as (or more) damaging, they are also less dramatic and therefore do not constitute a focus event to spur policy action.

Conclusion

Cities are essential actors to consider in adapting to climate change. The effects of climate change are highly variable within countries, and while national governments can issue top-down guidance, the precise needs are best identified by more local levels of government. While cities and municipalities can be more agile than countries at adopting policy change, they also have a wide variety of capacity. Support through international networks like the GCoM can be essential for gaining access to resources and financial support. Yet cities are not equally proactive at taking advantage of these networks. In this chapter, I have investigated why some cities—like Lagos and Durban—have been more active in taking advantage of international partnerships and pursuing climate adaptation strategies, while others—like Abuja and Bloemfontein—have not.

While each city under investigation in this chapter faces a unique set of circumstances, all are facing climate-related challenges that are likely to intensify. All have municipal governments with some degree of capacity, and all would benefit from putting adaptive measures in place to protect residents from the challenges that will arise from the changing climate. In Lagos and Durban, a local champion was integral in driving the process forward, and focus events underscored the urgency of action. In Lagos, Governor Fashola kept environmental concerns on the agenda through the duration of his governorship, using his centralized powers to generate a legacy that carried forward with his successor signing onto the GCoM. In Durban, Debra Roberts drove the process, though as a civil servant in a fragmented municipal government, she had to approach the task differently. In both cases, these local champions were persistent in addressing climate and other environmental issues for nearly a decade prior to joining the GCoM, leaving them well-placed to quickly achieve the benchmarks the programs set out.

In Abuja and Bloemfontein, there was no evidence of a local champion to shepherd the process. Abuja's history of municipal-led environmentalism has mostly consisted of harassing the poor in central urban spaces and demolishing informal settlements. The municipality has no history of large-scale climate planning or policy like Lagos or Durban did prior to signing onto the GCoM. Consideration of climate change is totally absent from the publicly available information about the Environmental Protection Board. Considering that Abuja only joined the Covenant in January 2021 (one year prior to the time of writing), it is unsurprising that they have not yet achieved any benchmarks. However, they also lack the legacy of planning evident in Lagos and Durban and have already fallen out of compliance with the program. Finally, in Bloemfontein, Mayor Manyoni did start a process of planning for climate adaptation by commissioning reports alongside signing onto the GCoM. However, he was voted out of office the following year, and it appears that nobody in the new government has taken on the mantle of climate action. In this case, there was a local champion—but he was there too briefly to institutionalize climate action.

One interpretation of this analysis is disheartening—if a local champion is what it takes to institutionalize climate action, then what happens in the cities where there isn't one, or where a promising actor gets ousted too soon? However, another interpretation is that meaningful action toward climate action is possible anywhere that someone is persistent enough to take it on and drive change.

Another important lesson is the power of focus events, and the challenges posed in areas that are poised to experience slow, creeping climate threats rather than sudden dramatic events. In both Lagos and Durban, the focus events that occurred had an immediate and dramatic effect on broad swaths of society—the wealthy were affected alongside the poor, and businesses suffered losses as well. In Abuja and Bloemfontein, the creeping climate threats related to drought and changing rain patterns disproportionately affect smallholder farmers, who tend to be poor and removed from municipal centers of political power. Awareness of climate change was limited across all four cities, indicating the ongoing importance of public-facing science to link climate change to immediately felt challenges—especially those that are less dramatic and predominantly affect vulnerable rural dwellers.

Nigeria and South Africa are not the only countries with cities that have earned badges through the GCoM—the Comoros, Mozambique, Tanzania, Ethiopia, Cote d'Ivoire, Uganda, and Cameroon each have at least one city that has earned at least three badges. Understanding what has propelled cities in these countries to begin taking adaptation actions is an important step toward encouraging and supporting more cities—especially in the most climatically vulnerable regions of the world—to make proactive adaptation plans.

Notes

1. Primwell, Nimi. 2021, August 1. "Lagos Floods." *CNN*.

2. Lagos State Government. 2019. "Lagos Climate Action Plan: Second Five Year Plan 2020–2025." https://cdn.locomotive.works/sites/5ab410c8a2f42204838f797e/content_entry5ab410faa2f42204838f7990/5ad0ab8e74c4837def5d27aa/files/C40_Lagos_Final_CAP.pdf?1626096978

3. eThekwini Municipality. 2019. "Durban Climate Action Plan 2019."

4. According to GDP per capita classification by the United Nations Development Program.

5. Calculation by author using Lagos State GDP/Lagos State population. Both figures are estimates, as official statistics are contested and sometimes conflate Lagos City with Lagos State. Lagos GDP estimate is from Pilling, David. 2018, March 25. "Nigerian Economy: Why Lagos Works." *Financial Times*. Lagos population estimate is from Campbell, John. 2012, July 10. "This Is Africa's New Biggest City: Lagos, Nigeria, Population 21 Million." *The Atlantic*. More conservative population estimates increase GDP per capita, but it remains within the upper-middle income category.

6. Estimate from Open Data Institute. 2019. "Mayors Dialogue on Growth and Solidarity: City Profile: Durban (eThekwini), South Africa." https://cdn.odi.org/media/documents/ hmi_mayors_dialogue_durban.pdf

7. Lagos State Government. 2019. "Lagos State Budget." Measured in 2019 dollars, per capita estimate based on population between 25–35 million.

8. KwaZulu-Natal Provincial Treasury. 2020. "Municipal Finance Management 3rd Quarter Review."

9. Accessed at https://www.rome2rio.com/labs/global-connectivity-ranking/

10. Princewell, Nimi. 2021, August 1. "Africa's Most Populous City Is Battling Floods and Rising Sea Levels and May Soon Be Unlivable, Experts Warn," *CNN*.

11. Lagos State Government. 2019, x.

12. Another incident of massive, damaging flooding hit Durban in April 2022: https://www.voanews.com/a/south-african-flood-victims-shelters-damaged-by-more-rains/6588616.html

13. Lagos State Government. 2019, xi.

14. eThekwini Municipality. 2019, 18.

15. *Ibid.*, 20.

16. Ekoro, Ekene. 2015, April 22. "Fashola, Diplomats Advocate Sustained Climate Change Mitigation." *All Africa*.

17. LSE Cities. 2018. "Governance Structure, Lagos." https://urbanage.lsecities.net/data/governance-structure-lagos

18. A *t*-test fails to reject the null hypothesis that the means are the same.

19. Personal correspondence with Anita Venter, researcher at the University of the Free State and founder of the Start Living Green initiative.

20. Vora, Shivani. 2021, June 22. "An Architect with an Eye on the Environment." *New York Times*. See also Cheeseman and Gramont 2017.

21. Lagos State Government. 2019, x.

22. Johnson, Ayodele. 2021, January 21. "How Africa's Largest City Is Staying Afloat." *BBC Future*.

23. Environmental Planning and Climate Protection Dept., Energy Office. 2014. "Durban Climate Change Strategy."

24. Most criticism has been about the disproportionate benefit to the wealthy rather than climate adaptation itself.

25. Fatunmole, Marcus. 2021. "Abuja Women Farmers at the Mercy of Changing Climate," *International Centre for Investigative Reporting* https://www.icirnigeria.org/abuja-wodmen-farmers-at-the-mercy-of-changing-climate

26. GDP per capita of $1,292, as estimated by Kingmakers, an economic intelligence firm based in Nigeria. Their projection is likely an underestimate. Budget numbers from Abuja Municipal Area Council 2019 Appropriation Bill, which indicates that the municipal area has an annual budget of about $23 million but can only raise $6.4 million in revenue, relying on loans and federal transfers for the rest.

27. See also Onuh-Yahaya, Zalnab. 2021, September 5. "Poor People Weren't Part of the Plan for Abuja." *Foreign Policy*.

28. "UniAbuja, NGO Collaborate to Create Awareness on Climate Change Impact—Director." *The Sun*. August 27, 2021. https://www.sunnewsonline.com/uniabuja-ngo-collaborate-to-create-awareness-on-climate-change-impact-director/

29. Per capita income according to Oxford Economics' Competitive Cities database, income classification according to the United Nations Development Program.

30. Mangaung Metro Municipality. 2020. "Preliminary Monthly Financial Report for the Period Ended 31 December 2019."

31. Municipal IQ. 2016, July. "Personality of the Month."

32. Myburch, Pieter-Louis. 2019, March 31. "Exposed: Ace Magashule's Murky Dealings." *Times Live*.

33. Personal correspondence, September 2021.

34. Centre for Environmental Management, North-West University. 2016. "Environmental Implementation and Management Plan for the Mangaung Metropolitan Municipality."

35. Office of the City Manager. 2020. "2019–2020 Mangaung Metropolitan Municipality Annual Performance Report." p. 129.

36. The office had twenty-nine employees and thirty-four vacancies (p. 134).

37. Mangaung Municipal Website. http://www.mangaung.co.za/planning-economic-development/environmental-management/

6

Advancing Gender Equality

Progress toward gender equality faces challenges worldwide. Despite myriad evidence that societies perform better across numerous indicators when women have the same rights and opportunities as men, women face disadvantages in nearly every country in the world. According to the United Nations Development Program's (UNDP's) Gender Inequality Index, which takes into account female reproductive health and gender gaps in political representation, educational attainment, and labor force participation, sub-Saharan Africa is the world's worst-performing region.[1] The maternal mortality ratio—550 deaths per 100,000 live births—is more than triple the second worst performing region (South Asia), while its adolescent birth rate—104.7 per 1,000 births—is nearly double the second worst performing region (Latin America). African women are the least educated group globally: only 28.8 percent of women have at least some secondary education, and there is an 11-point gap between men and women on this indicator. The only area in which African women outperform those in other regions is in labor force participation—63.5 percent of women work outside the home. Labor force participation is an important indicator because it reflects norms of women's presence in public spaces outside the home as well as their capacity for financial independence. However, it does not capture more nuanced elements of the labor market like women's concentration in lower-paid jobs.

Women also struggle in terms of their political presence and ability to advocate for themselves in public spaces. The Varieties of Democracy (V-Dem) project calculates an index of women's empowerment, which they define as "a process of increasing capacity for women," including "civil liberties, women's open discussion of political issues and participation in civil society organizations, and the descriptive representation of women in formal political positions." On this index, sub-Saharan Africa (index score of 0.69) only outperforms the Middle East/North Africa region (index score of 0.53). Taken together, the prospects for girls born in Africa are much worse than for those born in other regions. However, these indices mask a great deal of variation on the continent. There are numerous countries in which African women enjoy a greater degree of empowerment than those in other regions, particularly in terms of political representation. According to the V-Dem measure of women's political empowerment, twenty-six African countries score better than the world average.[2] Figure 6.1 illustrates African countries' combined performance on the UNDP and V-Dem indices, accounting for women's access to health care, political representation, educational attainment, and employment relative to men's.[3]

In this chapter, I proceed with a focus on Senegal and Rwanda, two countries with strong gender equality scores, to determine what they have in common that can explain their success. I then turn to most-similar case comparisons of Burundi (to Rwanda) and Guinea (to Senegal), two countries with important similarities to the main cases that have had less success promoting gender equality. More detail about case selection is available in the appendix.

Theories of Women's Empowerment and Gender Equality

There are few places in the world where women are functionally equal to men, but there is a lot of variation in the degree to which women are disadvantaged. Why is gender inequality so much more pronounced in some places than in others? The following section reviews ten theories, grouped into five categories, that seek to explain these disparities.

Sociocultural Theories

Popular understandings of gender inequality tend to reduce the issue to *patriarchy*: social, political, and economic systems in which men hold most resources and positions of power. While patriarchy is in some ways synonymous with gender inequality, there are some sociocultural characteristics that may contribute to women's ongoing subordination. Some have pointed out that Islam is associated with more overt patriarchy (Fish 2002; Groh and Rothschild 2012), possibly because Islam enumerates gendered duties and obligations that often become enshrined in civil law in majority-Muslim countries (Bop 2005, 1102). However, others have noted that interpretation of Islamic texts and treatment of women varies across Islamic sects (Donno and Russett 2004; Rizzo, Abdel-Latif, and Meyer 2007). Furthermore, many other religions also have patriarchal foundations that influence the legal field, including Pentecostal Christianity (Boyd 2014).

Figure 6.1 Gender Equality by Country

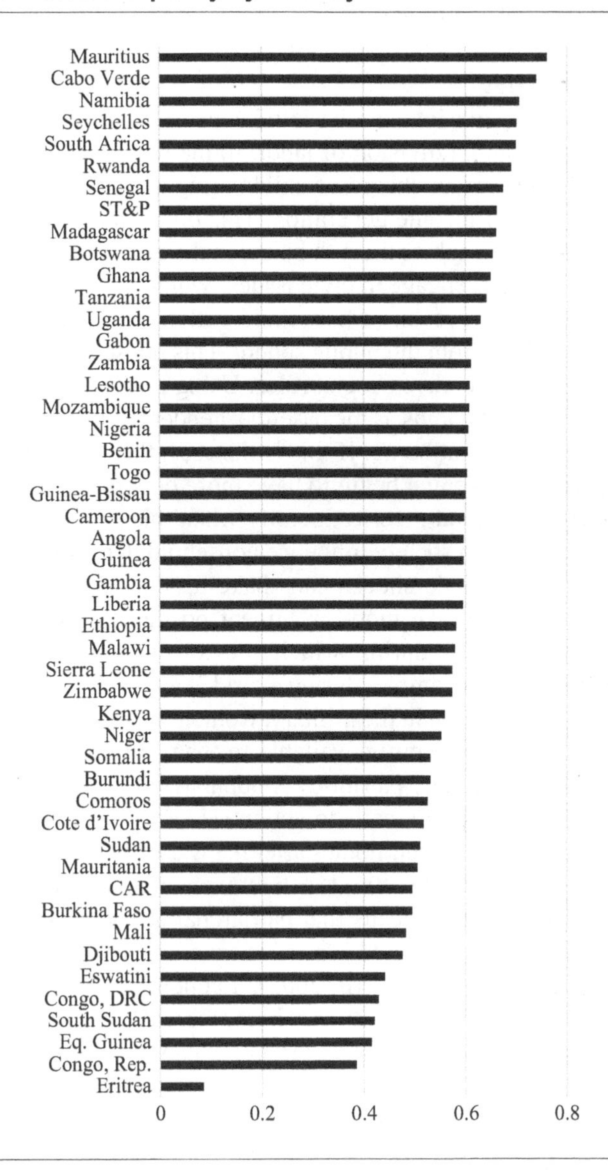

Many religions reinforce norms that uphold a social structure based on heterosexual nuclear families in which women are expected to perform most of the unpaid caretaking work within the household (Seguino 2011, 1309). Comparative research suggests that religiosity (the intensity of religious belief and practice), rather than any particular religion, is linked to the persistence of patriarchal attitudes (Schnabel 2016; Seguino 2011).

Structural Theories

Other explanations dig into the basis of women's and men's inequality, rooted in the household division of labor. In many places, in a traditional household, women are in charge of childrearing and housekeeping while men are in charge of income generation. This division of labor gives men financial control and enables them to be out in the public realm, where they might learn about and engage in civic issues. Women are more likely to be confined to the private realm of household without independent access to money and excluded from the public sphere. This household division crystallizes into distinct gendered social roles. Using this stylized understanding of traditional households as the baseline, gender inequality is a function of women being stuck at home. If this is the case, then patriarchal culture may dissipate when women begin to have more opportunities to leave the private sphere. Structural theories identify when this shift might begin, as macro-level changes in society influence household dynamics.

Sometimes, traumatic shocks can shake up the existing social order and enable women to take more prominent positions. These events can create critical junctures during which previously unthinkable changes become possible. For example, during World War II in the United States, with so many men serving in the military, women took jobs in factories that would have previously been unavailable to them. In this case, what had been unimaginable became patriotic, as popularized by Rosie the Riveter and other World War II–era calls to action (Honey 1985). While most of these women returned to their homes after the war ended, their experiences paved the way for changing attitudes about women in the workplace.

Modernization theory posits that patriarchal attitudes begin to soften with economic development and expanded economic opportunities outside households (Inglehart and Norris 2003). Economic modernization may reduce the demands on women's time at home (as washing machines replace handwashing of clothing, for example) while also expanding the need for labor (with the growth of the service economy). Economic development is associated with another theory, based on the demographic transition: a shift during which women go from having many children to only one or two, usually over the course of one or two generations. This change often occurs when the economy transforms from one in which many children is a boon (i.e., family-farm agriculture) to a major expense (i.e., an urbanized economy). If women spend less time on childrearing, then theoretically they have more time to undertake pursuits outside the home (Galor 2012).

Institutions, Civil Society, and Agency

Women's representation in political institutions, while itself a measure of women's empowerment, can begin to erode other dimensions of gender inequality. The regular and prominent appearance of women in public positions, known as descriptive representation, can sometimes generate other important sociopolitical changes. Descriptive representation can produce symbolic effects, as women's public appearances can begin to change attitudes about women's capabilities and also inspire other women to become more active in public life (Burnet 2011; Evans 2016). More women in positions of power can also result in substantive representation: women in office may promote policies that contribute to women's empowerment, such as antidiscrimination laws or policies addressing women's health issues (Mechkova and Carlitz 2021). Some suggest that any kind of women's representation is only meaningful in democratic contexts, as elected officials hold less power over policy in authoritarian contexts (Bauer and Burnet 2013); others highlight the importance of active women's civil society organizations working in coalitions to hold elected women accountable (Kang and Tripp 2018; Mechkova and Carlitz 2021), or the importance of other political leaders in preventing elected women from being tokenized (Hern n.d.). These theories and hypotheses are summarized in Table 6.1.

Most-Different Case Analysis: Rwanda and Senegal

Which of these theories can best explain improvements in women's empowerment and gender equality in African countries? In this chapter, I focus on a most-different case comparison of Rwanda and Senegal to evaluate these hypotheses.

Case Introduction: Rwanda and Senegal

Rwanda and Senegal both perform well on measures of gender equality despite taking different paths to producing such good outcomes. In Central Africa, Rwanda was the site of a genocide in 1994. By some estimates, immediately after the genocide, Rwanda's population was 70 percent women, and a significant portion of men were imprisoned. The extraordinary gender imbalance in society, plus the perception that women were less responsible for genocidal atrocities, led women to take a dominant role in rebuilding the Rwandan state. Women's representation in the labor force and politics dramatically increased, and in 2003 the government instituted a legislative quota to ensure women's ongoing political representation. While the quota only guarantees 30 percent of legislative seats for women,

Table 6.1 Theories of Gender Equality

Theory	Hypothesis
	Sociocultural
Islam	Women enjoy greater equality in non-Muslim majority countries.
Religiosity	Women enjoy greater equality in less religious countries.
Structural	
Critical junctures	Women enjoy greater equality when a traumatic shock to a country makes women's contributions more visible.
Modernization theory	Women enjoy greater equality in more developed economies.
Demographic transition	Women enjoy greater equality when the birth rate declines.
	Institutions
Symbolic representation	Women enjoy greater equality when the presence of women in prominent positions changes public attitudes about women's appropriate roles.
Substantive representation	Women enjoy greater equality when women in government enact policies that counter discrimination and improve women's lives.
Democracy	Women enjoy greater equality when elected women are able to implement policies in democratic contexts.
	Civil Society
Women's organizations	Women enjoy greater equality when women's civil society organizations actively hold elected women accountable.
	Agency
Political leadership	Women enjoy greater equality when political leaders support elected women and prevent their tokenization.

the proportion of seats they have won has continued to climb, reaching 64 percent in the lower house in 2013. Postgenocide Rwanda has also been marked by improvements in girls' access to school and maternal health, and legal reforms have made it easier for women to own land and control their own monetary assets.

Senegal, in West Africa, stands out in the region for its political stability since independence. While it was a one-party state for a time, Senegal introduced competitive elections in 1981. Lauded for its political stability, Senegal's history of gender equality is less impressive, in part due to women's low educational attainment and a hybrid legal system that disadvantaged women in inheritance and other civil matters (Camara 2007). However, in 2008, the government implemented a legislative gender quota that more than doubled women's legislative representation to 43 percent in 2010. During this period, women's political and civic participation also increased significantly (Hern 2020).

Identifying a Common Factor of Success

Rwanda and Senegal differ in many ways: Belgian versus French colonial histories, civil violence only in Rwanda, Central African highlands versus West African coast, primarily Christian versus Islamic—yet they have both experienced dramatic improvements in women's status over the past twenty years. The theories as applied to these two countries are summarized in Table 6.2. As the table illustrates, four hypotheses find support: both countries have evidence of descriptive representation generating both symbolic and substantive effects, women's civil society organizations, and political leadership supportive of women's empowerment.

Beginning with the sociocultural theories, the two countries differ on religion: Senegal is 95 percent Muslim, while Rwanda is majority Christian.[4] In Senegal, 97.2 percent of respondents to Afrobarometer's Round 4 stated that religion is "very important" to them, compared to 81.4 percent for the rest of the countries in the survey. Meanwhile, in Rwanda, only 40 percent reported to Wave 6 of the World Values Survey that religion was "very important" to them—far lower than the average of 74 percent reported in the other African countries sampled in that round.[5] Based on these two theories, Rwanda should perform significantly better than Senegal, so they cannot explain why both countries have fared well.

The structural theories do not perform any better. The idea of a traumatic shock creating a critical juncture holds some explanatory power in Rwanda (the genocide spurred a massive institutional overhaul), but Senegal had no such dramatic moment of change. Both Rwanda and Senegal are categorized by the UNDP as having low levels of human development and rank near the middle of African countries (Rwanda, ranked 24th of 53, performs slightly better than the continental median, while Senegal, ranked 33rd, performs slightly worse).[6] While birth rates are declining in both places, neither has undergone the demographic transition—each country's population is mostly rural, and the average number of children per woman is 4 in Rwanda, 4.7 in Senegal.[7]

Table 6.2 Theories as Applied to Rwanda and Senegal

Theory	Rwanda	Senegal	Conclusion
		Sociocultural	
Islam	Majority Catholic	Majority Muslim	Theory unsupported: predicts Senegal should struggle
Religiosity	Low	High	Theory unsupported: predicts Senegal should struggle
		Structural	
Critical junctures	Yes	No	Theory unsupported: predicts Senegal should struggle
Modernization theory	Low HDI	Low HDI	Theory unsupported: predicts both countries should struggle
Demographic transition	4 children/ woman	4.7 children/ woman	Theory unsupported: predicts both countries should struggle
		Institutions	
Symbolic representation	Yes	Yes	Supports theory
Substantive representation	Yes	Yes	Supports theory
Democracy	No	Yes	Theory unsupported: predicts Rwanda should struggle
		Civil Society	
Women's organizations	Yes	Yes	Supports theory
		Agency	
Political leadership	Yes	Yes	Supports theory

The institutional explanations are more promising. Both countries have elected large numbers of women in their legislative bodies, achieving a great degree of descriptive representation. Indeed, this metric is one reason both countries score well on measures of women's empowerment. However, as detailed subsequently, there is additional evidence that the presence of women in office has generated symbolic effects as well. Women have also been responsible for driving important policy changes in both Rwanda and Senegal, also described further. Importantly, regime type does not pass muster as an explanation in this case: while Senegal has a robust multiparty democracy, Rwanda's regime has become increasingly authoritarian since the end of the postgenocide transition. Both countries have active coalitions of women's organizations (as measured by Kang and Tripp 2018) that may contribute to the positive symbolic effects of women's representation, and both countries had presidents who offered strong support for quota legislation increasing women's descriptive representation.

The symbolic and substantive effects of women's descriptive representation, the presence of women's civil society organizations, and the support of political leadership all remain plausible theories for explaining improved outcomes in both Rwanda and Senegal. The following cases examine the part each played.

Rwanda

Rwandan society was completely devastated in a few short months by the 1994 genocide, in which over 10 percent of the population was ruthlessly slaughtered and many more were subject to rape and other atrocities. The violence came to an end when the Rwandan Patriotic Front (RPF), a militant group of exiled Tutsis[8] led by Paul Kagame, beat back government forces and took control of the capital city of Kigali. The decade that followed was marked by a painful process of reconciliation and rebuilding under a transitional government, which was ultimately replaced by an elected government under a new constitution in 2003.

Women played a dominant public role during this period. By some estimates, immediately after the genocide, women comprised 70 percent of the Rwandan population because so many men had been killed or exiled, and many of the remaining men were imprisoned for their crimes (Buss and Ali 2017, 568). Women picked up the pieces of the economy, knit communities back together, and busied themselves with healing the nation (Debusscher and Ansoms 2013). This was a clear instance of a traumatic event that generated a critical juncture: women's roles in the economy and society changed dramatically because of the genocide. During this time, they also became increasingly politically active (Herndon and Randell 2013). While Rwandan culture previously had little space for women in political life, the genocide shifted survivors' ways of thinking. The general perception was that women had been disproportionately victimized (many surviving women had been victims of sexual violence) and were bearing the brunt of both the genocide and rebuilding society, and therefore they deserved a say in constructing the political future (Powley 2003, 12). In addition, because a majority of *genocidaires* were men, people considered women as a group to be less responsible for the atrocities (Uwineza and Pearson 2009). Some also held the perspective that women's "feminine nature" made them nurturing and better at forgiveness, and therefore it was prudent to involve them in postgenocide governance (Powley 2003, 15).

This shift in public perception coincided with the rise of women's civil society organizations that began lobbying heavily for major changes. While women's civil society organizations had been strong in Rwanda prior to the conflict, their activities expanded dramatically in its aftermath to address the serious social and economic problems the country was experiencing (Longman 2006, 138). They insisted on changing land inheritance laws to make it easier for women to own land (a particularly important reform at a time when many women's male relatives were dead, exiled, or imprisoned), changing the classification of rape to a violent crime, and instituting a quota to ensure women's representation in government (Bauer and Burnet 2013; Powley 2006). Judith Kanakuze, a prominent civil society leader, was tapped for the constitutional commission in 2001, and the idea to include gender quotas in the new constitution has been attributed to her (Bauer and Burnet 2013, 107). In 1996, women created the Forum of Women Parliamentarians (FFRP), a nonpartisan caucus including all the women in parliament, which allowed them to organize collectively to privately lobby male parliamentarians one on one to support the quota and other laws to promote gender equality (Powley 2006, 8). Bauer and Burnet consider the coalition of women's groups to be central to the 2003 constitution explicitly codifying gender equality and instituting quotas across "all decision-making bodies" (2013, 107).

Kagame, leading the RPF, was supportive of these initiatives. Many suggest that he and other members of the RPF leadership had been influenced by women's involvement in the political sphere in Uganda (where members of the RPF had been exiled prior to the genocide), and women had long been integrated into RPF leadership (Powley 2003, 2006). As a result of women's active campaigning, the RPF instituted a system for reserving 30 percent of legislative seats for women, and further committed to involving women in the cabinet and other ministries (Bauer and Burnet 2013). The quota helped initially boost women's rate of election to the legislature, but soon they far exceeded the 30 percent minimum. The lower house of the Rwandan parliament elected 48 percent women in the first election under the new constitution in 2003, 56 percent in 2008, 64 percent in 2013, and 61 percent in 2018. Furthermore, the RPF under Kagame (who is still president) has continued to ensure women's involvement in the ministries, and since 2019 women constitute 52 percent of the cabinet.

While there is certainly still work to be done, women's quality of life has improved in other ways in Rwanda as well, in part due to new laws and policies implemented by the government. In addition to the land reform law and changing the criminal status of rape, the government has contributed to improvements in education and maternal health. Overall rates of education are still low in Rwanda, but the government has been working to address this issue by investing heavily in primary schools and ensuring girls have access to these schools (McLean Hilker 2011). Additionally, the government has undertaken health reforms to ensure that expectant mothers are better able to deliver and receive ante- and postnatal care in health centers: between 2005 and 2010, the percentage of Rwandan women delivering babies at health centers and hospitals increased from 18 percent to 60 percent with improved outcomes for infant mortality and children's nutrition as well (Pierce, Heaton, and Hoffmann 2014). On top of these changes, the female-dominated parliament has passed labor rights protecting pregnant and breastfeeding women and strengthened laws against domestic violence. Part of the reason women parliamentarians were able to accomplish these feats was working across party lines through the FFRP (Powley 2006).

In addition to these concrete improvements, there is evidence that attitudes about women in public spaces have changed over the decades since the genocide, at least in part due to women's increased political and economic participation. As described previously, women undertook additional economic activity in the postgenocide era and have maintained a higher labor force participation rate than men. Additionally, norms about women's contributions in the community and local political forums have shifted (Bauer and Burnet 2013). The structure of the Rwandan government includes mandatory meetings with local officials and community labor projects. Women officials at the local level have spurred "a sea change in attitudes toward women" (Burnet 2011, 315). While there is unfortunately limited data prior to the establishment of the new constitution, polling by the World Values Survey indicates that Rwandans attitudes about women political leaders continued to shift once they were in power. From 2007 to 2012, the percentage of Rwandans who disagreed with the statement "men make better political leaders than women" increased from 45 percent to 54 percent.[9] Women's visibility in political and economic roles has had important symbolic effects, increasing the amount that women participate in local meetings as well as popular perceptions of what women can do (Burnet 2011).

To say Rwanda performs well is not to say that it is perfect. Rwandan women are still underrepresented in secondary and tertiary education, and some rural Rwandan women view the parliamentarians as urban elites who know little of their lives (Bauer and Burnet 2013, 108; Debusscher and

Ansoms 2013, 1129). There are ongoing concerns that Kagame uses gender equality as a smokescreen to distract from his increasingly authoritarian administration, and that the women parliamentarians can do little but toe the party line (Buss and Ali 2017, 8). While many laud the increased visibility of women at local levels of governance, some women complain that the requirements around their participation just increase their unpaid labor (Burnet 2011). However, even accounting for these criticisms, Rwanda has made great strides toward women's empowerment and gender equality in political rights, public participation, and health and education outcomes. In this case, a well-organized and active coalition of women's groups, supported by the political leadership, pushed for lasting institutional change. The result was an increase in descriptive representation with some substantive outcomes and striking symbolic effects.

Senegal

Women's presence in politics and the labor force has increased dramatically in Senegal in recent years, which is surprising given the historical disadvantage women have faced. One of the legacies of France's colonial rule in Senegal is a large and persistent gender gap in educational attainment, and Senegalese women were less active in the nationalist movement and early-independence politics than they were elsewhere in Africa (Hern 2021). Customary and Islamic practices reinforced patrilineal inheritance, limiting the extent to which women could accumulate assets outside of marriage (Evans 2016). Yet Senegalese women have made great strides recently: the "parity" quota law ensures that nearly half of parliament is made up of women, the gender gaps in education and formal employment are shrinking, and legal changes have granted women new rights around inheritance and land ownership.

In Rwanda, a deeply traumatic shock broke open domestic politics and created an opportunity for women to influence new institutional design. No such rupture occurred in Senegal, which has enjoyed a stable political sphere since its independence in 1960. Under Léopold Senghor, the first president, Senegal was functionally a one-party state (though two "competing parties" were allowed to exist under extremely circumscribed conditions). Senegal became a true multiparty democracy in 1980, when Senghor retired and was succeeded by his prime minister, Abdou Diouf, who lifted restrictions on competing parties. The first true alteration in power came in 2000, when opposition candidate Abdoulaye Wade won the presidency. While some political reforms were made over this period, there were no dramatic upheavals; rather, the transition to a competitive system occurred seamlessly.

While women historically played a limited role in Senegalese politics, they had long been active in civil society. Organizations like the Association of Senegalese Women Lawyers (AJS) have been active since the 1970s, lobbying the government and working on legal reforms to better protect women's rights (Scales-Trent 2010). Grassroots organizations for women in Senegal abound. Binta Sarr, founder of the Association for the Advancement of Senegalese Women, noted that "here in Senegal you will hardly find a woman who is not organized, be it in a traditional association, a formalized women's group, an NGO, or an age group" (quoted in Sieveking 2007, 33). Many Senegalese women join *tontines*, savings and loans associations made up of other women that operate as informal banks and help insulate women against the monetary demands of their friends and relatives (Guérin 2006; Périlleux and Szafarz 2015).

Wade was elected in 2000 after running as a reformer, and he had espoused progressive ideas about social change in Senegal. Women's organizations in Dakar realized that he might provide an opportunity for women's political advancement, and the Senegalese Council of Women (COSEF) and AJS jumped to action. They recognized that to achieve legislative victories on things like reforming family law—which, among other things, gives husbands the exclusive right to choose where the family lives and stipulates that female heirs receive only half of what male heirs receive (Camara 2007, 790), they would need to increase the number of women in the legislature. Thus, they began to pressure the government to adopt a legislative gender quota that would make women's representation equal to men's (Hern 2020; Toraasen 2017). Their efforts were successful, and Wade signed the parity quota into law in 2010. Senegalese elect their representatives by voting for parties, and parties put forward lists of candidates that will gain seats depending on the percentage of votes the party receives. The parity law requires that parties alternate men and women on the list, guaranteeing that nearly half of those elected will be women (men are still overrepresented because they are almost always in the first spot on the list). The subsequent election, in 2012, nearly doubled the percentage of women in the legislature, from 22 percent to 43 percent. While this dramatic increase in descriptive representation was a victory in itself, the parity campaign and subsequent symbolic effects of its success have generated additional social and economic changes.

The influx of women into the legislature has changed the way that the urban elite view women in power, which has changed the way the parliament functions (Toraasen 2019). While closed male patronage networks used to keep the inner workings of Senegalese politics inaccessible to women (Beck 2003), women politicians are now using gendered norms around hospitality to cultivate their own support bases. As Emily Riley (2019) describes, women politicians have been able to cultivate their own networks through their presence at social events built around gift-giving and reciprocity; these social exchanges—at which women's presence is expected—have enabled women politicians to secure supporters in their communities. During the campaign for parity, COSEF's extensive grassroots campaign about the importance of women's involvement in politics coincided with an increase in women's political participation (Hern 2020). As in Rwanda, public attitudes about women as political leaders improved after the quota was implemented. According to the Afrobarometer, the percentage of Senegalese who think women should have the same chance as men to be elected into office increased from 64 percent in 2013 to 77.8 percent in 2017.[10]

During the same period, the gender gap in education began to decrease, and as of 2016, Senegalese girls were more likely to complete primary education than boys. Increases in girls' education coincided with an increase in their labor force participation as well (Malta, Martinez, and Mendes Tavares 2019). These across-the-board improvements can be attributed to several coincident phenomena: changes to certain parts of family law that were particularly disadvantageous to women, improved funding for education, an increase in descriptive representation in the legislature, and the activation of a broad grassroots network of women to promote women's involvement in politics and the economy. As in Rwanda, there is still plenty of room for improvement in Senegal. The gender gap in secondary and tertiary education is still large, women are still underrepresented in higher-paid jobs, and the legal changes guaranteeing women's ability to inherit land unevenly translate to action. However, there has been marked improvement in recent decades.

Rwanda and Senegal are very different but have experienced similar improvements over a similar period. Differences between the countries help eliminate some theories of gender equality, but the case evidence supported four hypotheses: in both countries, increases in descriptive representation generated important symbolic and substantive representation. Both countries had strong women's civil society organizations that were able to identify moments of opportunity to lobby for significant legal changes to improve women's legislative representation. In presidents Kagame and Wade, these groups had support from executives who were willing to follow through on these changes. The result in both cases was an effective legislative gender quota, resulting in an increase in descriptive representation, which translated to some limited substantive change and significant symbolic effects that rippled through society.

Most-Similar Cases: Burundi and Guinea

The foregoing comparison provided evidence in support of four hypotheses explaining Rwanda and Senegal's success: women's symbolic and substantive representation, active women's civil society organizations, and supportive political leadership. In both countries, well-organized women's civil society actors, supported by the president, were able to successfully increase their legislative presence through the implementation and enforcement of a gender quota. In both cases, the presence of women in parliament led to important symbolic representation alongside some substantive policy outcomes. To verify that this chain of events explains Rwanda and Senegal's relative success, the analysis now turns to two most-similar cases: Burundi (compared to Rwanda) and Guinea (compared to Senegal). Like Senegal and Rwanda, both these countries had active women's civil society organizations that succeeded in implementing a legislative gender quota. What is different, however, is that without strong support from the executive, these quotas have been poorly enforced. In Burundi, while the gender quota has increased women's descriptive representation, the president has blocked women legislators from changing laws that discriminate against women (and thus halting substantive representation). In Guinea, the gender quota has never been enforced at all. In these cases, women's progress has been stymied by political leaders who have kept their representation purely descriptive or refused to enable their descriptive representation at all.

Rwanda and Burundi

Rwanda and Burundi share many key historical details: neighbors and once part of the same colony of Ruanda-Urundi, they are similarly sized, share a similar ethnic demography, and were marked by similar forms of domestic conflict, including civil war with a genocidal component. Like Rwanda, Burundi emerged from this traumatic history and enacted a democratic constitution, though another characteristic they share is the increasingly authoritarian nature of the electoral regime. Despite their shared history, however, women's prospects are much worse in Burundi than in Rwanda. Burundi scores 0.58 on V-Dem's women's political empowerment index (compared to 0.79 in Rwanda), well below the continental average of 0.69. Similarly, Burundi scores 0.52 on the UNDP's Gender Inequality Index, indicating higher rates of inequality than in Rwanda (which scored

0.41). These scores reflect real differences in quality of life: Burundi has a higher maternal mortality ratio (712 per 100,000 live births, compared to 290 in Rwanda), adolescent birth rate (55.6 per 1000 births compared to 39.1 in Rwanda), and fewer women in Parliament (39 percent compared to 56 percent in Rwanda).

While both countries have a sizeable portion of women in parliament, in Burundi, women's legislative representation has not translated to the same symbolic or substantive gains as in Rwanda. Like in Rwanda, women's civil society organizations in Burundi organized a campaign to implement legislative gender quotas to improve women's political representation. These organizations had international support and a great deal of momentum, and ultimately succeeded in securing a 30 percent quota in the constitutional reform of 2005. Ostensibly, this law was similar to Rwanda's. However, there were some key differences in the way this law was enforced: unlike in Rwanda, in Burundi the government accepted the quota grudgingly, and while it has been respected at the national level, it has not been enforced at the local level (Martin de Almagro 2016, 118). In Rwanda, the presence of women in local government generated strong symbolic effects and started to change people's minds about women's leadership and participation in politics. In Burundi, however, it became clear that the government's commitment to including women in the political realm was superficial and likely resulted from international pressure.[11] When it came to passing legislation that would have tangible benefits to women—like reforming the land inheritance law to improve women's prospects for land ownership—Burundian president Pierre Nkurunziza stepped in and quashed the legislation. Women in parliament at the time explained that the law had failed because of "male resistance," which was bolstered by the executive branch (Saiget 2016).

Some suspect that because Burundi is still vulnerable to renewed conflict, President Nkurunziza is more interested in catering to political supporters who might be threatened by women's empowerment than enabling women's access to power (Saiget 2016, 373). This episode provides a stark counterpoint to similar land reform that passed in Rwanda, shepherded by the ruling party and President Kagame's leadership. Unlike in Rwanda, where women's political involvement has resulted in reforming the inheritance laws, improving access to maternal health care, and improved girls' school attendance, women's representation in Burundi has not translated into similar legislative or policy victories. Such challenges may be because, without the support of the ruling party or executive branch, "there still exists a tendency to see women as illegitimate or token politicians . . . and party culture expects women politicians to follow the lead of their male counterparts" (Byrne and McCulloch 2012). Thus, women's descriptive representation has translated to neither symbolic nor substantive representation.

This comparison suggests that the key difference between Rwanda and Burundi was the commitment of the executive and the ruling party to women's political empowerment, which determined how descriptive representation in the parliament translated to substantive or symbolic representation. In Rwanda, President Kagame and the RPF held a genuine commitment to women's active involvement in politics. Even from a cynical perspective, seeing Kagame's support of women as political opportunism, the effects of women's representation are tangible: increased participation in community governance, legislation to improve women's quality of life, and improvements on education and health indicators. In Burundi, the government's implementation of a gender quota was the result of international intervention rather than President Nkurunziza's support, and the government has made it clear that it is uninterested in women's substantive input. Without key allies in positions of power, the institutional changes in Burundi led to descriptive representation that was tokenizing rather than transformative.

Senegal and Guinea

Senegal and Guinea also have many similarities. They share a border, were both colonized by France, and gained independence two years apart. Both countries have women's civil society organizations working in coalition. However, while Senegal adopted and enforced a strong quota that ultimately resulted in symbolic representation for women, Guinea adopted a much weaker quota that the president has quite visibly never enforced. This lack of support from the country's political leadership undermined the ability of the quota to produce either descriptive or symbolic representation.

As in Senegal, Guinea experienced a period of one-party rule postindependence under its first president, Sékou Touré. Like other leaders at the time, President Touré incorporated women into politics by coopting their political energy into the party machinery (Ammann 2016, 44–45). Therefore, while women were involved in politics, they had little ability to express independent political ideas. Touré died in 1984, and his one-party regime was replaced by a military dictatorship under General Lansana Conté, who introduced multiparty elections in 1993. However, he won these elections, which were marred by irregularities, and continued to lead the country until his death in 2008. Conté was concerned about the way the international community perceived Guinea, and he therefore made a point of signing onto international treaties concerned with furthering women's rights. However, it appeared he did so less from a personal conviction about women's empowerment and more for the international optics (Ammann 2016, 46). Nevertheless, during the 1990s, women's groups in Guinea organized and created relationships with international organizations. For example, women politicians inspired by the organizing they had seen in Senegal created the Women's Political Party Organization (FPP) to coordinate women's actions in the political realm (Tripp, Konate, and Lowe-Morna 2006, 123). Conté's death in 2008 was followed immediately by a military coup, and the country's institutions were again reformed, ultimately resulting in the election of Alpha Condé in 2010.[12] This institutional reform included the new Electoral Law of 2010, which mandated a 30 percent gender quota for women (Asiedu et al. n.d.). Condé never enforced the quota—which relied on political parties voluntarily fielding female candidates—and women won only 21 percent of legislative seats in the 2013 elections.

After this election, women undertook additional organizing to strengthen the quota law. Women's civil society organizations, coalitions of women Guinean politicians, and international actors gathered to work on addressing its weaknesses.[13] The Forum of Women Parliamentarians, along with the UN Women, the UNDP, and the Canadian government, began to lobby the government to amend the electoral law to allow for gender parity. Modeled on Senegal's quota, the new law requires parties to alternate the gender of the candidates on their party lists.[14] With the help of international pressure, this law was passed in 2019. However, while the new electoral law provides a monetary incentive to parties who elect female candidates, there is no enforcement mechanism for parties who fail to do so. As a result, in the most recent election in 2020, the proportion of women in the legislature decreased to 17 percent. Women's civil society in Guinea was proactive and succeeded in shepherding through a gender quota, so why did Guinea's parity law lack any enforcement mechanism?

Ostensibly, President Alpha Condé was supportive of expanding women's political representation. In addition to adopting the improved quota, he proposed changes to the constitution to ban female genital mutilation and underage marriage and to reform divorce law to give women and men equal rights.[15] Yet critics have alleged that the constitutional changes were a smokescreen for the real goal of the constitutional reform, which was to allow Condé to reset his term limits and retain power. The constitutional referendum was marred by violence, and the opposition boycotted the subsequent legislative elections, partially explaining the lack of attention to women on the party lists. Condé's party won a supermajority, and he won a controversial (and previously unconstitutional) third term in 2020 in an election that the opposition boycotted, before being ousted in a coup in 2021.

Condé had a pattern of making statements and legal changes that superficially supported women's empowerment but were ultimately toothless. As in Burundi, these moves were intended to appease the international community and distract from his attempts to consolidate power. They were therefore designed to attract headlines but not to be enforced. Like Burundi, these moves also occurred in the context of political instability: Guinea's democratic institutions have yet to survive an alternation of power, and the future of its politics are in question at the time of writing.

These most-similar case comparisons indicate that active women's civil society organizations and improvements in descriptive representation do not automatically translate to symbolic and substantive representation. All four countries had active women's civil society organizations that successfully oversaw the adoption of legislative gender quotas. In both Rwanda and Senegal, the presidents' support for women in the legislature translated women's descriptive representation to symbolic and (some) substantive representation. In Burundi, a gender quota resulted in more women being elected to the parliament, but once there, they were constrained and unable to translate their positions to improved outcomes for women. In Guinea, the gender quota was adopted but never enforced. The main difference between Rwanda and Senegal, on the one hand, and Burundi and Guinea, on the other hand, was an executive who was willing to support women elected to the legislature and thereby enable symbolic and substantive representation. Taking the information from all four cases into account, the critical factors in Senegal and Rwanda were the support of political leadership in advancing women's descriptive representation, which helped translate it to symbolic and substantive representation.

Why were Kagame and Wade so much more supportive of women's political representation than Nkurunziza and Condé? While it is possible that Kagame and Wade just genuinely supported women's advancement more than Nkurunziza and Condé, it is difficult to assess a leader's true opinion on an issue like this. However, it is possible to evaluate the political incentives that each president faced. Because Senegal is a democracy and Rwanda is an authoritarian state, the nature of these incentives differ. As Bush, Donno, and Zetterberg (n.d., 2) point out, the international community rewards democracy, and autocracies that are economically dependent on the West have incentives "to enact reforms in policy areas that are related to democracy but pose few risks to regime survival." International pressure and financial incentives from donor countries make it prudent for autocrats to advance women's legal rights in their countries to curry favor with donor countries, but autocrats tend to advance women's rights only as much as they can without threatening their own power (Donno, Fox, and Kaasik 2022). Based on this logic, one would expect that the difference between Rwanda on the one hand and Burundi and Guinea on the other hand are the political risks and rewards of giving women real legislative power. For Senegal, as a democracy, one would expect electoral incentives for Wade from advancing women's legislative representation.

Kagame ascended to power with a great amount of international goodwill, as the international community was rightly embarrassed that their delayed action had enabled the Rwandan genocide. Kagame was well aware that his reputation as a progressive reformer would earn him ongoing international support, particularly as his administration became increasingly authoritarian. Importantly, Kagame was able to craft a political sphere in which decisionmaking is controlled by a small group of elites (Buss and Ali 2017, 8). Women in the Rwandan legislature have been criticized for toeing the party line and only bringing politically safe issues up for debate (Bauer and Burnet 2013, 109). Leaning into Rwanda's reputation as the only country in the world with a majority female parliament likely gave Kagame a great deal of cover to crack down on political dissent domestically, and the tightly controlled political arena prevents women's legislative access from threatening his power (Coffé 2012, 289). Kagame's support of women's legislative presence thus drew support for him internationally and bolstered his domestic support through women party loyalists.

As described previously, international pressure likely spurred Nkurunziza and Condé to support gender quotas in their countries, and each would have enjoyed reputational rewards for doing so. However, contextual differences would have made it more costly to enable women's true political advancement. In Burundi, the postwar peace was much more precarious than in Rwanda, and Nkurunziza's hold on power has been tenuous. The postwar constitution in 2005 created a transitional moment in which domestic women's coalitions and international pressure succeeded in establishing the quota. However, Nkurunziza has had less control over the political realm than Kagame, as opposition parties are able to assert some influence (Brand 2018, 7). Considering that members of Nkurunziza's ruling party are hostile to legislative advances that would benefit women, such as inheritance law reform, there are clear domestic political costs to supporting women's power within the legislature (Saiget 2016, 366). Nkurunziza's domestic political precarity became clear after the coup attempt and massive public unrest following the 2015 extension of his term limits. The government's heavy-handed crackdown led the United States and the European Union, the country's largest donors, to suspend aid—thereby removing significant financial incentives to keep up the façade of women's political empowerment.[16] Furthermore, the political crisis let Nkurunziza restructure his government, removing women from positions of power and replacing them with a council of "wise men" due to his perception that the moment "demanded" a tight male inner circle (Brand 2018, 18). In a politically precarious position, Nkurunziza thus faced greater political costs and fewer incentives to support women's meaningful contributions within the legislature once they were there.

Similarly, in Guinea, Condé's actions were clearly designed to bolster his support among the international community by paying lip service to—but never actually implementing—pro-women reforms. While courting international support, Condé was preoccupied with domestic political discontent. Economic mismanagement and corruption had made him unpopular, and disgruntlement was growing within his own government.[17] His response to this discontent was consolidation of power through constitutional reform. While there is no direct evidence of such, it is possible that the improvements to women's rights (in the new constitution) and the strengthened gender quota (adopted just before the constitutional referendum) were intended as a smokescreen to draw international support for his consolidation of power. In any case, women's hard-won gains were never implemented, as the 2020 election was marred by violence and opposition boycott and Condé was ousted in a coup shortly thereafter. In both Burundi and Guinea, the presidents were in such a precarious political position that the reputational gains they would have secured in the international community by truly promoting women's equality were inconsequential relative to the domestic threats they faced. On the contrary, Kagame—operating from a more secure position—enjoyed great reputational gains from women's political advancement, which for a long time obscured his deepening authoritarianism.

As the only president of a democracy in this chapter, Wade faced a different set of political incentives. It was in his interest to generate an electoral advantage for himself and his party. Because women's political participation was relatively low prior to the quota campaign, it was politically expedient to mobilize women to vote by expanding their impact in the legislature. Women were an under-mobilized political group when Wade came to power in 2000. Only 28 percent of Senegalese women voted in the 2005 elections, compared to 37% of men. Similarly, men were more likely to belong to a political party than women (30 percent compared to 24.4 percent, respectively).[18] Wade publicly supported the women's movement campaign for parity, providing funding and political backing, which rolled out in 2007. By 2008, women's voting rate and partisanship were equal to those of men (Hern 2020). Over that same period, the gender gap in support for President Wade's party closed—men's support was six points higher than women's in 2005, and only one point higher in 2008.[19] While Wade's party ultimately lost the presidency in 2012 amid other political controversies, he had clear electoral incentives to support women's legislative gains in the interest of mobilizing their vote. While it is possible that Kagame and Wade were genuinely committed to women's political advancement, it is also true that they had political incentives to expand women's legislative presence. However, Nkurunziza and Condé only had incentives to make superficial changes that looked good to the international community and were otherwise distracted by domestic political instability.

Conclusion

Women face significant challenges globally to their full involvement in economic and political life. These challenges are particularly pronounced in African countries, though in some places women have made great strides toward achieving equality with men. The cases of Rwanda and Senegal, both of which have experienced sustained improvement to women's status, provide some insights to the conditions that facilitate such improvements. In both countries, increases in descriptive representation led to symbolic representation and some substantive policy changes. However, as Burundi and Guinea illustrate, increasing the number of women in parliament (or passing a quota) does not necessarily improve women's symbolic or substantive representation. Political leadership (and the incentives to support women in the legislature) helps to explain why Rwanda and Senegal were able to translate descriptive representation into symbolic and substantive gains, but Burundi and Guinea were not. Rwanda and Senegal are not the only African countries with strong performance on women's empowerment and gender equality. Mauritius, Cabo Verde, Namibia, Seychelles, and South Africa also stand out as countries where women fare comparatively well. It would therefore be worthwhile to examine whether the processes that led to improvements in Rwanda and Senegal have also taken place in these countries.

In all four countries featured in this chapter. women's civil society organizations were important actors, highlighting gender inequities and lobbying the government to make changes. These groups formed coalitions and garnered support from international organizations, which bolstered their status and amplified their voices. However, only in Rwanda and Senegal were the executive and ruling party open to legal reforms and committed to improvements to women's status. In Rwanda, many have noted that Kagame and the ruling RPF party were influenced by their experiences in exile in Uganda, which was an early adopter of gender quotas (Powley 2006). In Senegal, President Wade was similarly committed to improving women's access to politics and shepherded through the strongest legislative gender quota in the region (COSEF 2011). They also both enjoyed relative political stability and had domestic political incentives to support women in the legislature. On the contrary, both Nkurunziza in Burundi and Condé in Guinea occupied politically precarious positions and had few incentives to support women in the legislature beyond courting international reputational gains. At least in the case of Burundi, there were clear political costs associated with supporting women that won seats in the legislature.

Inclusion of women in decisionmaking roles has coincided with important improvements for women and girls in both countries. In Rwanda, women's involvement has led to reform of inheritance laws that improve women's land rights, an expansion of girls' access to school, reform of laws around domestic violence, and dramatic improvements to maternal health. Additionally, women's inclusion in the legislature, cabinet, and local government have shifted attitudes about women as effective public servants, popularizing the perception that women are hard-working, less corrupt, and more altruistic in governance than their male counterparts (Herndon and Randell 2013). In Senegal, the increase in women's legislative presence has coincided with improvements in girls' educational attainment and women's employment, as well as reforms to inheritance and family law. Furthermore, the implementation of the quota coincided with an increase in women's political participation.

While the contexts of these changes in Rwanda and Senegal are completely different, the process in each country has contained similar elements: coalitions of local women's movements with international support, a sympathetic executive branch, the implementation of an effective quota, and subsequent legislative changes and symbolic effects that improve women's position in public life. Burundi and Guinea also had active women's civil society movements and legislative gender quotas without similar improvements, as they were thwarted by an unsympathetic executive. While these case comparisons suggest that a Western-style democracy is not a prerequisite for women's empowerment, they do highlight the importance of executives prioritizing women's legislative power, whether for intrinsic or instrumental reasons. Additionally, the comparison underscores that domestic political instability can reduce incentives for executives to support women's legislative power, undermining advances in women's political empowerment.

Notes

1. United Nations Development Program Gender Inequality Index Data, 2018.

2. Varieties of Democracy. "Women's Political Empowerment Index."

3. Combined performance determined by averaging the two indices, which each range from 0 to 1. The UNDP index was rescaled so that "1" indicated better performance on gender equality. The UNDP did not score eleven countries. To generate scores for those countries, I estimated the likely UNDP score based on the average difference between the UNDP and V-Dem scores (UNDP scores were on average 0.29 points lower than the V-Dem score). These scores should therefore be treated as rough estimates only. Countries for which this was necessary include Seychelles, Madagascar, Guinea-Bissau, Nigeria, Guinea, Comoros, Djibouti, Equatorial Guinea, Somalia, South Sudan, and Eritrea.

4. According to Round 4 of the Afrobarometer for Senegal and Round 5 of the World Values Survey for Rwanda. These surveys were carried out over the same period, but unfortunately neither survey includes both countries.

5. Other countries in Wave 4 of the World Values Survey: Ghana, Nigeria, South Africa, and Zimbabwe.

6. Based on UNDP country HDI rankings, 2018.

7. Data from the World Bank. 4.7 is Africa's continental average.

8. The genocide was perpetrated largely by the majority Hutu ethnic group, which controlled the government, against the Tutsi minority, though many Hutu perceived as too "moderate" were also victims.

9. Data from the World Values Survey, Rounds 5 (2007) and 6 (2012).

10. Data from the Afrobarometer, Rounds 5 (2013) and 7 (2017).

11. Unfortunately, data limitations prevent comparison over a longer time (as in Rwanda), but recent Afrobarometer data indicate that support for women's access to elected office, while relatively high, has declined slightly in recent years. The Afrobarometer estimated that support for women's equal access to office was about 74.9 percent in 2012 and 73.4 percent in 2015. The Afrobarometer does not conduct surveys in Rwanda, preventing direct comparison between the two countries.

12. Condé himself was ousted in a coup in 2021. The country's political future is uncertain at the time of writing.

13. National Democratic Institute. 2014, September 5. "Guinea Wins with Women." https://www.ndi.org/guinea-wins-with-women

14. UN Women. 2019, May 10. "Guinea Adopts Law on Parity, Securing Equal Representation for Women on Electoral Lists." https://www.unwomen.org/en/news/stories/2019/5/news-guinea-adopts-law-on-parity

15. France 24. 2020, April 2. "Guinean President Conde's Party Rightfully Won Violent March Elections: Electoral Commission." https://www.france24.com/en/20200402-guinea-conakry-alpha-conde-election-rally-guinean-people-rpg

16. Africa News. 2022, February 8. "EU Restores Aid to Burundi Despite Critics Issuing Warnings." https://www.africanews.com/2022/02/08/eu-restores-aid-to-burundi-despite-critics-issuing-warnings

17. Soudan, Francois. 2021, September 9. "Guinea: The Secret Story Behind the Fall of President Alpha Condé." *The Africa Report.* https://www.theafricareport.com/125796/guinea-the-secret-story-surrounding-the-fall-of-president-alpha-conde/

18. Afrobarometer, Round 3.

19. Afrobarometer, Rounds 3 and 4.

7

African Successes in Comparative Perspective

While African countries have faced numerous challenges related to governance, economic performance, and the production of public goods, many have also experienced success overcoming these obstacles. As I have demonstrated in this book, discussions of Africa as an undifferentiated continent mask a great deal of variation in national experiences. This book has covered a great deal of ground, both substantively and geographically, to illuminate the variety of experiences across African countries and to highlight successes in key arenas. It has showcased Gabon and Seychelles, which have achieved positive economic outcomes through policies of directed development; Botswana and Mauritius, which have maintained good governance through endogenous institutions and unifying leadership; Malawi and Guinea-Bissau, which have made remarkable strides in battling malaria through donors engaging local actors with national reach; Lagos, Nigeria and Durban, South Africa, which have taken strides toward planning a climate-resilient future, thanks to committed municipal champions and the mobilizing effect of focus events; and finally, Senegal and Rwanda, which have achieved large gains in women's empowerment through the substantive and symbolic effects of women's legislative representation, facilitated by supportive presidents.

One of my goals for the book was to showcase the diversity of the continent, in contrast to its monolithic representation in most popular media. In chapters on economic development and governance, I underscore how different the experience of colonialism was for different countries, and how much variation there has been in its aftermath. On one hand the cases of Gabon, Seychelles, Equatorial Guinea, and Sao Tome and Principe demonstrate how policy helped some countries overcome the negative economic consequences of colonialism, when leaders face political incentives to expand access to the economic realm. On the other hand, the cases of Botswana, Mauritius, Uganda, and Comoros illustrated how varied the nature of colonialism was, with important consequences around the way boundaries were drawn, the politicization of groups within new states, and whether it left precolonial institutions intact. Guinea-Bissau, Malawi, Sierra Leone, and Mozambique illuminate how much variation there is in public health challenges, even when considering only one disease, and the varied lingering effects of civil war. Lagos, Durban, Bloemfontein, and Abuja illustrate the different ways climate change will impact the continent, alongside the different strategies cities can employ to adapt to it. Finally, Rwanda, Senegal, Burundi, and Guinea illustrate how women's legislative representation has such a different impact across different political contexts, only translating to substantive and symbolic representation when the executive has political incentives to support it.

Aside from highlighting this diversity, I have also intentionally focused on success. As explained in the introduction, this focus is partly a corrective measure intended to balance the overwhelmingly negative coverage that Africa receives in journalism, pop culture, and academia. Aside from normative and philosophical reasons for focusing on success, there are also practical reasons. Understanding how some countries have performed well or made substantial advancements is essential for enabling improvements in the countries that continue to struggle. Determining why things went well in some places is as important as diagnosing what went wrong in others. When things do go well, rather than considering it exceptional, the most constructive response is to determine what went right and what lessons can be drawn for other cities and countries.

In the introduction to this book, I described three goals: centering African successes, highlighting Africa's diversity, and presenting an Africa-centered introduction to comparative politics. These first two goals have been addressed previously; in the rest of this concluding chapter, I turn to the third: what the study of Africa reveals about the theories, logic, and methods of comparative politics.

Theories of Comparative Politics Through an African Lens

To oversimplify, the goal of comparative politics is to use case comparison to determine which theories best explain an outcome of interest. Most theories in comparative politics can be grouped into categories focusing on structures, institutions, sociocultural forces, or personal agency. While scholars debate which types of theories are the most useful, the case analyses in this book indicate that different types of theories are better at explaining different types of outcomes.

Structures

Structural explanations focus on unchangeable circumstances, often beyond human manipulation. Structures can include things like a country's geography, resource wealth, or disease environment. Structures can affect outcomes because they shape a country's context in important ways. While structural explanations are prominent in examining African politics, they did not stand up to scrutiny in most cases presented in this book. Three chapters included explicit focus on structural theories: those explaining economic development, climate adaptation, and gender equality. Regarding economic development, scholars often use structural factors like geography and resources to explain economic performance, but none of these could explain why Seychelles and Gabon had achieved greater HDI than Sao Tome and Principe and Equatorial Guinea. Similarly, gender equality is often linked to structural factors like economic development or the demographic transition, but these theories could not explain why Rwanda and Senegal performed so much better than Burundi and Guinea in this matter. Structural features mattered more in the chapter on climate adaptation: the presence of dramatic, climate-related focus events helped explain why municipal governments of Lagos and Durban were so much more active than those in Abuja and Bloemfontein. Structural theories have been useful for comparing the performance of African countries to those on other continents, but because countries within Africa share many of the same structural features, these theories struggle to explain the variation in outcomes between African countries.

In some cases, however, structural features were important indirectly through their impact on other factors that mattered. In Chapter 2, whether presidents pursued directed developed was related to the logic of their political survival, which was determined by an eclectic set of structural circumstances (like whether the president was likely to live much longer). In Chapter 3, I found that good governance was related to endogenous institutions and unifying leadership, but the nature of colonial history influenced the extent to which unifying leadership was possible. In Uganda, the British built the colonial state around an amalgam of preexisting political groups, making unification much more challenging than in a place like Botswana. While the cases demonstrate that the actions of the first presidents were still important, structural features made unifying leadership more challenging for President Obote in Uganda than President Khama in

Botswana. Similarly, the lingering effects of civil war hampered malaria reduction campaigns in Sierra Leone and Mozambique, albeit through different mechanisms: the history of war in Sierra Leone decimated health infrastructure and contributed to a lack of trust in health practitioners, while in Mozambique lingering political antagonism has led to the uneven distribution of resources. Through different pathways, this history undermined efforts to achieve national reach of malaria reduction campaigns.

Institutions and Policy

Institutional explanations are prominent in political science, based on the observation that the rules governing a society are of grave importance for explaining what that society can accomplish. Institutions are a broad concept, but they are generally defined to include the formal rules that govern public spaces: constitutions, laws, and governing procedures. Governing institutions also produce policies. Policies are not the same as institutions and are often treated as a distinct category, but they are grouped together here for parsimony: institutions shape the way governments work, and governments produce policy. Institutional and policy-based theories were featured in all five substantive chapters in this book, and the hypotheses associated with them often found support across all cases within the chapters. Pursuing a policy of directed development was the only hypothesis that found support explaining economic development. Institutions that were at least partially endogenous (originating from within) helped explain why Botswana and Mauritius were able to achieve better governance than Uganda and Comoros. Women's symbolic and substantive representation in the legislature was what distinguished Rwanda and Senegal from Burundi and Guinea, plausibly explaining women's empowerment.

However, institutions are not always the only plausible explanation, and macrolevel institutional explanations about regime type fared poorly: whether a country was democratic or authoritarian could not explain economic development, public health outcomes, or gender equality (though it did indirectly shape rulers' political incentives to support women in the legislature). Furthermore, local government institutions did not explain why some cities were more proactive about climate adaptation, though the structure of local government did influence the way local champions had to approach climate-related policy. While institutions were important for many of the outcomes I examined in this book, they are not universally so.

Sociocultural Forces

Sociocultural forces are the social and cultural features of society that may influence outcomes. These include features like the level of social trust, the depth of social division, and cultural features with a clear relationship to political outcomes, like the dominant religion's attitude toward women. While sociocultural features are commonly invoked to explain political outcomes, they were rejected in every case comparison here. In all five chapters, I considered sociocultural explanations, but they failed to explain variation in economic development, quality of governance, public health outcomes, or women's empowerment. However, like structures, they were sometimes important indirectly in the way they influenced other factors. For example, sociocultural divisions were not broadly explanatory for challenges in implementing malaria prevention programs. However, they likely contributed to the regional concentration of resources in Mozambique, impeding the national reach of malaria programs. Similarly, sociocultural divisions did not explain poor governance. However, they provided fodder for divisive leadership in Uganda and Comoros. Sociocultural divisions were never determinative, but they sometimes influenced factors that were. While the sociocultural theories were broadly rejected in these cases, that does not mean that social or cultural factors are never important. It does suggest, however, that they are not destiny.

Agency and Leadership

The last theoretical category examines the role of individuals and leaders to shape outcomes through their personal agency. There is a long-running debate in political science about how important leadership is. Some believe that individuals can meaningfully shape political outcomes; others believe that people—even powerful leaders—are constrained by institutions and structures and therefore only have limited agency. Many of the cases in this book, however, illustrated how important leadership and individual agency can be. In four chapters, I considered agency-based explanations, and they were important for explaining outcomes in three. The development of good governance in Mauritius and Botswana, for example, was certainly helped by each country having leadership at independence that eschewed divide-and-conquer politics and instead pursued unification. Municipal climate action hinged on the action of a local champion willing to put climate on the agenda. Women's ability to translate descriptive representation to symbolic and substantive representation depended on the president's support of their efforts. In all these cases, leadership and the actions of individuals were important, though they were generally not the sole factor: their leadership was important in conjunction with institutional and structural factors in the case of governance, climate adaptation, and women's empowerment. In most cases, good leadership also coincides with political incentives supporting it.

Other theories defy categorization in these terms. For example, "engaging with local actors that have national reach" to address malaria does not fit comfortably in any of the previous categories, but it is a factor that regularly appears in public health–related political science and was an essential factor in the case analysis here. Similarly, international influences (like those affecting foreign aid flows) may be related to domestic policy (as in Chapter 6) or large-scale international relations (such as the Cold War, in Chapter 2).

These cases illustrate that no single theoretical approach can explain everything. Different types of theory are explanatory in different contexts. Moreover, these factors can interact in unpredictable ways. Sometimes, well-designed institutions can mitigate challenging structural or sociocultural factors. For example, gender quotas boosted women's legislative representation in Rwanda and Senegal, even though politics in both countries was historically male-dominated. Other times, however, institutional design seems to matter little at all. While municipal governments are designed differently in South Africa and Nigeria, these different institutional structures were immaterial for which cities pursued climate action. In each case, it was hard to predict which theories would remain plausible after comparison. Things that matter for explaining one outcome are irrelevant for another; a theory that works well in one country loses explanatory power in another. This unpredictability underlines the importance of considering as many theories as possible when trying to explain an outcome.

Revisiting the Strengths and Limitations of Comparative Case Analysis

To make the claims summarized in the previous section, I rely on the combination of most-different and most-similar case comparison to evaluate which theory or theories were most plausible for explaining each outcome. The logic of comparison provides a clear structure for determining whether a theory has support. If a hypothesis fails in one or more of the cases under comparison, then its related theory lacks support as a general explanation. Selecting cases that are most-similar or most-different provides additional analytic leverage, maximizing the number of theories that can be ruled out. In short, this method is effective at ruling out theories that cannot explain some outcome across multiple countries. However, this method also has its shortcomings.

The first and most obvious shortcoming is that this method only enables a researcher to test the theories they think of. It is always possible that some other factor the researcher failed to consider is what actually explains the outcome. This shortcoming is not unique to the comparative method—it is a problem for research in general. However, it bears mentioning. In each chapter I have considered a set of theories, drawn from existing literature, that spanned multiple theoretical categories. But the conclusions I draw are only as good as the theories considered are comprehensive. Each chapter may have unintentionally omitted important explanatory theories. The true explanation may be something that no researcher has thought of yet. Part of the project of ongoing research in each of these areas is to consider and test new ideas.

Next, the structure and methods applied in this book can provide evidence in support of theories and rule out other theories, but they cannot provide definitive, causal proof. In each chapter, I present one or a few theories that remain plausible after the gauntlet of comparison, with some evidence that supports them. However, failing to reject a theory is not the same thing as proving it. Political science has a range of other methodological tools, like experiments and process-tracing, that come closer to providing the type of evidence that might prove a theory to be correct. The distinction between "provides evidence in support of" and "proves" is important. When we find evidence in support of a theory, it increases our confidence that theory is correct, but it does not give us permission to stop considering other possibilities. In political science, and social science generally, it is important to remain open-minded about other possibilities when a theory has yet to be proven. Being cautious about the findings of a study—and open to new evidence that might disprove it—is a mark of good science.

Next, the goal of comparative case analysis is to determine which theory best explains an outcome in general—that is, across many country cases. This is one way of looking at the empirical world, where the goal of research is to find general truths that hold across many contexts. There are many reasons to approach social science this way, but it is not the only way to approach empirical research. For example, this way of approaching research might miss multiple pathways to an outcome or complex interactions between variables. To elaborate using an example from this book, Chapter 2 indicated that Seychelles and Gabon had one thing in common that contributed to their economic success: a policy of directed development. It is also possible, however, that there are several pathways to economic success that countries might follow. For example, one pathway might be free markets with a strong judicial system, while another pathway might be directed development with well-regulated corruption. In this example, two countries with nothing in common could achieve economic success. A comparative case analysis would be unable to reach this conclusion.

Finally, this style of comparative analysis reflects deterministic rather than probabilistic thinking. By looking for factors that are always present or absent to explain an outcome, the implication is that one factor (or a combination of factors) *determines* an outcome. For example, in Chapter 4, a deterministic argument would be that a focus event in a city with a local climate champion in government will necessarily lead to a proactive climate adaptation agenda. However, another way of looking at the world is probabilistic. A probabilistic argument is that the presence of a factor makes something *more likely* but does not determine it. For example, perhaps a focus event plus a local climate champion leads to climate adaptation policy 75 percent of the time, while cities without focus events or climate champions only adopt these policies 25 percent of the time. If you conducted a comparative case analysis and happened to select one of the 25 percent of cities with a focus event and a local champion that never adopted climate adaptation policies, then you would find no support for these theories, even though they lead to the policy 75 percent of the time (far more often than in cities that lack them). Evaluating probabilistic theories requires other methods, like large-N statistical analysis.

I include discussion of these shortcomings not to undermine the work of the previous five chapters but to urge caution in interpreting the results and to be clear about what this type of analysis can and cannot do. In each chapter, comparison provides evidence for one or a few theories. In many cases, this evidence is compelling, but it is not the final word. The big questions considered in this book are open subjects of ongoing research. Tentative conclusions should be interpreted as an invitation for ongoing investigation.

Things Don't Always Fall Apart

Published in 1959, Chinua Achebe's insightful and incisive novel *Things Fall Apart* invited readers to imagine how the onset of colonialism in Nigeria precipitated the unraveling of a community and way of life. In a stark departure from other popular literature about the African continent (for example, Joseph Conrad's grisly *Heart of Darkness*), Achebe depicted life in precolonial Nigeria as quotidian rather than dark and exotic, but he also illustrated how colonialism frayed the social and economic fabric of these communities. In the years since, media and scholarly portrayals of Africa have tended to focus on the negative. Some, like Robert Kaplan's apocalyptic essay "The Coming Anarchy," evoke Conrad's hyperbolic descriptions of chaos and death. Others, including much recent scholarly work, are more nuanced and careful, but—like Achebe—still focus on challenges.

The result is a pervasive sense of Afropessimism in pop culture, journalism, and scholarly work.

In this book, I center positive narratives about African countries not to detract from the real challenges they face, but as a corrective. African countries have experienced a great deal of hardship over the past 150 years, related to the continent's experiences with colonialism, integration into the global economy, the Cold War, and other global forces beyond the control of any single country or government. At the same time, many of these countries have made great strides and achieved social, political, and economic successes. African countries—like countries on any continent—experience success as well as hardship. While understanding the challenges that countries (and continents) face is important, understanding their successes is essential as well. Things don't always fall apart.

Appendix 1: Data Sources

Publicly available data sources used in this book are listed as follows, in alphabetical order.

Afrobarometer

The Afrobarometer collects public opinion data from over thirty African countries. Eight rounds of data are available, dating back to 1999 (fewer countries were included in earlier rounds). The Afrobarometer includes a wide swath of opinion questions on politics and economics. Each round in each country polls a nationally representative stratified random sample. Access at afrobarometer.org.

Institute for Health Metrics and Evaluation (IHME)

IHME is a research organization based at the University of Washington that compiles global health data into the Global Health Data Exchange. The database includes funding, intervention, and outcome information for a broad array of public health threats worldwide. Access at healthdata.org.

Interparliamentary Union (IPU)

The IPU is a prodemocracy organization of national parliaments. It maintains a database of the percentage of women in national legislatures globally, updated monthly. Access at ipu.org.

Legatum Institute

The Legatum Institute is a conservative-leaning think tank with the goal of supporting economic development. It produces the Legatum Prosperity Index, which is based on a compilation of other data sources (such as the Gallup World Poll and the World Health Organization). The methodology they use to construct this index and its subindices can be found in each published edition of the Prosperity Index. Access at li.com/about.

Organization for Economic Cooperation and Development (OECD)
The OECD is an organization of wealthy democracies. One of its functions is to maintain a database of economic information for all member countries and select nonmember countries. Data are primarily reported by governments and include metrics such as revenue sources and government spending. Access at stats.oecd.org.

Polity V
The Polity project scores countries according to their regime type on a scale of −10 (closed autocracy) to 10 (full democracy). The scores reflect the way executives are selected and constrained alongside the robustness of political competition. Access at systemicpeace.org.

United Nations Development Program (UNDP)
The UNDP is an agency under the United Nations that works to promote poverty alleviation and democracy. It compiles and calculates the Human Development Index, which includes average income, education, and life expectancy in each country. The data used to compile these indicators come primarily from the World Bank (see the following description). It also produces the Gender Inequality Index. Access at undp.org.

Varieties of Democracy
The Varieties of Democracy Project produces over 450 indicators measuring various aspects of democracy. Their indicators are based on information provided by country experts, which are then converted into continuous measurements of each concept using a Bayesian item-response theory estimation strategy. Access at v-dem.net.

World Bank
The World Bank is an international organization with the mission of reducing global poverty. One of its functions is data collection, primarily of indicators related to economic performance and development in each country. The World Bank relies on a variety of methods for producing these indicators, including household surveys and data produced by other international organizations such as the United Nations. A methodology statement accompanies each indicator to describe how it was produced. Access at data.worldbank.org.

World Values Survey (WVS) Association
The WVS is an international research program that regularly carries out nationally representative surveys over many countries to track political, social, and economic values over time. There have been seven waves of the survey since 1981. The survey now includes over 120 countries. Access at worldvaluessurvey.org.

Appendix 2: Case Selection

The following sections describe the criteria for case selection for each chapter in the order in which case selection occurred.

Economic Development

This chapter relied on the UNDP's Human Development Index to identify the most successful countries. There were five countries that achieved a score of 0.7 or higher, therefore qualifying as having a high level of human development according to the UNDP: Seychelles, Mauritius, Botswana, South Africa, and Gabon. Seychelles was an obvious choice as the country with the highest score. This selection eliminated Mauritius as a most-different case because, like Seychelles, it is a small island nation with similar colonial history and ethno-demography. Either Botswana, South Africa, or Gabon would have worked as a most-different case based on region and ethno-demography. However, Seychelles, Botswana, and South Africa all gained their independence from the British, while Gabon's colonial history was French, making it the most different from Seychelles.

To select a most-similar case for Seychelles, I limited the candidate cases to the other small island nations outside the top-scoring group: Cabo Verde, Sao Tome and Principe, Comoros, and Madagascar. None of these islands share Seychelles's colonial history. I eliminated Comoros and Madagascar because, having an indigenous population upon colonization, there are significant ethno-demographic differences in these groups. Cabo Verde or Sao Tome and Principe would therefore before similar, but Sao Tome and Principe had a lower score on HDI and therefore had a more different economic outcome, making it more appropriate for this comparison.

To select a most-similar case for Gabon, I limited the candidate cases to the countries that share Gabon's border: Cameroon, Equatorial Guinea, and the Republic of Congo. I eliminated Cameroon due to the important geographical difference that it does not have the degree of oil resources as Gabon. Either Equatorial Guinea or the Republic of Congo would have been appropriate most-similar cases, but for different reasons. While Congo and Gabon share a colonial history, Equatorial Guinea and Gabon are more similar in terms of their dynastic politics. I chose

Equatorial Guinea due to its lower score on HDI, making it more appropriate for this comparison.

Governance

This chapter relied on an average of the components of the World Governance Index in 2019 to identify top performers. On this scale, which ranges from –2.5 to 2.5, there is a clear cut-off point at 0. Seven countries had positive scores in 2019: Mauritius, Botswana, Cape Verde, Seychelles, Namibia, South Africa, and Ghana. Mauritius was an obvious choice, having by far the highest score. Selecting this country excluded Cape Verde and Seychelles from comparison, as they are too geographically similar (being small island nations). Botswana, Namibia, South Africa, and Ghana thus remain as possible most-different cases. Due to a history of settler colonialism, South Africa has similar race–class divisions as Mauritius. Any of the three remaining countries would make a suitable most-different case. I chose Botswana as the remaining country with the highest score.

Selecting a most-similar case to compare against Mauritius was straightforward: restricting selection to small island nations, Comoros has the worst score currently. Selecting a most-similar case for Botswana, however, was challenging. Its regional neighbors are inappropriate for comparison: South Africa and Namibia have strong governance, Zimbabwe had a different colonial experience as a settler colony, Mozambique and Angola were colonized by the Portuguese and had brutal, long-lasting civil wars. Zambia was a possible candidate, but its governance score (though negative) is not particularly bad. Continuing to move northward, Tanzania, Democratic Republic of Congo, Rwanda, and Burundi all had different colonial experiences. While Kenya was also a British colony, it had a large settler population, making its colonial experience different. Uganda is therefore the closest case with poor governance. While Botswana and Uganda are as similar as possible within the constraints of selection, the chapter acknowledges important differences in their experiences.

Women's Empowerment

This chapter relied on a combination of V-Dem's Women Political Empowerment Index and the UNDP's Gender Inequality Index. Performance on this combined index had no clear threshold delineating success, so the pool of the top ten most successful countries included Mauritius, Cabo Verde, Namibia, Seychelles, South Africa, Rwanda, Senegal, Sao Tome and Principe, Madagascar, Botswana, and Ghana. Of these, four (Mauritius, Seychelles, Sao Tome and Principe, and Botswana) had been discussed in earlier chapters, so I eliminated them. Given the disproportionate focus in earlier chapters on island nations, I also eliminated Cabo Verde and Madagascar. These rounds of elimination left Namibia, South Africa, Rwanda, Senegal, and Ghana. Of these remaining countries, Senegal is an obvious choice because of its status as the only former French colony and the only majority Muslim country. This selection eliminated Ghana, which shares Senegal's region, and Namibia and South Africa, which have similar political institutions. The most-different comparison case to Senegal is therefore Rwanda.

Selecting a most-similar pairing for Rwanda was straightforward. Burundi and Rwanda share key characteristics: they were a single polity prior to colonialism and had similar colonial and postcolonial political experiences as well as near identical ethno-demographic characteristics. Yet Burundi ranks much worse on the women's empowerment index. There were many possible pairings for Senegal. I first restricted the pool to countries that share a border with Senegal to maximize ethno-demographic similarities: Mauritania, Mali, Guinea, Guinea-Bissau, and the Gambia. I eliminated the Gambia and Guinea-Bissau because of their different colonial experiences, leaving Mali, Mauritania, and Guinea. All three were part of French West Africa and have considerably worse scores on the Women's Empowerment Index than Senegal. I ruled out Mali because, unlike Senegal, Mali experienced considerable political turmoil during the period under investigation. Both Mauritania and Guinea are far less democratic than Senegal, an important difference. However, Guinea's democracy was strengthening over the period of investigation while Mauritania's was weakening (per V-Dem's Electoral Democracy Index), and Guinea (like Senegal) is a secular state while Mauritania is an Islamic republic, so I selected Guinea as being more closely comparable. The coup ousting sitting president Condé did not occur until after the chapter was written.

Public Health

This chapter relied on percent reduction in malaria incidence from 2000 to 2018 as measured by the World Bank. To ensure that countries had a similar starting point, I limited the cases to the eighteen African countries that began the period with annual malaria incidence of more than 400 per 1,000 people. These countries were largely concentrated in West Africa. First, Guinea-Bissau was an obvious choice with the largest percent reduction—25 points greater than the next country. There were four countries with 40–50 percent reductions: Malawi, Ghana, Burundi, and Uganda. Ghana shares the same region as Guinea-Bissau and is therefore less suitable as a most-different case. Burundi and Uganda had less success but appear in other chapters in this book. Malawi, in a different region, with different demographics and political institutions, was the most different.

Selecting a most-similar case for Guinea-Bissau, I considered the three countries geographically closest: Guinea, Sierra Leone, and Liberia. I eliminated Guinea as it had much more success than the other two. Sierra Leone and Liberia both share similar characteristics with Guinea-Bissau: all three have histories of civil conflict and authoritarian leadership with recent gradually strengthening electoral systems. Sierra Leone and Liberia have similar histories as colonies set up to repatriate enslaved Africans and similar current ethnodemography. Either would have made an appropriate most-similar case. I ultimately selected Sierra Leone because it is closer to Guinea-Bissau and therefore the type of malaria each country experiences is more likely be similar.

There was only one option for a most-similar case for Malawi: Mozambique. While the two countries share a border, they are unfortunately dissimilar in their colonial histories and postcolonial politics. However, they are the only two countries in southern Africa that started the period with high malaria incidence. Importantly, they also shared the challenge that the malaria-transmitting mosquitoes in the region (1) are active earlier in the evening, making bed nets less effective, and (2) have developed insecticide resistance. These shared challenges make their public health requirements similar, though their other dissimilarities make comparison less useful.

Climate Adaptation

This chapter relied on data from the Global Covenant of Mayors regarding which African cities signed up and earned badges. The most badges an African city had earned was six, and four cities achieved this level of success. Three were in South Africa: Kwadukuza, Durban, and Johannesburg. There was little information about Kwadukuza, so I ruled it out. I selected Durban over Johannesburg in the interest of featuring a city that draws less attention. The next most-successful cities were in South Africa, Comoros, and Mozambique. I ruled out the other South African city as obviously not most-different, and Comoros and Mozambique because they were featured in earlier chapters. The next tier included Dar es Salaam, Lagos, Addis Ababa, and Cocody (Cote d'Ivoire). Any one of these would have been an appropriate most-different city. I eliminated Cocody due to lack of information. Upon looking into Dar and Addis, there were significant allegations of "greenwashing," and both are out of compliance with the Covenant. Therefore, I chose Lagos.

To select most-similar comparison cases, I looked at the other cities from the same country that had joined CGoM but made no progress. In South Africa, there were five options, of which I selected Bloemfontein because it was the only one that was comparably sized (the other cities were very small). For Nigeria, the two options were Abuja and Isoko South. I selected Abuja due to lack of available information about Isoko South.

Works Cited

Abdulahi, Mohamued Elyas, Yang Shu, and Muhammad Asif Khan. 2019, June. "Resource Rents, Economic Growth, and the Role of Institutional Quality: A Panel Threshold Analysis." *Resources Policy* 61: 293–303.

Acemoglu, Daron, Simon Johnson, and James A. Robinson. 2002. "Reversal of Fortune: Geography and Institutions in the Making of the Modern World Income Distribution." *The Quarterly Journal of Economics* 117, no. 4: 1231–1294.

Acemoglu, Daron, Suresh Naidu, Pascual Restrepo, and James A. Robinson. 2019. "Democracy Does Cause Growth." *Journal of Political Economy* 127, no. 1: 47–100.

Acemoglu, Daron, and James A. Robinson. 2012. *Why Nations Fail: The Origins of Power, Prosperity, and Poverty*. New York: Crown Publishers.

Achebe, Chinua. 1994. *Things Fall Apart*. New York Penguin Publishing Group.

Adama, Onyanta. 2018. "Urban Imaginaries: Funding Mega Infrastructure Projects in Lagos, Nigeria." *GeoJournal* 83, no. 2: 257–274.

Adamczyk, Christiane. 2011. "'Today, I Am No Mutwa Anymore': Facets of National Unity Discourse in Present-Day Rwanda." *Social Anthropology* 19, no. 2: 175–188.

Adedara, Ayodeji. 2020. "Ecological Identity in Governor Babatunde Fashola's Speeches on the Environment." *Lagos Notes and Records* 25, no. 1: 126–151.

Adida, Claire, Jessica Gottlieb, Eric Kramon, and Gwyneth McClendon. 2017. "Reducing or Reinforcing In-Group Preferences? An Experiment on Information and Ethnic Voting." *Quarterly Journal of Political Science* 12, no. 4: 437–477.

African Development Bank. 2016. *Gabon Joint 2016–2020 Country Strategy Paper and Country Portfolio Performance Review.*

Aide, Pedro et al. 2019. "Setting the Scene and Generating Evidence for Malaria Elimination in Southern Mozambique." *Malaria Journal* 18, no. 1: 1–11.

Ajibade, Idowu, Mark Pelling, Julius Agboola, and Matthias Garschagen. 2016. "Sustainability Transitions: Exploring Risk Management and the Future of Adaptation in the Megacity of Lagos." *Journal of Extreme Events* 3, no. 3: 1–25.

Albaugh, Ericka A. 2011. "An Autocrat's Toolkit: Adaptation and Manipulation in 'Democratic' Cameroon." *Democratization* 18, no. 2: 388–414.

Alesina, Alberto, Reza Baqir, and William Easterly. 1999. "Public Goods and Ethnic Divisions." *Quarterly Journal of Economics* 114, no. 4: 1243–1284.

Alesina, Alberto, and Eliana La Ferrara. 2005. "Ethnic Diversity and Economic Performance." *Journal of Economic Literature* 43, no. 3: 762–800.

Ali, Merima, Odd Helge Fjeldstad, and Ingrid Hoem Sjursen. 2014, December. "To Pay or Not to Pay? Citizens' Attitudes Toward Taxation in Kenya, Tanzania, Uganda, and South Africa." *World Development* 64: 828–842.

Almond, Gabriel, and Sidney Verba. 1963. *The Civic Culture: Political Attitudes and Democracy in Five Nations*. Princeton, NJ: Princeton University Press.

Althor, Glenn, James E. M. Watson, and Richard A. Fuller. 2016. "Global Mismatch Between Greenhouse Gas Emissions and the Burden of Climate Change." *Scientific Reports* 6: 1–6.

Ammann, Carole. 2016. "Everyday Politics: Market Women and the Local Government in Kankan, Guinea." *Stichproben. Wiener Zeitschrift für kritische Afrikastudien* 16, no. 30: 37–62.

Amone, Charles, and Okullu Muura. 2014. "British Colonialism and the Creation of Acholi Ethnic Identity in Uganda, 1894 to 1962." *Journal of Imperial and Commonwealth History* 42, no. 2: 239–257.

Arakelyan, Stella et al. 2021, December. "The Role of Trust in Health-Seeking for Non-Communicable Disease Services in Fragile Contexts: A Cross-Country Comparative Study." *Social Science and Medicine* 291: 1–10.

Aregawi, Maru et al. 2016. "Impact of the Mass Drug Administration for Malaria in Response to the Ebola Outbreak in Sierra Leone." *Malaria Journal* 15, no. 1: 1–13.

Arriola, Leonardo, Jed Devaro, and Anne Meng. 2021. "Democratic Subversion: Elite Cooptation and Opposition Fragmentation." *American Journal of Political Science* 115, no. 4: 1358–1372.

Arroz, Jorge Alexandre Harrison. 2017. "Social and Behavior Change Communication in the Fight Against Malaria in Mozambique." *Revista de saude publica* 51: 1–5.

Asiedu, Elizabeth, Claire Branstette, Neepa Gaekwad-Babulal, and Nanivazo Malokele. n.d. "The Effect of Women's Representation in Parliament and the Passing of Gender Sensitive Policies." Unpublished working paper.

Asiyanbi, Adeniyi P. 2015. "'I Don't Get This Climate Stuff!' Making Sense of Climate Change Among the Corporate Middle Class in Lagos." *Public Understanding of Science* 24, no. 8: 1007–1024.

Baker, Bruce. 2009. "Comoros: The Search for Viability." *Civil Wars* 11, no. 3: 215–233.

Bauer, Gretchen, and Jennie E. Burnet. 2013, November–December. "Gender Quotas, Democracy, and Women's Representation in Africa: Some Insights from Democratic Botswana and Autocratic Rwanda." *Women's Studies International Forum* 41: 103–112.

Beck, Linda. 2003. "Democratization and the Hidden Public: The Impact of Patronage Networks on Senegalese Women." *Comparative Politics* 35, no. 2: 147–169.

Bennett, Adam et al. 2013. "Mapping Malaria Transmission Intensity in Malawi, 2000–2010." *American Journal of Tropical Medicine and Hygiene* 89, no. 5: 840–849.

Benton, Adia. 2015. *HIV Exceptionalism: Development Through Disease in Sierra Leone*. Minneapolis: University of Minnesota Press.

Benton, Adia, and Kim Yi Dionne. 2015. "International Political Economy and the 2014 West African Ebola Outbreak." *African Studies Review* 58, no. 1: 223–236.

Bernhard, Michael, Tiago Fernandes, and Rui Branco. 2017. "Civil Society and Democracy in an Era of Inequality." *Comparative Politics* 49, no. 3: 297–309.

Berthe, Sara et al. 2014. "'When I Sleep under the Net, Nothing Bothers Me; I Sleep Well and I'm Happy': Senegal's Culture of Net Use and How Inconveniences to Net Use Do Not Translate to Abandonment." *Malaria Journal* 13, no. 357: 1–8.

Bhattacharyya, Sambit, and Roland Hodler. 2014, May. "Do Natural Resource Revenues Hinder Financial Development? The Role of Political Institutions." *World Development* 57: 101–113.

Blair, Robert A., Benjamin S. Morse, and Lily L. Tsai. 2017, January. "Public Health and Public Trust: Survey Evidence from the Ebola Virus Disease Epidemic in Liberia." *Social Science & Medicine* 172: 89–97.

Bop, Codou. 2005. "Roles and the Position of Women in Sufi Brotherhoods in Senegal." *Journal of the American Academy of Religion* 73, no. 4: 1099–1119.

Bor, Jacob. 2007. "The Political Economy of AIDS Leadership in Developing Countries: An Exploratory Analysis." *Social Science and Medicine* 64, no. 8: 1585–1599.

Boyd, Lydia. 2014. "Ugandan Born-Again Christians and the Moral Politics of Gender Equality." *Journal of Religion in Africa* 44, no. 3–4: 333–354.

Brand, Saskia. 2018. *Political Participation of Women in Burundi*. Ede, Nigeria: MDF Training and Consultancy Report.

Bratton, Michael. 1998. "After Mandela's Miracle in South Africa." *Current History* 97, no. 619: 214–219.

Brautigam, Deborah. 1997. "Institutions, Economic Reform, and Democratic Consolidation in Mauritius." *Comparative Politics* 30, no. 1: 45–62.

———. 1999. "The 'Mauritius Miracle': Democracy, Institutions, and Economic Policy." In Richard Joseph, ed., *State, Conflict, and Democracy in Africa*. Boulder, CO: Lynne Rienner.

Brautigam, Deborah, Odd Helge Fjeldstad, and Mick Moore. 2008. *Taxation and Statebuilding in Developing Countries: Capacity and Consent*. New York: Cambridge University Press.

Burnet, Jennie E. 2011. "Women Have Found Respect: Gender Quotas, Symbolic Representation, and Female Empowerment in Rwanda." *Politics and Gender* 7, no. 3: 303–334.

Bush, Sarah, Daniela Donno, and Pär Zetterberg. n.d. *Rewarding Women's Rights in Dictatorships*. Unpublished working paper.

Buss, Doris, and Jerusa Ali. 2017. "Rwanda: Women's Political Participation in Post-Conflict State-Building." In *The Oxford Handbook of Gender and Conflict*. Oxford: Oxford University Press.

Byrne, Siobhan, and Allison McCulloch. 2012. "Gender, Representation and Power-Sharing in Post-Conflict Institutions." *International Peacekeeping* 19, no. 5: 565–580.

Callander, Emilie J., and Stephanie M. Topp. 2020. "Health Inequality in the Tropics and Its Costs: A Sustainable Development Goals Alert." *International Health* 12, no. 5: 395–410.

Camara, Fatou. 2007. "Women and the Law: A Critique of Senegalese Family Law." *Social Identities* 13, no. 6: 787–800.

Campling, Liam, Hansel Confiance, and Marie-Therese Purvis. 2011. *Social Policies in Seychelles*. London: Commonwealth Secretariat.

Campos, Alicia. 2003. "The Decolonization of Equatorial Guinea: The Relevance of the International Factor." *Journal of African History* 44, no. 1: 95–116.

Carbone, Giovanni M. 2001. "Constitutional Alternatives for the Regulation of Ethnic Politics? Institution-Building Principles in Uganda's and South Africa's Transitions." *Journal of Contemporary African Studies* 19, no. 2: 229–252.

Carlucci, James G. et al. 2017. "Prevalence and Determinants of Malaria Among Children in Zambézia Province, Mozambique." *Malaria Journal* 16, no. 1: 1–13.

Carmin, Jo Ann, Isabelle Anguelovski, and Debra Roberts. 2012. "Urban Climate Adaptation in the Global South: Planning in an Emerging Policy Domain." *Journal of Planning Education and Research* 32, no. 1: 18–32.

Carroll, Barbara Wake, and Terrance Carroll. 1997. "State and Ethnicity in Botswana and Mauritius: A Democratic Route to Development?" *Journal of Development Studies* 33, no. 4: 464–486.

Carter, Miguel. 2018. *Vozes Do Povo: Guinea: Bissau's First Public Opinion Survey Summary of Main Results and Recommendations*. Bissau, Guinea-Bissau: DEMOS.

Casimiro, Sonia L. R., Janet Hemingway, Brian L. Sharp, and Michael Coleman. 2007. "Monitoring the Operational Impact of Insecticide Usage for Malaria Control on *Anopheles Funestus* from Mozambique." *Malaria Journal* 6, no. 142: 1–7.

Chang, Ha Joon. 2006. "Kicking Away the Ladder: The 'Real' History of Free Trade." In Anwar Shaikh, ed., *Globalization and the Myths of Free Trade: History, Theory, and Empirical Evidence*. New York: Routledge.

Chanock, Martin. 1985. *Law, Custom, and Social Order: The Colonial Experience in Malawi and Zambia*. New York: Cambridge University Press.

Charlier, Florence. 2016. *Cluster Country Program Evaluation on Small States: Seychelles Country Case Study FY07-15*. Washington, DC: World Bank.

Cheeseman, Nic. 2015. *Democracy in Africa: Successes, Failures, and the Struggle for Political Reform*. New York: Cambridge University Press.

Cheeseman, Nic, and Diane de Gramont. 2017. "Managing a Mega-City: Learning the Lessons from Lagos." *Oxford Review of Economic Policy* 33, no. 3: 457–477.

Cirera, Laia et al. 2020. "Moving Towards Malaria Elimination in Southern Mozambique: Cost and Cost-Effectiveness of Mass Drug Administration Combined with Intensified Malaria Control." *PLoS ONE* 15, no. 7: 1–17.

Coffé, Hilde. 2012. "Conceptions of Female Political Representation: Perspectives of Rwandan Female Representatives." *Women's Studies International Forum* 35, no. 4: 286–297.

Coleman, M., S. Casimiro, J. Hemingway, and B. Sharp. 2008. "Operational Impact of DDT Reintroduction for Malaria Control on Anopheles Arabiensis in Mozambique." *Journal of Medical Entomology* 45, no. 5: 885–890.

Corden, W. M. 1984. "Booming Sector and Dutch Disease Economics: Survey and Consolidation." *Oxford Economic Papers* 36, no. 3: 359–380.

COSEF. 2011. *Combats pour la parite: La campagne "avec la parite, consolidons la democratie."* Dakar: COSEF.

Crowder, Michael. 1982. *West Africa under Colonial Rule*. London: Hutchinson & Co.

Daniele, Vittorio. 2011. "Natural Resources and the 'Quality' of Economic Development." *Journal of Development Studies*, 47, no. 4: 545–573.

de Jager, Nicola, and David Sebudubudu. 2017. "Toward Understanding Botswana and South Africa's Ambivalence to Liberal Democracy." *Journal of Contemporary African Studies* 35, no. 1: 15–33.

de Smith, S. A. 1968. "Mauritius: Constitutionalism in a Plural Society." *The Modern Law Review* 31, no. 6: 601–622.

de Sousa Pinto da Fonseca, Liliana et al. 2021. "Malaria Prevention Knowledge, Attitudes, and Practices in Zambezia Province, Mozambique." *Malaria Journal* 20, no. 293: 1–10.

Debusscher, Petra, and An Ansoms. 2013. "Gender Equality Policies in Rwanda: Public Relations or Real Transformations?" *Development and Change* 44, no. 5: 1111–1134.

Dionne, Kim Yi. 2011. "The Role of Executive Time Horizons in State Response to AIDS in Africa." *Comparative Political Studies* 41, no. 1: 55–77.

———. 2018. *Doomed Interventions: The Failure of Global Responses to AIDS in Africa*. New York: Cambridge University Press.

Dionne, Kim Yi, and Boniface Dulani. 2013. "Constitutional Provisions and Executive Succession: Malawi's 2012 Transition in Comparative Perspective." *African Affairs* 112, no. 446: 111–137.

Donno, Daniela, Sara Fox, and Joshua Kaasik. 2022. "International Incentives for Women's Rights in Dictatorships." *Comparative Political Studies* 55, no. 3: 451–492.

Donno, Daniela, and Bruce Russett. 2004. "Islam, Authoritarianism, and Female Empowerment: What Are the Linkages?" *World Politics* 56, no. 4: 582–607.

Dos Anjos Luis, António, and Pedro Cabral. 2016. "Geographic Accessibility to Primary Healthcare Centers in Mozambique." *International Journal for Equity in Health* 15, no. 1: 1–13.

Dulani, Boniface, and Kim Yi Dionne. 2014. "Presidential, Parliamentary, and Local Government Elections in Malawi, May 2014." *Electoral Studies* 36: 218–225.

Dulani, Boniface, Adam S. Harris, Jeremy Horowitz, and Happy Kayuni. 2021. "Electoral Preferences Among Multiethnic Voters in Africa." *Comparative Political Studies* 54, no. 2: 280–311.

Dunning, Thad. 2008. *Crude Democracy: Natural Resource Wealth and Political Regimes*. Cambridge: Cambridge University Press.

Edwards, Zophia. 2018. "No Colonial Working Class, No Post-Colonial Development: A Comparative-Historical Analysis of Two Oil-Rich Countries." *Studies in Comparative International Development* 53, no. 4: 477–499.

Elischer, Sebastian. 2013. *Political Parties in Africa: Ethnicity and Party Formation*. New York: Cambridge University Press.

Embalo, Birgit. 2012. "Civil–Military Relations and Political Order in Guinea-Bissau." *Journal of Modern African Studies* 50, no. 2: 253–281.

Englebert, Pierre. 2002. *State Legitimacy and Development in Africa*. Boulder, CO: Lynne Rienner.
Englebert, Pierre, and Kevin C. Dunn. 2019. *Inside African Politics*. 2nd ed. Boulder, CO: Lynne Rienner.
Enguita-Fernàndez, Cristina et al. 2021. "Trust, Community Health Workers and Delivery of Intermittent Preventive Treatment of Malaria in Pregnancy: A Comparative Qualitative Analysis of Four Sub-Saharan Countries." *Global Public Health* 16, no. 12: 1889–1903.
Enria, Luisa et al. 2021, October. "Bringing the Social into Vaccination Research: Community-Led Ethnography and Trust-Building in Immunization Programs in Sierra Leone." *PLoS ONE* 16, no. 10: e0258252.
Epo, Boniface Ngah, and Dief Reagen Nochi Faha. 2020. "Natural Resources, Institutional Quality, and Economic Growth: An African Tale." *European Journal of Development Research* 32, no. 1: 99–128.
eThekwini Municipality. 2019. *Durban Climate Action Plan 2019*.
Evans, Alice. 2016. "'For the Elections, We Want Women!': Closing the Gender Gap in Zambian Politics." *Development and Change* 47, no. 2: 388–411.
Evans, Ruth. 2016. "Gendered Struggles over Land: Shifting Inheritance Practices among the Serer in Rural Senegal." *Gender, Place and Culture* 23, no. 9: 1360–1375.
Fanthorpe, Richard. 2006. "On the Limits of Liberal Peace: Chiefs and Democratic Decentralization in Post-War Sierra Leone." *African Affairs* 105, no. 418: 27–49.
Fatton, Robert. 1995. "Africa in the Age of Democratization: The Civic Limitations of Civil Society." *African Studies Review* 38, no. 2: 67–99.
Ferree, Karen, and Jeremy Horowitz. 2010. "Ties That Bind? The Rise and Decline of Ethno-Regional Partisanship in Malawi, 1994–2009." *Democratization* 17, no. 3: 534–563.
Filho, Walter, ed. 2021. *African Handbook of Climate Change Adaptation*. New York: Springer US.
Fish, Michael S. 2002. "Islam and Authoritarianism." *World Politics* 55, no. 1: 4–37.
Foss, Ann. 2018. "Divergent Responses to Sustainability and Climate Change Planning: The Role of Politics, Cultural Frames and Public Participation." *Urban Studies* 55, no. 2: 332–348.
Fox, Ashley M. 2014. "AIDS Policy Responsiveness in Africa: Evidence from Opinion Surveys." *Global Public Health* 9, no. 1–2: 224–248.
Frankel, Jeffrey. 2016. "Mauritius: African Success Story." In Sebastian Edwards, Simon Johnson, and David N. Weil, eds., *African Successes, Volume IV: Sustainable Growth*, edited by, 295–342. Chicago, IL: The University of Chicago Press.
Frynas, Jędrzej George. 2004. "The Oil Boom in Equatorial Guinea." *African Affairs* 103, no. 413: 527–546.
Frynas, Jedrzej George, Geoffrey Wood, and Ricardo M. S. Soares de Oliveira. 2003. "Business and Politics in Sao Tome e Principe: From Cocoa Monoculture to Petro-State." *African Affairs* 102, no. 406: 51–80.
Funada-Classen, Sayaka. 2013. *The Origins of War in Mozambique: A History of Unity and Division*. London, Oxford: African Minds.

Gabbay, Rony. 1988. "Tourism." In Reginald Thomas Appleyard and Rabindra Nath Ghosh, eds., *Indian Ocean Islands Development*, 205–226. Canberra: Australia National University.

Gadjanova, Elena. 2017. "Ethnic Wedge Issues in Electoral Campaigns in Africa's Presidential Regimes." *African Affairs* 116, no. 464: 484–507.

Gallup, John Luke, Jeffrey D. Sachs, and Andrew D. Mellinger. 1999. "Geography and Economic Development." *International Regional Science Review* 22: 179–232.

Galor, Oded. 2012. "The Demographic Transition: Causes and Consequences." *Cliometrica* 6, no. 1: 1–28.

Gerring, John, Strom Thacker, and Rodrigo Alfaro. 2012. "Democracy and Human Development." *Journal of Politics* 74, no. 1: 1–17.

Gerstl, Sibylle et al. 2010. "Long-Lasting Insecticide-Treated Net Usage in Eastern Sierra Leone—The Success of Free Distribution." *Tropical Medicine and International Health* 15, no. 4: 480–488.

Geymonat, Sophia Aureoles. 2019. "The Other Voice of Climate Change: A Case Study of Community-Based Adaptive Capacities, Through the Analysis of Activists Networks, Building Resilience in South Africa." Unpublished Thesis, Linnaeus University.

Ghebremusse, Sara. 2018. "Good Governance and Development in Botswana—The Democracy Conundrum." *Law and Development Review* 11, no. 2: 913–938.

Glentworth, Garth, and Ian Hancock. 1973. "Obote and Amin: Change and Continuity in Modern Uganda Politics." *African Affairs* 72, no. 288: 237–255.

Good, Kenneth. 1999. "Enduring Elite Democracy in Botswana." *Democratization* 6, no. 1: 50–66.

Greer, Scott, Elizabeth King, Elize Massard da Fonseca, and Andre Peralta-Santos. 2021. *Coronavirus Politics: The Comparative Politics and Policy of COVID-19*. Ann Arbor, MI: University of Michigan Press.

Grindle, Merilee S. 2004. "Good Enough Governance: Poverty Reduction and Reform in Developing Countries." *Governance* 17, no. 4: 525–548.

———. 2017. "Good Governance, R.I.P.: A Critique and an Alternative." *Governance* 30, no. 1: 17–22.

Groh, Matthew, and Casey Rothschild. 2012. "Oil, Islam, Women, and Geography: A Comment on Ross (2008)." *Quarterly Journal of Political Science* 7, no. 1: 69–87.

Guérin, Isabelle. 2006. "Women and Money: Lessons from Senegal." *Development and Change* 37, no. 3: 549–570.

Gunder Frank, Andre. 1978. *Dependent Accumulation and Underdevelopment*. New York: New York University Press.

Gyimah-Boadi, Emmanuel. 1996. "Civil Society in Africa." *Journal of Democracy* 7, no. 2: 118–132.

Habyarimana, James, Macartan Humphreys, Daniel N. Posner, and Jeremy M. Weinstein. 2007. "Why Does Ethnic Diversity Undermine Public Goods Provision?" *American Political Science Review* 101, no. 4: 709–725.

Haggard, Stephen. 1990. *Pathways from the Periphery: The Politics of Growth in the Newly Industrializing Countries*. Ithaca, NY: Cornell University Press.

Hanson, Jonathan K., and Rachel Sigman. 2021. "Leviathan's Latent Dimensions: Measuring State Capacity for Comparative Political Research." *Journal of Politics* 83, no. 4: 1495–1510.

Hassan, Hamdy A. 2009. "The Comoros and the Crisis of Building a National State." *Contemporary Arab Affairs* 2, no. 2: 229–239.

Helmke, Gretchen, and Steven Levitsky. 2004. "Informal Institutions and Comparative Politics: A Research Agenda." *Perspectives on Politics* 2, no. 4: 725–740.

Hern, Erin A. 2020. "Gender and Participation in Africa's Electoral Regimes: An Analysis of Variation in the Gender Gap." *Politics, Groups, and Identities* 8, no. 2: 293–315.

———. 2021. "Colonial Education and Women's Political Behavior in Ghana and Senegal." *African Studies Review* 64, no. 1: 217–241.

———. n.d. *Executive Leadership and Effective Gender Quotas in Africa*. Unpublished working paper.

Herndon, Gerise, and Shirley Randell. 2013. "Surviving Genocide, Thriving in Politics: Rwandan Women's Power." *Cosmopolitan Civil Societies: An Interdisciplinary Journal* 5, no. 1: 69–96.

Hershey, Christine L. et al. 2017. "Malaria Control Interventions Contributed to Declines in Malaria Parasitemia, Severe Anemia, and All-Cause Mortality in Children Less than 5 Years of Age in Malawi, 2000–2010." *American Journal of Tropical Medicine and Hygiene* 97, no. Suppl. 3: 76–88.

Holtz, Timothy H. et al. 2002. "Insecticide-Treated Bednet Use, Anaemia, and Malaria Parasitaemia in Blantyre District, Malawi." *Tropical Medicine and International Health* 7, no. 3: 220–230.

Honey, Maureen. 1985. *Creating Rosie the Riveter: Class, Gender, and Propaganda During World War II*. Amherst: University of Massachusetts Press.

Hope, Kempe Ronald. 2000. "Decentralisation and Local Governance Theory and the Practice in Botswana." *Development Southern Africa* 17, no. 4: 519–534.

Horowitz, Donald L. 1993. "Democracy in Divided Societies." *Journal of Democracy* 4, no. 4: 18–38.

Horowitz, Jeremy, and Kathleen Klaus. 2020. "Can Politicians Exploit Ethnic Grievances? An Experimental Study of Land Appeals in Kenya." *Political Behavior* 42, no. 1: 35–58.

Hughes, Sara. 2017. "The Politics of Urban Climate Change Policy: Toward a Research Agenda." *Urban Affairs Review* 53, no. 2: 362–380.

Hunter, Nina. 2012. "The Economic and Gender Consequences of South Africa's Home-Based Care Policy." *Social Policy and Administration* 46, no. 6: 654–671.

Hutchins, Harry et al. 2020. "A Survey of Knowledge, Attitudes, and Practices Regarding Malaria and Bed Nets on Bubaque Island, Guinea-Bissau." *Malaria Journal* 19, no. 412: 1–15.

Infante-Amate, Juan, and Fridolin Krausmann. 2019, February. "Trade, Ecologically Unequal Exchange and Colonial Legacy: The Case of France and Its Former Colonies (1962–2015)." *Ecological Economics* 156: 98–109.

Inglehart, Ronald, and Pippa Norris. 2003. *Rising Tide: Gender Equality and Cultural Change around the World*. New York: Cambridge University Press.

Jensen, Nathan, and Leonard Wantchekon. 2004. "Resource Wealth and Political Regimes in Africa." *Comparative Political Studies* 37, no. 7: 816–841.

Jerven, Morten. 2010. "Accounting for the African Growth Miracle: The Official Evidence—Botswana 1965–1995." *Journal of Southern African Studies* 36, no. 1: 73–94.

Johnson, Chalmers. 1982. *MITI and the Japanese Miracle: The Growth of Industrial Policy, 1925–1975*. Stanford: Stanford University Press.

Kabwegyere, Tarsis B. 1974. *The Politics of State Formation: The Nature and Effects of Colonialism in Uganda*. Nairobi: East African Literature Bureau.

Kandeh, Jimmy D. 2008. "Rogue Incumbents, Donor Assistance and Sierra Leone's Second Post-Conflict Elections of 2007." *Journal of Modern African Studies* 46, no. 4: 603–635.

Kang, Alice J., and Aili Mari Tripp. 2018. "Coalitions Matter: Citizenship, Women, and Quota Adoption in Africa." *Perspectives on Politics* 16, no. 1: 73–91.

Kanyeihamba, George W. 2010. *Constitutional and Political History of Uganda*. 2nd ed. Kampala, Uganda: LawAfrica Publishing.

Kareem, Buyana et al. 2020. "Pathways for Resilience to Climate Change in African Cities." *Environmental Research Letters* 15, no. 7: 1–17.

Kasenally, Roukaya. 2011. "Mauritius: Paradise Reconsidered." *Journal of Democracy* 22, no. 2: 160–169.

Kasozi, Abdu B. 1994. *The Social Origins of Violence in Uganda, 1964–1985*. Montreal: McGill-Queen's University Press.

Kavanagh, Matthew, and Renu Singh. 2020. "Democracy, Capacity, and Coercion in Pandemic Response—COVID-19 in Comparative Political Perspective." *Journal of Health Politics, Policy, and Law* 45, no. 6: 997–2012.

Kelsall, Tim. 2008. "Going with the Grain in African Development?" *Development Policy Review* 26, no. 6: 627–655.

Klaus, Kathleen, and Matthew I. Mitchell. 2015. "Land Grievances and the Mobilization of Electoral Violence: Evidence from Côte d'Ivoire and Kenya." *Journal of Peace Research* 52, no. 5: 622–635.

Kofoed, Poul-Erik et al. 2007. "Different Doses of Amodiaquine and Chloroquine for Treatment of Uncomplicated Malaria in Children in Guinea-Bissau: Implications for Future Treatment Recommendations." *Transactions of the Royal Society of Tropical Medicine and Hygiene* 101, no. 3: 231–238.

Kohler, Iliana V. et al. 2022, March. "Curtailing Covid-19 on a Dollar-a-Day in Malawi: Role of Community Leadership for Shaping Public Health and Economic Responses to the Pandemic." *World Development* 151.

Kok, Maryse C. et al. 2017. "Optimising the Benefits of Community Health Workers' Unique Position between Communities and the Health Sector: A Comparative Analysis of Factors Shaping Relationships in Four Countries." *Global Public Health* 12, no. 11: 1404–1432.

La Porta, Rafael, Florencio Lopez-De-Silanes, and Andrei Shleifer. 2008. "The Economic Consequences of Legal Origins." *Journal of Economic Literature* 46, no. 2: 285–332.

Lagos State Government. 2019. *Second Five Year Climate Action Plan: 2020–2025*.

Lange, Matt. 2009. *Lineages of Despotism and Development: British Colonialism and State Power*. Chicago: University of Chicago Press.

Leonard Boyle, Emma. 2017. "Was Idi Amin's Government a Terrorist Regime?" *Terrorism and Political Violence* 29, no. 4: 593–609.

Letsa, Natalie Wenzell, and Martha Wilfahrt. 2020. "The Mechanisms of Direct and Indirect Rule: Colonialism and Economic Development in Africa." *Quarterly Journal of Political Science* 15, no. 4: 539–577.

Levi, Margaret. 2020. *Of Rule and Revenue*. Berkeley: University of California Press.

Lieberman, Evan S. 2009. *Boundaries of Contagion: How Ethnic Politics Have Shaped Government Responses to AIDS*. Princeton, NJ: Princeton University Press.

Lijphart, Arend. 2004. "Constitutional Design for Divided Societies." *Journal of Democracy* 15, no. 2: 96–109.

Lindemann, Stefan. 2010. *Exclusionary Elite Bargains and Civil War Onset: The Case of Uganda*. London: Crisis States Research Centre.

Llop-Girones, Alba, and Sam Jones. 2021. "Beyond Access to Basic Services: Perspectives on Social Health Determinants of Mozambique." *Critical Public Health* 31, no. 5: 533–547.

Longman, Timothy. 2006. "Rwanda: Achieving Equality or Serving an Authoritarian State?" In Gretchen Bauer and Hannah Britton, eds., *Women in African Parliaments*. Boulder, CO: Lynne Rienner.

Lydon, Ghislaine. 2005. "Writing Trans-Saharan History: Methods, Sources and Interpretations Across the African Divide." *Journal of North African Studies* 10, no. 3–4: 293–324.

———. 2015. "Saharan Oceans and Bridges, Barriers and Divides in Africa's Historiographical Landscape." *Journal of African History* 56, no. 1: 3–22.

Makina, Anesu, and Theresa Moyo. 2016. "Mind the Gap: Institutional Considerations for Gender-Inclusive Climate Change Policy in Sub-Saharan Africa." *Local Environment* 21, no. 10: 1185–1197.

Malesky, Edmund J., and Krislert Samphantharak. 2008. "Predictable Corruption and Firm Investment: Evidence from a Natural Experiment and Survey of Cambodian Entrepreneurs." *Quarterly Journal of Political Science* 3, no. 3: 227–267.

Malta, Vivian, Angelica Martinez, and Marina Mendes Tavares. 2019. *A Quantitative Analysis of Female Employment in Senegal*. IMF Working Papers.

Mamdani, Mahmood. 1996. *Citizen and Subject: Contemporary Africa and the Legacy of Late Colonialism*. Princeton, NJ: Princeton University Press.

Martin de Almagro, Maria. 2016, August 25. "Negotiating Gender Security: The Transnationalism of Local Activist Discourses in Post-Conflict Burundi and Liberia," In *Gender and Race Matter: Global Perspectives on Being a Woman* 107–125.

Mathanga, Don P. et al. 2005. "Reduction of Childhood Malaria by Social Marketing of Insecticide-Treated Nets: A Case-Control Study of Effectiveness in Malawi." *American Journal of Tropical Medicine and Hygiene* 73, no. 3: 622–625.

———. 2012. "Malaria Control in Malawi: Current Status and Directions for the Future." *Acta Tropica* 121, no. 3: 212–217.

Mathanga, Don P., and Cameron Bowie. 2007. "Malaria Control in Malawi: Are the Poor Being Served?" *International Journal for Equity in Health* 6, no. 22: 1–6.

Mawby, Spencer. 2020. *The End of Empire in Uganda: Decolonization and Institutional Conflict, 1945–79*. New York: Bloomsbury Publishing.

Mazrui, Ali A. 2019. "Ethnic Tensions and Political Stratification in Uganda." In Brian M. du Toit, ed., *Ethnicity in Modern Africa*, 47–68. New York: Routledge.

Mbileni, Charity. 2015. *Draft Climate Change Adaptation and Mitigation Strategy for Mangaung Metropolitan Municipality*.

McCoy, Kaci D. et al. 2021. "Are Malaria Transmission-Blocking Vaccines Acceptable to High Burden Communities? Results from a Mixed Methods Study in Bo, Sierra Leone." *Malaria Journal* 20, no. 183: 1–12.

McDonnell, Erin Metz. 2020. *Patchwork Leviathan: Pockets of Bureaucratic Effectiveness in Developing States*. Princeton, NJ: Princeton University Press.

McFerson, H. M. 2009. "Governance and Hyper-Corruption in Resource-Rich African Countries." *Third World Quarterly* 30, no. 8: 1529–1547.

———. 2010. "Poverty Among Women in Sub-Saharan Africa: A Review of Selected Issues." *Journal of International Women's Studies* 11, no. 4: 50–72.

McLean Hilker, Lyndsay. 2011. "The Role of Education in Driving Conflict and Building Peace: The Case of Rwanda." *Prospects* 41, no. 2: 267–282.

Mechkova, Valeriya, and Ruth Carlitz. 2021. "Gendered Accountability: When and Why Do Women's Policy Priorities Get Implemented?" *European Political Science Review* 13, no. 1: 3–21.

Miguel, Edward. 2004. "Tribe or Nation?: Nation Building and Public Goods in Kenya versus Tanzania." *World Politics* 56, no. 3: 327–362.

Mill, John Stuart. 2020. *A System of Logic, Ratiocinative and Inductive*. Frankfurt, Germany: Outlook Verlag GmbH.

Montgomery, Catherine M., Khátia Munguambe, and Robert Pool. 2010. "Group-Based Citizenship in the Acceptance of Indoor Residual Spraying (IRS) for Malaria Control in Mozambique." *Social Science and Medicine* 70, no. 10: 1648–1655.

Morgan, Ashey et al. 2019. *Policy Summary: The Nexus of Fragility and Climate Risks*. Washington, DC: USAID.

Muller-Crepon, Carl. 2020. "Continuity or Change? (In)Direct Rule in British and French Africa." *International Organization* 74, no. 3: 707–741.

Mwendera, Chikondi A. et al. 2019. "Challenges to the Implementation of Malaria Policies in Malawi." *BMC Health Services Research* 19, no. 19: 1–9.

Nageon de Lestrang, Joel. 1988. "The Fisheries of Seychelles." In *Indian Ocean Islands Development*, edited by Reginald Thomas Appleyard and Rabinda Nath Ghosh, 172–185. Canberra: Australia National University.

Nnedu, Obinna et al. 2010. "Syndromic Diagnosis of Malaria in Rural Sierra Leone and Proposed Additions to the National Integrated Management of Childhood Illness Guidelines for Fever." *American Journal of Tropical Medicine and Hygiene* 82, no. 4: 525–528.

North, Douglass. 1990. *Institutions, Institutional Change, and Economic Performance*. New York: Cambridge University Press.

North, Douglass C., and Barry R. Weingast. 1989. "Constitutions and Commitment: The Evolution of Institutions Governing Public Choice in Seventeenth-Century England." *The Journal of Economic History* 49, no. 4: 803–832.

Nthomang, Keitseope. 2004. "Relentless Colonialism: The Case of the Remote Area Development Programme (RADP) and the Basarwa in Botswana." *Journal of Modern African Studies* 42, no. 3: 415–435.

Nunn, Nathan. 2009. "The Importance of History for Economic Development." *Annual Review of Economics* 1: 65–92.

Ojedokun, Usman, Yetunde O. Ogunleye, and Adeyinka A. Aderinto. 2021. "Mass Mobilization for Police Accountability: The Case of Nigeria's #EndSARS Protest." *Policing: A Journal of Policy and Practice* 15, no. 3: 1894–1903.

Oluwafemi, Lasisi Shamusideen. 2019. "Knowledge, Attitude, and Practical Response of Adult Population to Global Campaign on Climate Change in Lagos State, Nigeria." *Education Quarterly Reviews* 2, no. 4: 789–798.

Omara-Otunnu, Amii. 1987. *Politics and the Military in Uganda, 1890–1985*. New York: Saint Martin's Press.

Ombga, Luc Desire. 2009. "On the Duration of Political Power in Africa." *Comparative Political Studies* 42, no. 3: 416–436.

Ostheimer, John. 1973. "Political Development in the Comoros." *The African Review* 3, no. 3: 491–506.

Otiso, Kefa M. et al. 2011. "Airline Connectivity as a Measure of the Globalization of African Cities." *Applied Geography* 31, no. 2: 609–620.

Palermo, Valentina et al. 2020. "Assessment of Climate Change Mitigation Policies in 315 Cities in the Covenant of Mayors Initiative." *Sustainable Cities and Society* 60: 1–14.

Pasquini, Lorena. 2020. "The Urban Governance of Climate Change Adaptation in Least-Developed African Countries and in Small Cities: The Engagement of Local Decision-Makers in Dar Es Salaam, Tanzania, and Karonga, Malawi." *Climate and Development* 12, no. 5: 408–419.

Perera, Suda, E. Houston Shearon, Paul Jackson, and Heather Lyne de Ver. 2018. "*What Enables or Disables Leadership for Transformational Change in Africa?*" Research Paper 55, Uongozi Institute.

Périlleux, Anais, and Ariane Szafarz. 2015. "Women Leaders and Social Performance: Evidence from Financial Cooperatives in Senegal." *World Development* 74: 437–452.

Pierce, Hayley, Tim B. Heaton, and John Hoffmann. 2014. "Increasing Maternal Healthcare Use in Rwanda: Implications for Child Nutrition and Survival." *Social Science and Medicine* 107: 61–67.

Pieterse, Pieternella, and Tom Lodge. 2015. "When Free Healthcare Is Not Free: Corruption and Mistrust in Sierra Leone's Primary Healthcare System Immediately Prior to the Ebola Outbreak." *International Health* 7, no. 6: 400–404.

Pitcher, Anne. 2021. "Mozambique Elections 2019: Pernicious Polarization, Democratic Decline, and Rising Authoritarianism." *African Affairs* 119, no. 476: 468–486.

Pitcher, Anne, Mary H. Moran, and Michael Johnston. 2009. "Rethinking Patrimonialism and Neopatrimonialism in Africa." *African Studies Review* 52, no. 1: 125–156.

Porteous, Obie. 2022 *Research Deserts and Oases: Evidence from 27 Thousand Economics Journal Articles on Africa*. https://onlinelibrary.wiley.com/doi/10.1111/obes.12510

Posner, Daniel N. 2004a. "Measuring Ethnic Fractionalization in Africa." *American Journal of Political Science* 48, no. 4: 849–863.

———. 2004b. "The Political Salience of Cultural Difference: Why Chewas and Tumbukas Are Allies in Zambia and Adversaries in Malawi." *American Political Science Review* 98, no. 4: 529–545.

Poupko, Eliezer S. 2017. "An Exploratory Study of Constitutional Design in Three Island States: Seychelles, Comoros, and Mauritius." *Journal of Contemporary African Studies* 35, no. 3: 324–348.

Powley, Elizabeth. 2003. *Strengthening Governance: The Role of Women in Rwanda's Transition*. Washington, DC: Hunt Alternatives Fund.

———. 2006. *Rwanda: The Impact of Women Legislators on Policy Outcomes Affecting Children and Families*. New York: United Nations Children's Fund.

Putnam, Robert. 1993. *Making Democracy Work: Civic Traditions in Northern Italy*. Princeton, NJ: Princeton University Press.

Ramtohul, Ramola. 2020. "Women's Political Representation in Small Island Developing States: A Comparative Analysis of Mauritius and Seychelles." *Small States & Territories* 3, no. 1: 83–98.

Reckien, Diana et al. 2018. "How Are Cities Planning to Respond to Climate Change? Assessment of Local Climate Plans from 885 Cities in the EU-28." *Journal of Cleaner Production* 191: 207–219.

Reed, Michael. 1987. "A Neo-Colonial Enclave of Enduring French Interest." *Journal of Modern African Studies* 25, no. 2: 283–320.

Reilly, Benjamin. 2001. *Democracy in Divided Societies: Electoral Engineering for Conflict Management*. New York: Cambridge University Press.

Ricart-Huguet, Joan. 2021. "Colonial Education, Political Elites, and Regional Political Inequality in Africa." *Comparative Political Studies* 54, no. 14: 2546–2580.

———. 2022. "The Origins of Colonial Investments in Former British and French Africa." *British Journal of Political Science* 52, no. 2: 736–757.

Rich, Jeremy. 2007. *A Workman Is Worthy of His Meat: Food and Colonialism in the Gabon Estuary*. Lincoln: University of Nebraska Press.

Riedl, Rachel Beatty. 2018. "Institutional Legacies: Understanding Multiparty Politics in Historical Perspective." In Nic Cheeseman, ed., *Institutions and Democracy in Africa: How the Rules of the Game Shape Political Developments*, 41–60. New York: Cambridge University Press.

Riley, Emily Jenan. 2019. "The Politics of Terànga: Gender, Hospitality, and Power in Senegal." *Political and Legal Anthropology Review* 42, no. 1: 110–124.

Rizzo, Helen, Abdel-Hamid Abdel-Latif, and Katherine Meyer. 2007. "The Relationship Between Gender Equality and Democracy: A Comparison of Arab Versus Non-Arab Muslim Societies." *Sociology* 41, no. 6: 1151–1170.

Roberts, Debra. 2015. "City Action for Global Environmental Change: Assessment and Case Study of Durban, South Africa." In *The Routledge Handbook of Urbanization and Global Environmental Change*. New York: Routledge.

Roberts, Debra, and Sean O'Donoghue. 2013. "Urban Environmental Challenges and Climate Change Action in Durban, South Africa." *Environment and Urbanization* 25, no. 2: 299–319.

Robinson, Amanda Lea. 2016. "Internal Borders: Ethnic-Based Market Segmentation in Malawi." *World Development* 87: 371–384.
Robinson, Ashton. 2019. "Seychelles: Prospects, Probity and Legacy–Governance Under Transnational Pressures." *Round Table* 108, no. 3: 307–326.
Robinson, James A., and Q. Neil Parsons. 2006. "State Formation and Governance in Botswana." *Journal of African Economies* 15, no. Suppl. 1: 100–140.
Rodney, Walter. 1982. *How Europe Underdeveloped Africa*. Washington, DC: Howard University Press.
Rodrigues, Amabelia et al. 2008. "Changing Pattern of Malaria in Bissau, Guinea-Bissau." *Tropical Medicine and International Health* 13, no. 3: 410–417.
Rodríguez, Daniela C., Hastings Banda, and Ireen Namakhoma. 2015. "Integrated Community Case Management in Malawi: An Analysis of Innovation and Institutional Characteristics for Policy Adoption." *Health Policy and Planning* 30, no. Suppl. 2: ii74–ii83.
Rodrik, Dani. 2012. In *In Search of Prosperity: Analytic Narratives on Economic Growth*. Princeton, NJ: Princeton University Press.
Ross, Michael L. 2012. *The Oil Curse: How Petroleum Wealth Shapes the Development of Nations*. Princeton, NJ: Princeton University Press.
———. 2015. "What Have We Learned About the Resource Curse?" *Annual Review of Political Science* 18: 239–259.
Sa, Ana Lucia, and Edalina Rodrigues Sanches. 2021. "The Politics of Autocratic Survival in Equatorial Guinea: Co-Optation, Restrictive Institutional Rules, Repression, and International Projection." *African Affairs* 120, no. 478: 78–102.
Saiget, Marie. 2016. "(De-)Politicising Women's Collective Action: International Actors and Land Inheritance in Post-War Burundi." *Review of African Political Economy* 43, no. 149: 365–381.
Sandbrook, Richard. 2007. "Astute Governance Promotion Versus Historical Conditions in Explaining Good Governance: The Case of Mauritius." In *Exporting Good Governance: Temptations and Challenges in Canada's Aid Program*. Waterloo, Ontario: Wilfrid Laurier University.
Scales-Trent, Judy. 2010. "Women Lawyers, Women's Rights in Senegal: The Association of Senegalese Women Lawyers." *Human Rights Quarterly* 32, no. 1: 115–143.
Schnabel, Landon. 2016. "Religion and Gender Equality Worldwide: A Country-Level Analysis." *Social Indicators Research* 129, no. 2: 893–907.
Seay, Laura E. 2013. "Effective Responses: Protestants, Catholics, and the Provision of Health Care in the Post-War Kivus." *Review of African Political Economy* 40, no. 135: 83–97.
Sebudubudu, David, and Bertha Z. Osei-Hwedie. 2006. "Pitfalls of Parliamentary Democracy in Botswana." *Africa Spectrum* 41, no. 1: 35–53.
Seguino, Stephanie. 2011. "Help or Hindrance? Religion's Impact on Gender Inequality in Attitudes and Outcomes." *World Development* 39, no. 8: 1308–1321.
Seibert, Gerhard. 2006. *Comrades, Clients, and Cousins: Colonialism, Socialism, and Democratization in Sao Tome and Principe*. Leiden: Brill.
Sharp, Elaine B., Dorothy M. Daley, and Michael S. Lynch. 2011. "Understanding Local Adoption and Implementation of Climate Change Mitigation Policy." *Urban Affairs Review* 47, no. 3: 433–457.

Shaw, Mark. 2015. "Drug Trafficking in Guinea-Bissau, 1998–2014: The Evolution of an Elite Protection Network." *Journal of Modern African Studies* 53, no. 3: 339–364.

Sieveking, Nadine. 2007. "'We Don't Want Equality; We Want to Be Given Our Rights': Muslim Women Negotiating Global Development Concepts in Senegal." *Africa Spectrum* 42, no. 1: 29–48.

Simon, Hannah. 2016. "Understanding the Polarisation of Environmental and Social Activism in South Africa." *South African Journal of Science* 112, no. 11–12: 1–2.

Sokoloff, Kenneth, and Stanley Engerman. 2000. "History Lessons: Institutions, Factor Endowments, and Paths of Development in the New World." *Journal of Economic Perspectives* 14, no. 3: 217–232.

Steynor, Anna et al. 2020. "Learning from Climate Change Perceptions in Southern African Cities." *Climate Risk Management* 27: 1–8.

Strauss, Scott. 2006. *The Order of Genocide: Race, Power, and War in Rwanda.* Ithaca, NY: Cornell University Press.

Sumich, Jason. 2010. "The Party and the State: Frelimo and Social Stratification in Post-Socialist Mozambique." *Development and Change* 41, no. 4: 679–698.

Tayler-Smith, Katie et al. 2011. "Free Treatment, Rapid Malaria Diagnostic Tests and Malaria Village Workers Can Hasten Progress toward Achieving the Malaria Related Millennium Development Goals: The Médecins Sans Frontières Experience from Chad, Sierra-Leone and Mali." *Journal of Public Health in Africa* 2, no. 1: 50–53.

Taylor, Ian. 2003. "As Good as It Gets? Botswana's 'Democratic Development.'" *Journal of Contemporary African Studies* 21, no. 2: 215–231.

———. 2006. "The Limits of the 'African Miracle': Academic Freedom in Botswana and the Deportation of Kenneth Good." *Journal of Contemporary African Studies* 24, no. 1: 101–122.

———. 2019. "France a Fric: The CFA Zone in Africa and Neocolonialism." *Third World Quarterly* 40, no. 6: 1064–1088.

Teixeira, Aurora, and Sawelerk Nascimento. 2019. "FDI in Small States and Unattractive Markets: The Case of São Tomé and Príncipe." *Journal of Contemporary African Studies* 37, no. 4: 351–378.

Thaut Vinson, Laura. 2020. "Disaggregating Ethnicity and Conflict Patterns: Evidence from Religious and Tribal Violence in Nigeria." *Ethnopolitics* 19, no. 1: 19–44.

Thompson, Paul, Henry Wissink, and Zintle Siwisa. 2019. "The 'Seychelloisation' of the Seychelles Labour Market: Policy and Constraints of Island Labour Market Reform." *Island Studies Journal* 14, no. 2: 81–96.

Thomson, Anna et al. 2011. "Low Referral Completion of Rapid Diagnostic Test-Negative Patients in Community-Based Treatment of Malaria in Sierra Leone." *Malaria Journal* 10, no. 94: 1–7.

Toraasen, Marianne. 2017. *Gender Parity in Senegal—A Continuing Struggle.* Report, Christian Michelsen Institute.

———. 2019. "Gender Parity and the Symbolic Representation of Women in Senegal." *Journal of Modern African Studies* 57, no. 3: 459–481.

Toto Same, Achille. 2008. *Mineral-Rich Countries and Dutch Disease: Understanding the Macroeconomic Implications of Windfalls and the Development*

Prospects—The Case of Equatorial Guinea. World Bank Policy Research Working Paper.

Tripp, Aili Mari. 2016. "Women's Mobilisation for Legislative Political Representation in Africa." *Review of African Political Economy* 43, no. 149: 382–399.

Tripp, Aili Mari, Dior Konate, and Colleen Lowe-Morna. 2006. "Sub-Saharan Africa: On the Fast Track to Women's Representation." In Drude Dahlerup, ed., *Women, Quotas and Politics*. New York: Routledge.

Uittenbroek, Caroline J., Leonie B. Janssen-Jansen, and Hens A.C. Runhaar. 2016. "Stimuli for Climate Adaptation in Cities: Insights from Philadelphia—an Early Adapter." *International Journal of Climate Change Strategies and Management* 8, no. 1: 38–56.

Ursing, Johan et al. 2007. "Chloroquine Resistant P. Falciparum Prevalence Is Low and Unchanged Between 1990 and 2005 in Guinea-Bissau: An Effect of High Chloroquine Dosage?" *Infection, Genetics and Evolution* 7, no. 5: 555–561.

———. 2009. "Chloroquine Is Grossly Overdosed and Overused but Well Tolerated in Guinea-Bissau." *Antimicrobial Agents and Chemotherapy* 53, no. 1: 180–185.

———. 2014. "Malaria Transmission in Bissau, Guinea-Bissau Between 1995 and 2012: Malaria Resurgence Did Not Negatively Affect Mortality." *PLoS ONE* 9, no. 7: 1–8.

Uwineza, Peace, and Elizabeth Pearson. 2009. *Sustaining Women's Gains in Rwanda: The Influence of Indigenous Culture and Post-Genocide Politics.* Report, The Institute for Inclusive Security.

Verisk Maplecroft. 2021. *Environmental Risk Outlook 2021.*

Vicente, Pedro C. 2010. "Does Oil Corrupt? Evidence from a Natural Experiment in West Africa." *Journal of Development Economics* 92, no. 1: 28–38.

Vigh, Henrik. 2009. "Conflictual Motion and Political Inertia: On Rebellions and Revolutions in Bissau and Beyond." *African Studies Review* 52, no. 2: 143–164.

Vinck, Patrick et al. 2019. "Institutional Trust and Misinformation in the Response to the 2018–19 Ebola Outbreak in North Kivu, DR Congo: A Population-Based Survey." *The Lancet Infectious Diseases* 19, no. 5: 529–536.

Vittorio, Danielle. 2011. "Natural Resources and the 'Quality' of Economic Development." *Journal of Development Studies* 47, no. 4: 545–573.

Walker, Iain. 2007. "What Came First, the Nation or the State? Political Process in the Comoro Islands." *Africa* 77, no. 4: 582–605.

Wallerstein, Immanuel. 2004. *World Systems Analysis: An Introduction*. Durham, NC: Duke University Press.

Wang, Lili et al. 2021. "A Household-Based Cross-Sectional Survey of Knowledge, Awareness and Practice Regarding Malaria in Western Area Rural District, Sierra Leone." *Frontiers in Public Health* 9.

Weszkalnys, Gisa. 2008. "Hope & Oil: Expectations in São Tomé e Príncipe." *Review of African Political Economy* 35, no. 117: 473–482.

Wigley, Simon, and Arzu Akkoyunlu-Wigley. 2017. "The Impact of Democracy and Media Freedom on Under-5 Mortality, 1961–2011." *Social Science & Medicine* 190, no. 10: 237–246.

Wijaya, Nurrohman, Vilas Nitivattananon, Rajendra Prasad Shrestha, and Sohee Minsun Kim. 2020. "Drivers and Benefits of Integrating Climate Adaptation

Measures into Urban Development: Experience from Coastal Cities of Indonesia." *Sustainability (Switzerland)* 12, no. 2: 1–16.
Wilkinson, Annie, and James Fairhead. 2017. "Comparison of Social Resistance to Ebola Response in Sierra Leone and Guinea Suggests Explanations Lie in Political Configurations Not Culture." *Critical Public Health* 27, no. 1: 14–27.
Wondji, Charles S. et al. 2012. "Impact of Pyrethroid Resistance on Operational Malaria Control in Malawi." *Proceedings of the National Academy of Sciences of the United States of America* 109, no. 47: 19063–19070.
Woo-Cumings, Meredith, ed. 1999. *The Developmental State*. Ithaca, NY: Cornell University Press.
Wood, Geoffrey. 2004. "Business and Politics in a Criminal State: The Case of Equatorial Guinea." *African Affairs* 103, no. 413: 547–567.
World Bank. 2018. *Poverty and Shared Prosperity 2018: Piecing Together the Poverty Puzzle*. Washington, DC: World Bank.
World Health Organization. 2020. *World Malaria Report*. Geneva: WHO.
Wrong, Michela. 2021. *Do Not Disturb: The Story of a Political Murder and an African Regime Gone Bad*. New York: PublicAffairs.
Yates, Douglas. 2014. "Port-Gentil: From Forestry Capital to Energy Capital." In Joseph Pratt, Martin Melosi, and Kathleen Brosnan, eds., *Energy Capitals: Local Impact, Global Influence*. Pittsburgh, PA: University of Pittsburgh Press.
Yeganeh, Armin Jeddi, Andrew P. McCoy, and Todd Schenk. "Determinants of Climate Change Policy Adoption: A Meta-Analysis." *Urban Climate* 31, (March 2020): 1–26.
Young, Crawford. 2012. *The Postcolonial State in Africa: Fifty Years of Independence, 1960–2010*. Madison, WI: University of Wisconsin Press.
Zgambo, Maggie, Balwani Chingatichifwe Mbakaya, and Fatch Welcome Kalembo. 2017. "Prevalence and Factors Associated with Malaria Parasitaemia in Children under the Age of Five Years in Malawi: A Comparison Study of the 2012 and 2014 Malaria Indicator Surveys (MISs)." *PLoS ONE* 12, no. 4: 1–13.

Index

About the Book

What does it take for African countries to achieve political and economic successes? Scholarship on Africa tends to focus on the barriers to reaching desired outcomes. While recognizing that these barriers are very real, Erin Hern takes a contrary, unabashedly optimistic approach: rather than treating countries that perform well as "miracles," she seeks to normalize their success, analyzing the performance of those that have made good choices in the face of adverse circumstances.

Hern shows how most-similar and most-different cases can be used to test major explanatory theories. Making the topic accessible to nonexperts, in each of five issue chapters she highlights two countries that have performed well, evaluates which theories can best explain their successes, and then turns to two shadow cases (countries that have not performed as well) to evaluate whether those theories remain plausible. Including an opening chapter that introduces the theory and methods of comparative politics, this provocative book is ideal for classroom use.

Erin Accampo Hern is associate professor of political science in the Maxwell School, Syracuse University.